Praise for Post-Gay? Post-Christian?

Post-Gay? Post-Christian? is a twenty-first-century treatise that was begging to be written. Debbie Thurman took up the challenge of "going where angels fear to tread," and readers will be the better for her soul-searching and meticulously researched work. On the surface, this book may appear to be simply an evangelical encyclical against "the gay agenda." Look again. Thurman calls out the Church to be the Church in every sense, and that also means being the arm of compassion to a community that feels it has been effectively shut out of it. Can we do this with both truth and grace? Thurman believes we can. She painstakingly shows us just how convoluted the postmodern gay culture war has become and how complex the individual struggle is for those who are torn by it. Thurman leaves no stone unturned as she enlightens readers and asks them to take up the challenge of being "salt and light" to a culture in desperate need of it.

Dr. Jim Garlow
Senior Pastor, Skyline Wesleyan Church
San Diego

"A timely book! Debbie Thurman handles a difficult topic with wisdom and grace!"

Anne Paulk
Author of *Restoring Sexual Identity:
Hope for Women Who Struggle with Same-Sex Attraction*

"The American family is under attack to such an extent that our entire moral center and every issue that stems from that center are on a precipice. While we deliberate in the humanistic halls of equality for same-sex marriage and whether gays are discriminated against in the same way blacks have been, our society is systematically becoming unhinged from its moorings. We must stop it! *Post-Gay? Post-Christian?* is a great tool to help Christians understand this dilemma and respond according to a biblical worldview. Debbie Thurman has essayed important principles thoroughly and researched them to provide a well-balanced treatise. Every pastor and elder should use this book to respond to our culture. Every Christian should read this to impact the community in which they live."

Bishop Harry R. Jackson, Jr.
Senior Pastor of Hope Christian Church
(Washington, D.C. area)
Founder and President, High Impact Leadership Coalition

Debbie Thurman's personal story is one full of grace and redemption. As an accomplished writer and minister, she has used her experience to see others helped and healed. I wholeheartedly share her desire to see the church equipped to disciple all who struggle with sexual brokenness and, therefore, I am pleased to recommend her and this book.

Alan Chambers
President, Exodus International

POST-GAY?
POST-CHRISTIAN?

ANATOMY OF A CULTURAL
AND FAITH IDENTITY CRISIS

DEBBIE THURMAN

Cedar House Publishers
Monroe, Virginia

Published by Cedar House Publishers
P. O. Box 399
Monroe, VA 24574-0399
www.cedarhousepublishers.com

Unless otherwise indicated, all Scripture quotations are taken from the HOLY BIBLE, NEW INTERNATIONAL VERSION®. NIV®. Copyright © 1973, 1978, 1984 by the International Bible Society. Used by permission of Zondervan. All rights reserved.

Cataloging-In-Publication Data

Thurman, Debbie.
  Post-gay? Post-Christian? : anatomy of a cultural and faith identity crisis / Debbie Thurman.
    p. ; cm.
  Includes bibliographical references and index.
  ISBN: 978-0-9676289-6-7
  1. Homosexuality~Religious aspects~Christianity. 2. Gay rights~Religious aspects~Christianity. 3. Gay liberation movement~United States~History. 4. Ex-gay movement~United States. I. Title.

BR115.H6 T48 2011
261.835/766   2010913790

Printed in the United States of America
Cover Design by Natalie Fowler

For Russ, my one-flesh soul mate

Amor vincit omnia.

"Here I am! I stand at the door and knock.
If anyone hears my voice and opens the door,
I will come in and eat with him, and he with me.
To him who overcomes, I will give the right
to sit with me on my throne, just as I overcame
and sat down with my Father on his throne.
He who has an ear, let him hear
what the Spirit says to the churches."

Revelation 3:20-22

Contents

Acknowledgments

This book had been percolating in me for some time before I actually began putting the words into concrete form. At its midpoint, God clearly spoke to my heart and told me to "lay it on the altar" for a season. I did not question his wisdom, but obeyed, knowing he would give me direction in his time. That's just what happened. When God told me to take it up again, a light shown on the path before me, confirming he had a purpose for this book. So, above all, I thank my Lord and Master. Not only did he heal me from the insidious pain and confusion of a significant struggle with same-sex attraction, but he also entrusted me with a heart of reconciliation toward others who struggle—as well as those who don't. My twofold message of appreciation is first, for the people who helped me get to the point of even writing this book, and second, for those who helped fan its embers into whatever flame it represents.

My dear husband, Russ, is God's sweetest gift to me. That he found the strength, faith, and love to stand by me through a dark decade of intermittent depression—a life-or-death struggle at its nadir—would have been miraculous enough. Adding to that the grace to forgive my later rebellious indiscretions and walk the tortuous road with me toward marital restoration is beyond amazing. I stand in awe of what our God has done. Our story is a testament to his holy design for marriage. How he loves us!

A special thanks must go to my mom and to my former

pastor's wife, Vonnie, both of whom wrapped their arms of grace around me when I, with great trepidation, revealed my struggle to them in 1995. Their loving responses, though I am sure they labored to understand it all, ministered incredible healing to my soul. Bless you both! And how could I ever thank my awesome counselor, Diane, enough? She was a godsend. I forever will be grateful for the divine insight and compassion she brought to our year of intense counseling sessions. Also in that 1990s group belongs my former pastor, Larry Osborne, the only person at North Coast Church in Vista, California (a church worthy of being missed greatly) to whom I confessed my struggle while asking him to hold me accountable. No, he did not run me off or uncomfortably hold me at arm's length. He responded with true Christian love and concern. He is an amazing pastor and leader.

I wish to express my profound gratitude for my late pastor, Jerry Falwell, who took the news of my past struggle in stride and encouraged me as I began to explore this new ministerial territory. It was "Doc" Falwell who blessed and helped launch my umbrella ministry, Sheer Faith, and its inaugural book a decade ago. He was a fatherly cheerleader and mentor, and I will forever miss him. I hope his prayers, both for me and for Christ's beloved Church, will prove prophetic. He and I were just beginning to discuss the sexual identity conundrum in the Church and the respective roles God was calling us to play in the Third Millennium when he suddenly went home to be with the Lord in May 2007.

I also owe much to my counseling mentor, the late Dr. Daryl Pitts, who had a vision for Freedom Ministry at Thomas Road Baptist Church soon after I arrived there, and allowed me to have a role in shaping it and serving in it. Daryl received the diagnosis of ALS (Lou Gehrig's Disease) graciously, and lived out his final days with a joy and faith that deeply touched all who knew him. I likewise truly appreciate the women struggling with same-sex attraction who allowed me to disciple them during my latter work with Freedom Groups ministry. They faithfully came, week after week, baring their souls and teaching me more about God's grace in the process as I humbly and imperfectly sought to reflect his truth. I pray each of them continues to find the peace and healing they seek. I remain humbled by their trust and their courage.

I have been especially blessed with the wise counsel of my own gifted husband. He is my rock and my sounding board when I need him to be. Hon, you are the best! Who else could love me, warts and all, as you do? Russ and our daughters, Jenni and Natalie, (who received the shocking news that their mom once "walked on the gay side" with maturity and grace) comprise the Sheer Faith/Cedar House team. How blessed are we to have all that talent and support in the family! We may no longer all live under the same roof, but we are of one heart, one accord.

Lastly, I thank my fellow "formers"—those brothers and sisters in Christ who have traded their complex struggles with same-sex attraction for wholeness and holiness, or are moving through God's sanctifying grace toward that place, whatever it may look like. They have drawn closer to the true lover of their souls, as he has to them, and they have stayed the course. You know who you are. It isn't easy to come out of that "closet" and publicly testify to God's healing grace, but some of you boldly and compassionately have done so, to the glory of his kingdom. Success—not just what the world calls success—may appear to some of my brothers and sisters to be a mere pinpoint on the horizon, even an impossible destination to reach. But God searches and knows each heart. He never fails to help his afflicted people find contentment when they seek him.

The world shouts its cadence, but the lover of Christ marches to a different drummer. "In this world you will have trouble. But take heart! I have overcome the world" (John 16:33).

Introduction

For me to offer anything approaching a definitive book on how the Church, the culture, and the gay rights movement have impacted each other, I would have to be a social scientist, psychologist, theologian, and historian. Were I to wrap that package in the experience of having walked on both the homosexual and heterosexual sides of the tracks, so much the better. I do claim the latter qualification. As a longtime social observer and chronicler, I have bulging files of data. I even have two books in the psychology genre to my credit. I suppose I could be called a journeyman psychologist. I have kept copious notes from decades of Bible study, sermons, teaching, and general reading. I've been a mom for 24 years and a wife for 29. Perhaps more importantly for the subject matter at hand, I have participated in many meaningful conversations with people from all walks of life, both gay and straight, over the past several years. Life is a potent teacher—a harsh taskmaster at times.

If any super-authority in all the above-cited disciplines truly exists in the human realm, I salute you. I believe my education—in both an academic and hard-knocks sense—qualifies me to open a sizable window into a touchy topic, but one that keeps insisting on defining this present age in particular ways. Therefore, I press on. And I trust in the God who made me and fitted me for my work.

Are we a "post-gay" society? What does that even mean? Furthermore, should we care? I believe the answer to the first question is "No." To the last question I answer, "Yes." I need to make it abundantly clear that I am not advocating some strategy in this book for Christians to win the "culture war" or project their will (or what they may perceive as God's will), Dominionist-style, onto the sociopolitical landscape. I am very much vested, however, in Christians being equipped to debate biblical truth in the public square and to speak up, as is their constitutional right, when they believe this nation is being harmed by those who would impose a seemingly godless form of government—or ungodly social mores— on us. Just as much, I long to see the Church be the Church in every sense. That means speaking and living both grace and truth in the world, and helping the lost or missing-in-action come to understand the power of redemption through Jesus Christ.

In one sense, this book is the outgrowth of my sojourn in what we perfunctorily call "ex-gay ministry," but what is increasingly being referred to as more of a post-gay journey to wholeness or a realizing of one's identity in Christ while yet a struggler. We must be careful, however, when using the term post-gay as it is mostly a secular invention. It did not originally mean what some former gays want it to mean today. In a sociological sense, it is meant to describe that time when the ball is over and no one cares anymore who came with whom, i.e., when gay is no longer a big deal. It is a big deal, however—just not in all the ways it is presented to be. Naturally, the journey to post-gay, whatever your definition, does not look the same for any two people. Mine started long ago in my youth.

Many questions exist for those trying to come to terms with homosexuality in all its rainbow hues. I am but one among those seeking answers. My Christian worldview naturally informs my cultural outlook. I happen to believe it ought never to be the other way around. That it is for growing numbers of people, inside and outside the Church, has created a sticky dilemma for all of society. Who can make sense of it all? This book attempts to do just that. Believing in a long-overdue, truly Christian response to homosexuality, as well as an appropriate and helpful gay response to the Church, I am going where angels fear to tread. God help me!

As this book was conceived, I saw it as a way of articulating a deep-seated frustration and a call to stand for truth. To me, it seemed that too many God-fearing people had allowed their eyes to be blinded to the dark side of a secular sociopolitical agenda, of which gay rights appeared to have become the fulcrum. I feared for the Church—feared our salt would become tasteless and be thrown out; that we would be assimilated by toothless, godless doctrines and become lukewarm spittle in the mouth of Christ, our Bridegroom. But then I thought about how much we'd already done just that, without even dealing with the gay question. I love the Church, despite her faults—and there are many. I love her salt-of-the-earth people who continually worship, pray, and serve—in good times and bad—in congregations of all shapes and sizes across this great land and abroad. Yet, I cannot dwell on this diverse family of God for long without thinking about the prodigals—the confused, the marginalized—"the least of these." There are many subgroups of people who slip between the cracks in the very place where they should be made to feel most welcome. Our sexual-identity-confused or gay-identifying brothers and sisters are foremost among them.

If our identity is to be found in the creating, sustaining Godhead—Father, Son, and Holy Spirit—how do we relate to and minister to those who appear to place so high a premium on their sexuality that it defines them in ways most others cannot understand? We know we have adulterers, fornicators, and sinners of all stripes congregating, working, and even teaching the innocent and vulnerable in our churches and communities. Why don't they seek to have their identities affirmed in their sinfulness (or proclivity to it) or publicly celebrate it? Why don't we figuratively drag them out into the street, with stones in our hands? Why aren't we as visibly exercised over the high rates of divorce and the usual sexual sins, even among Christians, as we are over the smaller numbers of people pushing gay marriage? Many of the faithful may logically wonder just what makes homosexuality different, somehow worthy of special consideration (or special condemnation) among the plethora of predispositions or temptations we Christians may acquiesce to. Why do some move beyond their sexual identity confusion and others find doing so virtually impossible, even when they sincerely seek God's will for their lives? Can't the same be said of other forms of sin-bondage?

"Come to me, all you who are weary and burdened, and I will give you rest," Jesus promises. But how many of us who are supposed to be "Jesus with skin on" have forgotten how to make our church homes places of refuge and reconciliation? We cannot have that without exhorting the lost sheep to repent after coming as they are to the Christ who waits for them with open arms. Still, we must be looking always to keep our own houses in order, lest the "planks" that accumulate in our eyes wall us off from those we are seeking to "save." It is Jesus who does the saving, of course. He draws through us as we comfort and forgive those with the same comfort and forgiveness he has given us. His well is deep while ours is pitifully shallow. Jesus is all about the well and its water while we, unfortunately, are too often about the buckets we use to draw the water. That needs to change. Around that certain conviction, then, a broader vision for this book took shape.

We must realize that the suffering experienced by those who see (but don't necessarily accept) themselves as homosexual, bisexual, or transgender—or who are just not sure where they fit into the spectrum of "sexual identity"—is indeed real and agonizing. I know because I've been one of them. By the way, so has Jesus, in a sense. He knew all the temptations and bore all the sins of the world so he could identify with them, and in doing so, hammered the final nail into the sin-death coffin. Even with their fate sealed, Satan and his fallen angels battle on for the heart and soul of mankind. The so-called culture war, of which the gay revolution has become a major part, is a bloody manifestation of the Enemy's and mankind's rebellion. It is ripping at the fabric of who we are, threatening to further tear families, churches, communities, governments—all of civilization—apart. We are in its grip, like it or not. No, I don't think we have arrived at that post-gay or post-Christian place some see as inevitable yet. That space-bound ship has not yet broken through the atmosphere. It is rocketing forward, however. It ought to be clear that neither appeasing nor demonizing from either side will resolve this conflict because it is soul-deep.

We hear about those who desire to "build bridges" between the Church and the gay community. I get where they are coming from, although I don't agree with all their tactics. That bridge has long existed, of course. His name is Jesus. People—some well-meaning and others mean-spirited—have only made the chasm deeper and wider. How do we teach our children God's plan for human sexuality and marriage when at every turn they are confronted with "everybody's doing it" heterosexual promiscuity or the gay rights gospel? How will gay-affirming people, longing both to understand themselves and be understood by others, make their way to the Church of Christ, which has shut them out in so many ways?

Regardless of what other nations perceive themselves to be, the United States is a nation with its roots firmly planted in a Judeo-Christian heritage and its law-informing precepts. We have allowed ourselves to be seduced by the revisionist notion that we are not and never were a God-fearing nation, strongly influenced by the Christian faith. This "revelation" works to the advantage of any ideology that seeks to deconstruct and redefine the traditional family. When we abandon our foundation—and healthy families are the bedrock of all civilization—we leave it vulnerable to those who would rebuild upon it with something far less stable, or even disastrous. If we don't understand how we were deceived, we will be unable to see our way back to sanity. Not all that has come out of this Pandora's box (or closet) can go back in, however. It began with the sexual revolution of the sixties and grew uglier and more divisive with the rise of no-fault divorce and abortion-on-demand. We, the people, grew more and more selfish while the Church waited with folded hands and pious lips and was assimilated, in part, by the secular culture. Just as God's chosen people did in days of old, we have allowed idols to sit on the high places and we refuse to tear them down.

The gay culture war has spawned a cultural and spiritual coup that has all but enthroned a new moral order in the Western world. The ripples have spread far and wide, creating an "Us vs. Them" mentality, though both sides are riddled with sin. How many of us have the resolve to mount the "high places" and remove the idols—all of them? Judging by the shouting contests all around us, plenty are motivated. Too many are blinded or narrowed by self-righteous anger, however. That applies to both sides. I recently heard a pastor make an astute observation: with as many as half of marriages purportedly ending in divorce, and the gay population likely being somewhere between 2 and 5 percent, we ought to center our focus much more on the 50-percent problem than the 5-percent one. The Church has failed miserably to uphold God's plan for marriage. We cannot blame the gay rights push for that.

Are we ready to take the real Jesus—all of him—into the byways of the world? Are we willing to stand firm on the changeless truth of his Word, while humbly serving the very people we have wounded? I pray so.

Debbie Thurman
October 2010
Monroe, Virginia

One

Gay Revolution:
From Stonewall to Soulforce

The summer of 1969 saw several history-making events. My generation—Baby Boomers—commemorated the fortieth anniversaries of each with varying degrees of fanfare in 2009. Those old enough to remember can recall the Apollo 11 lunar mission and Neil Armstrong's televised "giant leap for mankind" onto the moon's surface in July of 1969. That year's August Woodstock music festival was a pop-culture phenomenon that elicits unique memories for many. Much less known outside the gay community is another event that occurred that June at an otherwise obscure gay bar in New York's Greenwich Village—the Stonewall Inn. It might be considered a "giant leap" for the gay movement, whose early activists, no doubt, saw gaining legitimate minority status in the hearts and minds of average citizens as akin to flying to the moon. Sadly, many Boomers who lived through that era are gone now, lost to the tragic holocaust of AIDS. In the early morning hours of June 28, eight police officers raided the Stonewall Inn, ostensibly because it had no liquor license. Such raids at gay bars had been commonplace for years. What made this one different is that, for the first time, militant gays fought back—in a big way.

Accounts differ as to how the Stonewall riots began. Urban legend has it that the bar's 200 or so patrons were in an unusually volatile mood following Judy Garland's death a week earlier. A good many of the 20,000-plus mourners attending her funeral— she was an icon of sorts to the gay community—were said to be gay men. Perhaps angry homosexuals, some of whom were already experienced anti-Vietnam war or anti-establishment protesters, just snapped from years of harsh treatment and decided to make a stand. For whatever reason, a full riot broke out and spilled over into the next several days. Initially, the overwhelmed police force barricaded itself inside the empty bar, which the protesters almost set ablaze at one point. The beleaguered cops had to be reinforced by the Tactical Patrol Force (TPF), an elite riot-control squad specially trained to disperse the war protestors of that day.

So began, more or less, the postmodern gay revolution. A gay magazine in New York published a special riot edition, featuring a story entitled, "The Hairpin Drop Heard Round The World." A short time after Stonewall, the Gay Liberation Front (GLF)—a precursor to later militant gay organizations—formed. The following summer, on the anniversary of the riots, the first gay pride march with 10,000 participants took place in the Big Apple. The last week or so in June continues to be recognized as Gay Pride Week, while June is Gay Pride Month, by a year-2000 declaration of former President Bill Clinton. Gays get another month of special observation, however. October 11 is National Coming Out Day, and the entire month of October is GLBT (gay, lesbian, bisexual, transgender) Awareness Month, focusing on various gay icons and their historic contributions. One wonders what may be next on the gay-rights horizon, since the calendar still has ten more months to be claimed.

In April 1972, I visited the city that never sleeps for the first time on my high school senior trip. Our group stayed in the historic Taft Hotel in midtown Manhattan. From an upper story window, my roomies and I witnessed one of New York's still-nascent gay pride parades taking place on the street below. The next evening, we went to see Lauren Bacall in "Applause" on Broadway. We sat bug-eyed during the scene where a chorus line of presumably gay actor-waiters, clad in nothing but checkered aprons and tap shoes form the waist down, table-danced to raucous applause during the title number. That fall, I enrolled as a freshman at an elite Virginia women's college. When I tried out for the basketball team, I got yet another reminder that I was "no longer in Kansas." The coach was as butch as they come, and too many of the other players, peppering their speech with a non-stop chorus of F-words and sporting mannish mannerisms, left me feeling as if I didn't get the memo. I decided they didn't need my basketball skills. I was more than a little wary of whatever game they were playing. Colleges back then did not have to deal with athletes openly touting a "gender identity" that was different from their sex, as they do today.

The growing gay culture also had invaded the classroom. My sociology professor took the better part of class one day to describe for us in joyful detail the lesbian "wedding" of two friends he had attended in Washington, D.C. the previous weekend. I worked with his wife in my part-time library job and actually got to meet said couple when they visited her there. I remember one of them having a rainbow "Gay power for gay lovers" patch—a fad of that era—sewn onto her back jeans pocket. Not long after that, I was sorting the library's mail when out of its plain, brown wrapper fell the latest issue of *Playboy*, its cover graced by two amorous, doe-eyed coeds. A cover line unabashedly asked, "Should I sleep with my roommate"? Fortunately, I didn't have one since I lived at home and commuted to classes. I wondered just how many of my classmates were conducting that social experiment. It was hard to get the *Playboy* image out of my mind.

Home was not exactly the picture of bliss for me. My parents had divorced a few years earlier. My dad was an alcoholic, laboring at recovery but with a long journey still ahead of him. Mom worked hard to hold everything together. My younger brother routinely embarrassed me by carousing around the campus with the son of one of my professors, dabbling in drugs and generally living la vida macho, seventies-style, with willing students. Otherwise, he was at home, playing his psychedelic music as loud as possible, sending me to the campus library until closing time late at night. Still, I am probably quite fortunate to have lived at home during my college years. Otherwise, I fear I too would have fallen to the many temptations that were all around me. It was a different world on campus. As it was, I was having trouble staying chaste in a long-distance relationship with the boyfriend whom I naïvely believed I would marry after we graduated.

I babysat for a family that lived just up the street from me. The liberated mother of two—a Northern transplant to our sleepy, little college town who had married a local boy—left the infamous feminist tome, *Women Unite: Our Bodies, Ourselves*, out in plain sight for me to secretly read after the children were in bed. My head was spinning with confused images. Raised in a conservative, church-going community—with a Southern Baptist upbringing since birth—I was caught between two worlds. There was no escaping the ubiquitous sexual revolution, with its strong feminist and homosexual undertow. I knew, although no one else did, that I was in danger of being carried out to sea by it. Twenty years would pass, half of which I spent cycling in and out of major depression, the other half fighting the homosexual temptations that depression had dulled, before I dared to taste the forbidden fruit. The agony that came with capitulating to that sin was like a knife repeatedly piercing my heart—far worse than the pain of unrequited desire.

Those wounds healed ever so slowly through solid counseling and other support, which included much prayerful time I spent prostrate before God, seeking his face and his will for my life. Eventually, mercifully, I came to see myself in the whole image of God. That healing formed a hope and compassion in me that I am compelled today to extend to others like me—especially those brought up as Christians—who are similarly struggling with same-sex attraction. Many of them remain hidden in their secret closets or cloistered in small, accepting communities. Others have come out and live as openly gay men and women while some choose celibacy. A growing number of them are now Christian activists seeking "freedom for lesbian, gay, bisexual, and transgender people from religious and political oppression"—in other words, full acceptance by the Church for homosexuality as a "gift" from God. The one thing we all know, regardless of how we interpret Scripture, is that we never actually chose the terribly conflicted feelings we have known. They are so complex as to be somewhat beyond our comprehension, despite the oversimplified and scientifically or biblically unsupported explanations we have been spoon-fed by the media and gay activists and even those Christian extremist groups bent on exposing the "lies from the pits of hell" of gay affirmation. For me, it is sufficient to accept this brokenness as a symptom of a fallen, sinful world. That means only one legitimate solution exists for reconciling its confusion and pain: Jesus Christ.

The Gates of Hell Are Pushing

Flash forward about 25 years from my college days to this same part of Central Virginia—Jerry Falwell country—and a sunny Sunday morning in October 1999. On the sidewalks outside Falwell's Thomas Road Baptist Church in Lynchburg—my church, as of earlier that year—stands a gathering of Christian gay protestors and their supporters. They are part of Soulforce, the nonviolent but subtly militant gay activist organization led by Rev. Mel White, former evangelical ghostwriter for Falwell and other prominent Christians. The group has managed to get Falwell to agree to a meeting between representatives of the Christian gay and local church communities in an attempt to tone down the "anti-gay rhetoric" they say has issued forth from the pulpit at Thomas Road and other conservative churches for too long. Most churchgoers that morning enter through side doors or politely walk by, smiling and largely ignoring the equally polite protestors. A few stop and speak with them, some of those conversations leading shortly afterward to a web-based project called Bridges Across the Divide. Some national, regional, and local news media folk mill about. The much-ballyhooed meeting goes off with only a few hitches (the Church leadership does not allow the two groups to "break bread" together, for instance, citing scriptural injunctions). Falwell preaches a somewhat conciliatory sermon that morning, but elects not to broadcast it later to the nation over "The Old Time Gospel Hour" television program. In the end, nothing changes. Falwell is not "converted" to pro-gay theology (although I know he continued to have great compassion for his old friend, White), hell does not freeze over, and Soulforce just paints a bigger target on the "religions right."

We've come a long way, baby—from a ghetto subculture of closeted gays and lesbians taking root predominantly in cities like San Francisco, New York City, and New Orleans, to out-and-about, progressive Christian gays, fomenting a movement that is splintering mainline church denominations and is coming ever closer to bridging the ideological gap in the minds of many Americans. We're in a full political, cultural, and spiritual war waged by influence-peddling activists, lobbyists, and the media. A main objective—the coveted spoils of this war—is the right to constitutionally define the ancient institution of marriage, either as it has been traditionally or broadened by judicial fiat or legislative sleight-of-hand to include same-sex couples and more, altering the socio-political landscape forever. Many gays just want mainstream legitimacy. Problematically for them, many others still want to keep the sassy, edgy, party-loving image. The gay-rights movement can appear to be a tug-of-war between the two elements. Conservative sociologists and many biblically literate Christians fervently believe legally sanctioned gay marriage will do the already-embattled family no favors, and could well be its fatal blow. The result, goes the reasoning, would be unprecedented upheaval for all civilization, for which a married mom and dad rearing children is the essential building block. Liberal sociologists and activists argue that traditional marriage has long been in a precarious freefall (the divorce rate was already at 33 percent in the fifties) and that allowing homosexuals to marry and even raise children will not further erode traditional families, well-reasoned counter-arguments notwithstanding. What ought to be obvious no longer is for many because we have moved ever farther away in this postmodern era from moral clarity and truth.

There is even a socialist/anarchist sub-voice within homosexual activism that questions why gays should ever want to emulate the patriarchal bastion of oppression they perceive marriage as representing. Perhaps that's why the lesbian couple whose lawsuit brought us gay marriage in Massachusetts in 2003 eventually filed for divorce. The other states that are slowly affirming and codifying same-sex marriage—five so far, not counting the several more recognizing gay civil unions or the two states whose voters fought back and won—may as well stand by for a new wave of divorces and the heart-rending child custody battles they will breed as the courts are asked to rule with a set of laws intended to cover heterosexual marriages. California remains locked in a back-and-forth pattern, with its fate likely to be decided by the U.S. Supreme Court. Transgender issues aside, traditional custody disputes don't deal with ex-men or ex-women as warring parents. However, some prominent legal cases have arisen when one same-sex spouse or partner has opted to renounce homosexuality and claim a God-ordained right as the legitimate parent of a child brought into that union, via artificial insemination, a surrogate arrangement, or a previous heterosexual marriage. It is most common in lesbian unions that go sour. The most prominent so far has been the seven-year ongoing battle over custody and visitation involving a now-8-year-old child in the Lisa Miller-Janet Jenkins (*Miller v. Jenkins*) case. This case involves two states—Vermont, a gay marriage state and Virginia, a state with a particularly strong one-man, one-woman constitutional marriage amendment and a Marriage Affirmation Act. Miller is the child's biological mother who chose a relationship with Jesus Christ over homosexuality after being in a brief civil union with Jenkins, an avowed lesbian. Just how abundant are longtime-monogamous same-sex unions, such as those the media enthusiastically parade in front of us? No one knows.

The Great Cover-up?

Another rallying cry for both sides of this cultural debate is on the HIV/AIDS front. AIDS was a hot topic again in 2006, the 25th anniversary of its emergence as a serious public health problem. Men having sex with men (MSM) remain at the highest end of the risk scale for the HIV virus and were responsible for 50-70 percent of known infections in the U.S., as of 2006 when the latest data was analyzed by the Centers for Disease Control and Prevention (CDC). The CDC (MMWR) report, "HIV Prevalence Estimates—United States, 2006," details data "suggesting that HIV prevalence in the United States increased by approximately 112,000 (11.3

percent) from 2003 to 2006." HIV in the black MSM population is nearly twice as prevalent as it is in the white MSM population, and it is proliferating in the black heterosexual population, as well. Except for pockets, the worldwide pandemic is not receding and is affecting increasing numbers of women, children, and various ethnic groups. Cultural differences and moral sentiment/stigma vary from country to country, making the virus' spread more difficult to contain. Money remains an issue, even though the cost of newer antiretroviral drugs has decreased. Some complain of the lack of funds to finance research and development of more vaccines, needed because of the adaptability of the various HIV viral strains. Yet AIDS research gets considerably more funding per victim than any other deadly disease. Others maintain too much money is being siphoned off by profiteering drug companies, is wasted on ineffective public education programs, or is tied up in the ideological wars between funding factions. Those advocating stronger abstinence-based programs are dismissed as proselytizers and science bashers. The evidence shows the ABC—Abstinence, Be Faithful, Condoms—approach to HIV prevention works dramatically better than the "safe-sex" condom approach alone. Uganda saw a substantial reduction in HIV/AIDS rates during the first eight to ten years of this approach, from 15 percent of the population infected to only 5 percent. Kenya's rate of reduction also has been impressive.[1]

　　But Uganda has been in a heated battle over gay rights and HIV/AIDS policies. Faith and science are at war there, with lots of U.S. aid on the line. Uganda's HIV rates, which went from the highest in all of Africa to the lowest, proving that a population can be motivated to change risky behaviors, have been climbing again. In this largely Christian nation, some ultra-conservative elements have sought draconian legislative measures aimed at wiping out their "gay problem" by targeting not only "serial offenders"—those who have even consensual gay sex with one or more partners—or predatory "defilers," but also those who sympathize too much with homosexuals for the national comfort level. Homosexuality is a serious "crime against nature" to many Ugandans. Some government officials in Uganda, as well as some fiery, indignant church leaders, have even pushed for the death penalty for those found guilty of certain "aggravated" sexual offenses—having sex with a minor or a disabled person or exposing a sexual partner, consensual or not, to HIV. International pressure, including outcries from some prominent American evangelicals and the U.S. Department of State, has kept this battle on the international radar. Life imprisonment already exists in Uganda for certain heterosexual and homosexual offenses, including "defilement" or adults having sex with persons under the age of 18. Singling out gays for harsher punishment than heterosexuals committing the same offenses is not likely to fly in a country where archaic tribal rituals and serial infidelity still greatly multiply human suffering.

South Africa, a country that has pushed condoms as AIDS prevention more than any other in Africa, had the highest rate of HIV infections in the world as of 2005, according to the 2006 UNAIDS Report of the Global AIDS Epidemic. A 2005 study by the Human Sciences Research Council showed that 10.8 percent of the South African population was then infected with HIV/AIDS.[2] Those numbers have continued to increase, especially in older women, who, it is reasoned, are more victimized by cultural ignorance and ingrained sexual practices than younger women, among whom HIV infection rates have dropped some. Craig Timberg, writing for The Washington Post, reported in March 2007, "Researchers increasingly attribute the resilience of HIV in Botswana—and in southern Africa generally—to the high incidence of multiple sexual relationships." He further concluded, "Soaring rates of condom use have not brought down high HIV rates. Instead, they rose together, until both were among the highest in Africa."[3] The 2008 UNAIDS report offers the sobering assessment that "... prevention programs, especially in countries with concentrated epidemics, fail to reach many people at high risk of exposure to HIV, including a majority of men who have sex with men and injecting drug users."[4] In the U.S., the gay community attempts to downplay its role in the spread of HIV infections, and younger populations of gay men, as well as some minority populations, are not as well-informed on preventive measures as they should be.

The South African government chose to provide unlimited condoms free of charge. Well-manufactured condoms are about 80-90 percent effective in preventing the HIV virus, if used properly and consistently. That's the big "if" that argues against their exclusive use, other moral questions aside. If people can't control their sexual impulses, how do we expect them (especially teens) to be disciplined in condom use? The latex prophylactic is also less effective than touted against other sexually transmitted diseases. Abstinence until marriage and faithfulness to one's spouse are—how often must it be repeated?—100 percent effective in preventing all STDs. The U.S. President's Emergency Plan for AIDS Relief (PEPFAR), first proposed by President Bush in his 2003 State of the Union address, originally contained a proviso that roughly one-third of its allotted funds would be spent on fidelity and abstinence-based prevention education. Congress has all but removed that requirement from the program, while dramatically increasing the funding for drugs and condoms.

Gay rights advocates even fight among themselves over how best to prevent and treat HIV infections. Divided in principle and practice, each side points fingers at those they consider to be political sell-outs. In gaydom, they have been called "Uncle Toms." The latest five-year strategy released by PEPFAR in December 2009 proposed reducing the HIV infection rate by 12 million cases.

An article in *The Lancet*, the esteemed British medical journal, in March 2010, however, pointed out in no uncertain terms the "deep gulf" within the prevention community, which makes this goal untenable:

> One camp sees that multiple sexual partnerships drive infection in generalised epidemics in eastern and southern Africa, dispersed through the broad population. The other emphasises the large number of already infected individuals, particularly the many existing discordant couples, and stresses widespread HIV testing. But careful examination of these complex generalised epidemics reveals a crucial role for both components, and provides a basis for a unifying approach.[5]

In a *Lancet* commentary, in which Shelton replied to a letter concerning HIV myths, he said, "We are failing to focus properly on the key driver of these generalised (as opposed to concentrated) HIV epidemics: concurrent sexual partnerships." He further pointed out that "the latest UNAIDS annual report does not even mention concurrent partners or partner reduction, and the 2007 report of the Global Health Prevention Working Group barely notes it." And he concludes "the major prevention strategy emerging in the 1980s—the most-at-risk strategy—has been highly successful in helping contain concentrated epidemics with more modest funding."[6]

The Kinsey Connection

It is interesting to go back and review the run-up to the Stonewall era in the gay movement, known then as the "homophile" movement. One influential figure was Frank Kameny, a homosexual scientist who had been fired from a government job in the 1950s McCarthy era. Deciding that the government had "declared war" on him, he became a full-fledged gay rights activist, to the extent possible in those days. Less-radical homosexual activists had been trying to get someone within the medical/mental health establishment to acquiesce and push for reversing the long-held view of homosexuality as a disordered condition. "The prejudiced mind is not penetrated by information, and is not educable," said Kameny.[7] True, and applicable to both sides in the debate we continue to engage in today. Kameny dismissed the "experts" who disagreed with him and undertook his own PR campaign. Taking his lead from the black civil rights movement, as Mel White later would do in establishing Soulforce, he said, "I do not see the NAACP and CORE worrying about which chromosome and gene produced a black skin, or about the possibility of bleaching the Negro." Playing off the "Black is beautiful" slogan, Kameny—he would go on to run for Congress as an openly gay candidate in 1971—coined another: "Gay is good."[8] It is Kameny who takes credit for convincing us that 10 percent of the general population is homosexual. "I personally created the '10-percent figure' in late 1960 for use in my position to the U.S. Supreme Court, in my own case," he said in a letter to the *Washington Blade* on September 6, 2002. "The figure was based upon a reasonable and plausible, intentionally conservative and understated interpretation of the Kinsey data, which were the only statistics then available."

Ah, Kinsey. Social scientists have many a bone to pick with his research. Some sources maintain his data was more conservative than generally depicted—that he supposedly claimed only 4 percent of the adult male population and about 2 percent of females were exclusively homosexual. Kameny's arbitrary 10 percent figure, then, is overblown even by Kinseyan standards. It is Kinsey who gave the sexual continuum theory and the bisexuality movement their initial impetus. He claimed that as many as 37 percent of the male population have had at least one homosexual encounter. Of course, most of his sexual research subjects were prison inmates. The ones that weren't infants or children, that is.

Dr. Judith Reisman and Edward Eichel's 1990 book, *Kinsey, Sex, and Fraud: The Indoctrination of a People*, deconstructed Alfred Kinsey's research. A 1989 book entitled *AIDS: Sexual Behavior and Intravenous Drug Use*, from the National Academy of Science, originally supporting Kinsey's work, recanted:

> It has long been recognized that one of the greatest faults of the Kinsey research was the way in which the cases were selected; the sample is not representative of the entire U.S. population or of any definable group in the population. This fault limits the comparability and appropriateness of the Kinsey data as a basis for calculating the prevalence of any form of sexual conduct.[9]

More Kinsey bad news appeared in James H. Jones' 1997 book, *Alfred C. Kinsey: A Public/Private Life*:

> The man I came to know bore no resemblance to the canonical Kinsey. Anything but disinterested, he approached his work with missionary fervor. Kinsey loathed Victorian morality. ... He was determined to use science to strip human sexuality of its guilt and repression. He wanted to undermine traditional morality, to soften the rules of restraint. ... Kinsey was a crypto-reformer who spent his every waking hour attempting to change the sexual mores and sex offender laws of the United States.[10]

Hijacking the Mental Health System

As the 1960s and seventies progressed, the gay movement took on the militant, socialist character of the anti-war, anti-establishment, and feminist movements. In 1973, gay activists found their (somewhat reluctant) man inside the medical establishment. Dr. Robert Spitzer, pressured by the literal taking over of the American Psychiatric Association's convention that year by militant gays, spearheaded the move to eliminate homosexuality from the list of diagnosable mental disorders. This was another benchmark for gay rights—a revolution within the revolution—that set the stage for the gay cultural gains made in the three ensuing decades. Of course, 1973 was a banner year for anarchists as that was also the year of *Roe v. Wade,* the historic Supreme Court decision that found the right to privacy in the Constitution and formed another defining cultural and moral battle. Once the APA did an about-face—only roughly one-third of its members tacitly voiced approval through a later vote—other organizations within the medical establishment began to capitulate like dominoes and trumpet homosexuality as normal, acceptable behavior. Gay was good. Science had declared it so.

In their 2005 book, *Destructive Trends in Mental Health: The Well-Intentioned Path to Harm,* psychologists Nicholas Cummings (past president of the American Psychological Association) and Rogers Wright lament "the ascent of social activism over open-minded scientific inquiry and quality care in the current mental health establishment."[11] Cummings and Wright describe themselves as "lifelong liberal activists," so they are hardly conspiratorial conservative mouthpieces. Cummings was part of the first task force that championed the mental health needs of gays, lesbians, and bisexuals. However, the authors come out strong against the current direction of the mental health establishment when dealing with homosexuality:

In the current climate, it is inevitable that conflict arises among the various subgroups in the marketplace. For example, gay groups within the APA have repeatedly tried to persuade the association to adopt ethical standards that prohibit therapists from offering psychotherapeutic services designed to ameliorate "gayness" on the basis that such efforts are unsuccessful and harmful to the consumer. Psychologists who do not agree are termed homophobic. Such efforts are especially troubling because they abrogate the patient's right to choose the therapist and determine therapeutic goals. They also deny the reality of data demonstrating that psychotherapy can be effective in changing sexual preferences in patients who have a desire to do so.[12]

To its credit, the American Psychological Association did recently acknowledge through its Task Force on Appropriate Therapeutic Responses to Sexual Orientation that religiously mediated efforts toward sexual orientation change could be helpful for those whose same-sex attractions are incongruent with their faith or religious worldview. Still basically anti-change in philosophy, the APA nonetheless conceded that statistically significant numbers of people seeking help through faith-based counseling or support groups for unwanted same-sex attraction do move in a positive direction along the scale of change, or more readily accept celibacy as an option.

It is not just psychology and psychiatry that have been politically hijacked out of the medical establishment by gay activists. Medicaid has even paid for controversial sex-change ("reassignment") surgeries in some states, costing taxpayers as much as $85,000 per surgery. The state of Washington decided in 2006 to halt Medicaid funding of such surgeries at about the same time its state Supreme Court voted to uphold its voters' ban on gay marriage.[13]

I find it most intriguing that depression has become more and more medicalized as a clinical impairment over the past 30 years while homosexuality has become more normalized. Today, growing numbers in the medical community are realizing the mistake in taking sorrow, a necessary and even useful human condition, and trying to treat it medically and psychologically or mask it altogether. While some depression is clinical and related to other physical ailments, much of it is not. Taking the possible developmental and clear health-risk factors out of the homosexual medical literature for political expediency is as wrong as throwing open the pharmaceutical flood gates and enslaving untold numbers of depressed "patients" to drugs. To call homosexuality per se a "mental illness" when many on the GLBT spectrum appear otherwise normal, functional, and ostensibly happy, would clearly be a stretch in postmodern culture. But can we be sure there is no inherent pathology in homosexuality? Can we really declare normal a condition whose sexual behaviors run counter to every natural law mankind has long known and that is accompanied by some serious health risks? The medical establishment has an obligation, for the sake of public health if for no other reason, to closely examine its current positions on homosexuality. That jury remains out, weighing the evidence, popular sentiment and politics notwithstanding. Gay rights activists, of course, tend to turn purple with anger and cast their opponents in the most hateful terms when confronted with the unsavory facts. Extremists on the other side of the fence spit out their accusations with equal contempt.

After the medical establishment came on board with the gay movement, the public education system was the next target for gay propaganda. In 1987, the GLBT Educators Caucus was established within the liberal National Education Association (NEA). This opened the door for various gay-themed educational programs to enter the classroom, many being initially pushed in California, one of the gayest bellwether states. Staunch California conservatives came out swinging. They threatened to pull their children out of public schools and made their voices heard in boisterous school board meetings as they fought against blatant gay propaganda in the classroom. Christian child psychologist James Dobson began to urge his huge constituency of Focus on the Family radio program listeners to contact state representatives and voice their objections to questionable education policies and legislation that grew more prevalent into the nineties. The battle, often played out in the courts through legal challenges to controversial statutes, kept California's and other states' constitutional attorneys busy.

Creating Homophobia and "Suspect" Status

In 1989 (the year Kinsey was first debunked), a rather radical, if arcane, pro-gay book, *After the Ball: How America Will Conquer its Fear and Hatred of Gays in the 90's* by Marshall Kirk and Hunter Madsen, appeared. It advocated a tri-partite strategy for helping America to conquer its unsavory homophobia and to accept gay as normal: desensitize, jam, and convert the "bigots." The book has been widely misquoted, although why I cannot say. There is more than enough incriminating material in it without rearranging it. The book could have benefited from some rewriting, since the two authors seemed enamored with stilted phrasing. They suggested a massive, but unrealistic advertising campaign to help secure their objectives. They considered that they would be accused of "exchanging one false stereotype for another equally false." They maintain, however, that "it makes no difference that the ads are lies; not to us, because we're using them to ethically good effect. ..."

The authors spend a good deal of the book pointing out the ways in which the gay community is a house of cards. They maintain the gay community is ruled by "too many fiefdoms." Interestingly, Kirk and Madsen claim there is (was) a "permanent identity crisis" in the gay community, that gays "compartmentalize their notion of self into two halves, like a split personality—part gay and part non-gay—and hold that the latter part is really more representative." The authors discuss the factors that "discourage the we-feeling among gays," such as the social chasm between gay males and females and the discomfort their forced political intimacy engenders. They also point out the division within the male gay camp, and call it the "R-types" (those manly gays who can pass themselves off as straight) vs. the "Q-types" or "homosexuals on display." Despite all these problems, Kirk and Madsen propose a propagandistic image makeover for gays, though they seem to question from the outset that it will work. "Our effect is achieved without reference to facts, logic, or proof," they state.

Whether this was an organized strategy for social change or the historical convergence of pro-gay trends and attitudes, today we see that the methods for bringing about critical changes in public attitudes and policies related to gay rights have played out better than Kirk, Madsen, and other activists could have imagined. The assertions Kirk and Madsen made that: (1) "Gays don't feel an urgent need to liberate themselves and transform their society by eliminating homohatred," and (2) "Gays don't see themselves as members of a valuable and cohesive cultural group worth fighting for," today are laughable.[14] The gay ethos now pervades institution after institution. It has taken biblical truth captive and is redefining our cultural mores, while many in the Church fret and fume or are stymied by paralysis of analysis. Not wanting to either appear intolerant of their gay brothers or sisters or incur the wrath of their fellow truth-dividing, Bible-reading

Christians, many just pretend not to notice anything is amiss. Others have leapt over the transom and have come to equate love and compassion with full acceptance of homosexuality, taking sin right out of the equation.

Since 1972, when gay rights activists first marched on Washington, D.C., demanding to be recognized as a bona-fide minority group—and even more so after they marched again in 1993—their social change tent, Church or no Church, has grown enormously. Here is a basic run-down of both federal- and state-level gains for gay rights:

Affirmative Action/Minority Status for Gays:

More and more cities with gay rights legislation in force (San Francisco and Denver were two of the first) have instituted affirmative action goals for gay city employees.

Federal Grants for Gay-as-Normal Sex Education Curriculum:

From 1993-1995, nearly $38 million in federal grant money was given to promote gay-related "health studies" in America's public schools. In 2006 and 2007, California made sweeping pro-gay changes in curriculum and public education policies, and other states have followed.

Federal Discrimination Aid for Gay Advocacy Organizations:

By 1982, an exhaustive study had revealed that the federal government was providing 58 percent of funding for all American homosexual advocacy organizations. It is commonly known that per-case federal spending on AIDS research (which here in the United States has a skewed benefit to gay males) far exceeds spending on research for other diseases producing comparable or much larger mortality rates.

Non-Discrimination Against Gays in Insurance Coverage:

Gay rights lobbyists were largely responsible for AIDS being declared a "disability" under the Americans with Disabilities Act (1991). Thus, AIDS has become the world's first 100-percent fatal disease to be protected by "minority rights," thus making non-discrimination against AIDS sufferers mandatory for employers and insurers.

Child Custody, Adoption, Visitation, Foster-Parenting Rights for Gays:

In November 1995, the New York Supreme Court, noting "fundamental changes" in the American family, ruled (4-3) that neither heterosexual nor homosexual couples have to be married to adopt a child together. In July 1996, the Washington, D.C. Court of Appeals ruled that homosexual unmarried couples in "committed relationships" are permitted to adopt children under District law. Other states have followed suit. A Vermont court declared in 2003 that an unrelated, non-adoptive, lesbian civil union partner was a "parent" to the child born to the other partner. These are the tip of the iceberg.

Legalization of Same-Sex Marriages:

Hawaii was the first state whose Supreme Court heard a gay marriage case in 1993. The court reinstated an earlier lawsuit by three gay couples that had been thrown out by a circuit court judge. As public policy analyst Whitney Galbraith observed, "The key to the [Hawaii Supreme Court's] decision [regarding same-sex "marriage"] was the court's declaring same-sex couples to be part of a 'suspect class.'" If gays are indeed part of a suspect class, they should not be denied such privileges as marriage either, the argument goes.[15] Though Hawaii subsequently passed a sate constitutional amendment authorizing its legislature to ban gay marriage (which it did), the prior court rulings there opened the door for other states to pursue similar pro-gay-marriage options. Hawaii's legislature authorized civil unions in 2010, but the governor refused to sign the bill into law, viewing it as "marriage by another name."

In November 2003, the Massachusetts Supreme Judicial Court became the first in the nation to rule in favor of gay marriage. In May 2008, California's Supreme Court joined suit, but its decision was overturned by voters six months later and then reinstated by a federal judge. Four additional states (Connecticut, New Hampshire, Vermont, and Iowa) and the District of Columbia have since codified same-sex marriage, in one way or another. Maine's legislature passed a gay-marriage bill in 2009, but voters turned it back, as California had done the previous year. New Jersey recognizes same-sex civil unions (Illinois is headed there) while Oregon, Washington, California, Colorado, Nevada, Hawaii, Wisconsin, and Maryland currently have domestic partnership laws similar to civil unions.

Syndicated columnist Mike Royko, not exactly a conservative, wrote more than a decade ago that gays were hardly the oppressed minority they claim to be. They are arguably less so today:

> [Homosexuals'] difficulties look pretty meager compared to those of the poor, the uneducated, and the unemployed. It may be a politically incorrect risk to disagree with those hundreds of thousands of homosexual demonstrators who gathered in Washington, but, no, this decade will not be 'The Gay '90s.' That's because there are so many people in this country who have far worse problems than do homosexual men and lesbians.[16]

The Little Rainbow Schoolhouse

Edging ever closer to its "gaytopia," California led up to its landmark 2008 gay marriage ruling with several earlier banner legislative years for gay rights. "The 2005-2006 legislative session in California broke the record for the most lesbian, gay, bisexual, and transgender rights bills ever passed by a state legislature in our nation's history," touted Geoff Kors, executive director of Equality California, which brought the lawsuit that state justices heard before ruling in favor of gay marriage.[17] In 2006, the California legislature was compelled to vote on a bill, introduced by openly gay Democratic State Senator Sheila Kuehl of Santa Monica, that would mandate school children be given "age-appropriate" and positive instruction about the contributions of "people who are lesbian, gay, bisexual or transgender, to the economic, political, and social development of California. ..." Gov. Schwarzenegger made good on his vow to veto even a revised version of the bill (political posturing in an election year, perhaps?). At the height of the controversy, almost 90,000 faxes opposing the bill were sent from pro-family Californians to the offices of state assemblymen in one 24-hour period, according to Focus on the Family, which led the pro-family charge.[18]

That bill had another stealth companion that managed to work its way through the California legislature along party lines and was signed into law by Schwarzenegger in the summer of 2006. It gives the state superintendent of public instruction the power to withhold state funds for any school district deemed to be discriminating against gays, and scrutinizes classroom instruction, Big Brother-style. Dan Walters, State Capitol columnist for *The* Sacramento Bee, wrote of this move, "Treating all people, regardless of sexual orientation, with absolute equality is one thing. In seeking such equality in marriages and other fields, gay rights advocates, it could be said, are occupying the moral high ground.

There's nothing moral about legally mandating propaganda of any kind in the classroom."[19] While Walters' statement about gay activists owning the "moral high ground" is improperly accepted as axiomatic among most members of the press, his aptly expressed sentiment about propaganda in the classroom is not gaining traction in liberal-leaning California.

In the fall of 2007, Schwarzenegger was fighting two firestorms—the literal blazing inferno that burned a half-million acres of the state and the backlash from a bill long desired by gay rights activists that he finally signed into law: SB 777. The bill prohibits anything "discriminatory" from being said in California classrooms about homosexuality. The implication is that it will be mainstreamed as normal behavior into curriculum. As California goes, so goes the nation, historically.

Many California families, predictably, have begun a new wave of defections from public schools, and even from the near-bankrupt state, itself. Gov. Schwarzenegger chose not to fight the state Supreme Court's ruling on gay marriage, despite its overturning of the people's 61-percent-majority mandate in 2000's Proposition 22 vote. The people had the final say again, however.

Political Expediency and Our Children

There is little doubt that the exponential growth of school Gay-Straight Alliance (GSA) clubs has impacted the rush for teens to identify as gay, lesbian, bisexual, transgender, or "questioning," regardless of how well-intentioned these clubs may be or how much actual anti-gay bullying goes on in schools. School bullying hit the national agenda as a problem sorely needing to be confronted in the fall of 2010 after a series of heart-wrenching student suicides, some from gay or perceived-gay youth. Confused students are encouraged to find their label from among those on the GLBTQ spectrum. Popular youth fiction (such as the book

Misfits) and other media influences through MTV and network programming aimed at teens are contributing to the problem. In 2007, we saw the first-ever transgender high school students running for prom queen/king in California (one—a "drag queen" looking lovelier than some of the real girls—even won). This wave has not yet begun to crest. Are kids just thinking this is amusing and harmless counter-culture stuff? At least one lawsuit against a school district was filed by a female student who says she was humiliated when, among other things, only a handful of students showed up at her high school's alternative prom. It was organized for the gay-identified students who were barred from attending the official one as same-sex couples.

A large youth problem yet to be dealt with is just coming to light. Recent studies are finding that gay-identified teens, and especially girls who say they are bisexual, are at much higher risk for depression and suicide than previously known. One such study came from the University of British Columbia's McCreary Research Centre, which found that bisexual teen girls are nearly four times as likely to attempt suicide as straight girls and three times as likely as gay teen boys.[20] Bisexuality, or experimentation with it, is clearly on the rise among teens, especially girls. It is common knowledge among students, and my own daughters, while still in high school—a Christian school—confirmed it existed among their peers.

Another noteworthy study published in the *American Journal of Preventive Medicine* in October 2005 found that risky behavior in the form of sex, alcohol, and drugs causes the most teen depression.[21] Conventional wisdom had thought just the opposite—that sex and drugs were forms of self-medication for already-depressed teens. Commenting on the study in a November 30, 2005 article for *The Christian Post* and other publications, Dr. Warren Throckmorton, professor of psychology at Grove City College in Pennsylvania, said that depression may be "the new sexually transmitted disease" among teens. The two-year study, authored by Dr. Denise Hallfors of the Pacific Institute for Research and Evaluation in Chapel Hill, North Carolina, showed that girls experimenting with sex of any kind were three times more likely to be depressed than those who abstain from all sexual activity (12 percent versus 4 percent). For sexually promiscuous teen girls, the results were shocking: 44 percent of girls with multiple sexual partners during the study period experienced depression.[22] Hallfors concluded, "Parents, educators, and health practitioners now have even more reason to be concerned about teen risk behaviors and to take action about alcohol, drugs, and sex."[23]

"Morally Straight"?

Gay rights activists have taken aim at any institution they believe is vulnerable to their threats and "bullying" tactics, and that now even includes churches or anything remotely para-church. They have set their sights on the Boy Scouts of America with a vengeance, attempting repeatedly to force the century-old organization to allow gay scouts and gay scoutmasters to join—a violation of its moral code. The Scouts win some and lose some. In an ironic turn of events following a lawsuit filed on behalf of a Christian Good News Club in a California school district, claiming the club should be allowed free use of school district facilities because the Boy Scouts were afforded that courtesy, the court ruled against both organizations and began charging the Scouts a rent fee. "Now there will be no discriminatory treatment between evangelists and Boy Scouts," Jose Gonzales, an attorney for the San Diego Unified School District, was reported as saying in *The Union-Tribune.* [24]

The Boy Scouts won two prior legal battles in San Diego, being allowed to continue leasing land for a camp in historic Balboa

Park, and an aquatic center on Fiesta Island, while Philadelphia, the "City of Brotherly Love," handed them what initially had appeared to be a staggering defeat. There, where the Scouts' third-largest council, the Cradle of Liberty Council, has had its headquarters for 80 of the venerable organization's 100 years, the openly gay city solicitor and other activists tried to force the Scouts out of the building they built with their own hands in 1923 but had given back to the city in an agreement to lease the offices for $1 a year "in perpetuity." The city found a way to get around the U.S. Supreme Court's 2000 ruling in support of the Scouts' right to exclude openly gay scouts and scoutmasters from membership and to make the Scouts pay for it, since they own the property the historic building sits on. They sought to make the Philly council pay the fair market value in rent for their building of $200,000 per year or vacate. The Scouts filed a lawsuit and, after more than two years, the case was finally decided in their favor.

"With violence on the rise, you'd think a program teaching integrity to 40,000 boys would be the last thing to go. But this city insists on putting political correctness first," lamented a Family Research Council radio commentary, when the news of the Scouts' Philly battle first broke.[25] An editorial appearing in the online edition of *Investor's Business Daily* ("Scouts Honor," Oct. 19, 2007) asked, "Isn't it hypocritical, though, to be intolerant in the name of tolerance, to say that it's wrong to disapprove of the lifestyles of others but OK to condemn the religious and moral beliefs of others?" The editorial further stated, "If America is about anything, it's about the right to hold beliefs and views with which others disagree, the right to express and act on those views, and the right to freely associate with others holding similar views. That's not bigotry; it's true diversity." Alas, many gay activists and their media champions don't get that.

Ironically, one of the amicus briefs supporting the Boy Scouts was filed by members of Gays and Lesbians for Individual Liberty. They pointed out that "infringement of the freedom of association would harm all Americans, but it would particularly threaten the welfare of gay and lesbian Americans." Were they worried they might be forced to allow heterosexuals into their group or merely upholding the same standard for all?

While disgruntled gays have many legitimate complaints of mistreatment or discrimination, creating homo-hysteria or using hyperbole to inflate their woes will only earn them derision. Not every institution they dislike is fomenting homophobia or "spiritual violence." Some are, to be sure. Others are just repeating old, worn talking points. It is incumbent on the Church and Christian organizations to take the lead in seeking to diffuse this crisis. What many see as an era of gay proliferation that has gone too far others see as an opportunity to bind old wounds and find a place of peaceful co-existence in which both sides seek to understand each other in the light of Scripture. God will judge what is in our hearts. He expects more from us than mere good intentions.

Two

Ideological Rift Within the Church: Revolution vs. Regeneration

Shortly before his death in 1984, evangelical theologian and apologist Francis Schaeffer said, "Tell me what the world is saying today and I'll tell you what the Church will be saying seven years from now."[1] The world is speaking loudly and clearly. Sadly, the Church is following suit, and Shaeffer's seven-year window has been condensed in the twenty-first century. While many hide their heads in the sand, the Church is under assault by postmodernist and secularist groups whose tactics are a subtle—and sometimes not-so-subtle—form of totalitarian coercion. We need to be clear that not all gays and lesbians fall into this category, but some do. Their influence is clearly felt. The Church is an essential pillar of the culture that many gay activists covet for their own. To the extent that the Church is slouching toward apostasy, such militants already own it. The larger gay community has a love-hate relationship with Christendom, and we, the Church, are partly to blame for that.

In the fall of 1960, while the infantile gay revolution was

still trying to organize, Nikita Khrushchev famously pounded his shoe on a United Nations podium to drive home his threat of a Soviet takeover of America: "We will bury you!" Do radical gay rights organizations similarly desire to bury the Church of Jesus Christ in what we may call a subversive, cultural cold war? Ben Patrick Johnson, a board member for the gay rights group Equality California, eerily echoed the Soviet premier's infamous warning as he railed against the Capital Resource Institute, a family-defending Christian organization in a May 2007 e-mail.[2] Khrushchev, referring back to his comment at a later date, is reported to have said, "Of course, we will not bury you with a shovel. Your own working class will bury you." That is an equally chilly reminder to both Church and State that either is capable of falling to its own political correctness, if it conforms to the secular or quasi-Christian thinking invading it.

No Bridge Over These Troubled Waters

By 2006, Mel White's Soulforce—the standard bearer for the Christian gay movement—had been handed over to the next generation, for the most part. The organization may have had some genuine and laudable desires in its earlier days to bridge the gap between straight and gay Christendom. At least it helped spawn some unheralded attempts at such. But an underlying bitterness, an ache that is hard to disguise sometimes, seems to propel Soulforce forward. The group is known for its Equality Rides of gay and lesbian college students and a few other supporters to Christian colleges and military academies. Members also have participated in sit-ins at military recruiting centers around the country, protesting the U.S. Armed Forces' Clinton-era "Don't Ask, Don't Tell" policy, now on the verge of being rolled back. In 2008, Soulforce targeted mega-churches in the interval between Mothers and Fathers Days with the biblically antithetical message that homosexual "families" are allowed in God's plan, too. No longer having Jerry Falwell to target as a principle adversary—one has to imagine that was, in part, because of White's previous friendship with Falwell—Soulforce activists continued to speak out against James Dobson and Focus on the Family for spreading "spiritual violence" against gays. Today, Dobson is decoupling himself in retirement from FOTF somewhat, and has a new radio program with his son Ryan that may find itself at odds with the gentler image FOTF has been projecting under new leadership. What rankles Christian gays most is the message Dobson and company long preached in the name of "truth-in-love" to struggling homosexuals and their families, especially through the 12-year-old Love Won Out conferences. That message is that "change"—a regenerated heart leading to a transformed life and varying degrees of healed sexuality—is possible and that significant numbers of those formerly in bondage to same-sex attractions are living testaments to it.

Love Won Out recently moved under the umbrella of Exodus International, the Christian referral organization for those seeking to better understand or move beyond homosexuality. Some prefer the term post-gay to ex-gay to describe those on this particular journey because ex-gay too easily implies a complete and radical change in sexual orientation, and fewer people are coming to believe such a thing is possible. Radical, nonreligious (or so it appears) gays largely carry the flag for the gay rights movement. They are increasingly flanked, however, by gay-affirming churches, by gay Christians, and by some vocal "ex-ex-gays," or those who attempted change, mostly through Exodus-sanctioned ministries, and decided transformation was not possible for them. Early activists likely could not have imagined such an alliance.

While the medical and mental health establishments already are highly influenced by pro-gay sympathy and public, taxpayer-funded education is on the way to being the second cultural pillar under gay ownership, the Church has not truly capitulated—yet. Mainline denominations have been under heavy attack and some have fallen, however. The Episcopal Church, part of the worldwide Anglican Communion, was the first domino to go down, in large part. Rev. Eugene Robinson of New Hampshire became the first openly gay Episcopal bishop to be consecrated in 2003. In 2006, the church narrowly elected Rev. Katharine Jefferts Schori as its presiding bishop. Not only does she validate the Christian feminist movement for many, but she also is decidedly pro-gay in her views and public statements. Roberts was joined in 2010 by an openly lesbian bishop in California, Rev. Mary Glasspool.

Anglican journalist David Virtue, in a June 2006 commentary, pointed out the hypocrisy of "progressive" Episcopalians and their "inclusion" myth: "For over 40 years we have watched as traditionalists have been denied acceptance to seminaries and to holy orders because they did not toe the 'progressive' line and they have been made to feel unwelcome, isolated, and alienated out of their parishes by the so-called 'tolerance' of the progressives." Not only have these liberal church leaders been intolerant and anything but inclusive in their actions toward fellow Episcopalians, but they also "have used the media for their own political ends, making orthodox priests look like fundamentalists and worse, when all the orthodox ever wanted to do was behave like classical Anglicans, a tradition that goes back to Thomas Cranmer," said Virtue.[3]

One of the most succinctly stated, commonsense Christian commentaries on postmodern sexuality I have seen was offered by Rev. Tim Holt, senior pastor of Seacoast Vineyard Church in the Faith and Ethics column appearing in the op-ed pages of Myrtle Beach, South Carolina's *The Sun News* in July 2006. Holt had this to say:

God does not bend his will or ways to accommodate our inclinations. We must, as uncomfortable as it may be, begin to allow ourselves to be lovingly bent toward a posture that reflects God's will.

If indeed certain persons are inclined toward same-sex attraction because of heredity, then I would see that as a result of our fallenness [sinful nature]. ... We all must learn to live within the confines, at least as followers of Jesus, of where God is leading us.

Bottom line, we cannot as followers of Jesus allow ourselves to create theology based on our own desire to accommodate those we care about.

Does that mean we refuse to respect, love, and care for others who fit into this discussion? Absolutely not! Can we love, serve, and at the same time confront and help one another walk out of our broken areas and into God's will? I certainly hope so. That's the Church I love and want to be a part of.[4]

I believe the above view resonates with significant numbers of evangelical Christians, an oft-caricatured and misunderstood part of the Church, now even divided to some extent within as conservatives and liberals debate back and forth about what the term evangelical means. Each group tends to tar the other with a broad and sometimes-malicious brush. We are still a long way from the Ephesians 4 unified body of believers Paul exhorted the Church to be. By the way, check out Paul's use of the Greek word *anechomenoi* (tolerating or forbearing), clearly implying patience in its context in Ephesians 4:2-3. Paul was exhorting Christians to be patient with or tolerant of one another's weaknesses, for the sake of unity. In fact, our patience is to reflect how God deals with us. Paul used the Greek word *Anoche* in Romans 2:4, translated tolerance or forbearance, in reference to God's patience. But the perfectly legitimate word "tolerance" today to many has come to mean acceptance of beliefs contrary to our own, even if they espouse tenets antithetical to biblical teaching. Patience implies tactful restraint rather than acquiescence. Further, the mainstream media, being largely biblically illiterate, cannot differentiate between bickering "churchiness" and real doctrinal disparity within the body. Jesus Christ is coming back to judge his Church and all the earth, of course. The book of Revelation, supported by Old and New Testament exegeses, makes this clear.

The sentiment expressed by Rev. Holt is almost never seen in the media as being an expression of conservative, compassionate Christianity. Yet, this exact attitude reigns inside the churches that welcome struggling homosexuals within their congregations and counseling ministries as they seek to lovingly hold them accountable and disciple them on the road to wholeness. Other more "progressive" churches believe their congregations should be fully accepting of their GLBT parishioners rather than lovingly compelling them to repent, as they should for all sinners in their midst. Gay believers long to worship in both atmospheres, but many will not even set foot in a conservative church. I have heard tales of oppression, outings, and congregational censuring of gays in some of these churches that make me shake my head in sorrow. Of course we must give the entire gospel message, "offensive" truth and all, to those we really care about. No one coming to a church should expect not to hear about sin and repentance. But must we force gays to do what to them amounts to eating a scorpion, stinger first? We add insult to injury by then winking at other "more normal" sinners in our midst. Oh, we Christians have perfected a smugness all our own.

It is difficult to get our finger on the real pulse of the Church, even in the U.S. these days. Research organizations like the Barna Group and the Pew Forum on Religion and Public Life attempt to measure the beliefs and practices within major religious and nonreligious groups, as well as among the various denominations of both Catholic and Protestant church-goers or identifiers. Their surveys are instructive and probably fairly approximate the true picture. It is not an encouraging one, in many respects. While certain self-identifying traits among those who claim to be Christian may be predictable and common to most subgroups (i.e., church attendance or prayer), others have become less so. Even among evangelicals—those who typically accept the absolute authority of Scripture and Jesus as the resurrected Son of God—a gradual creep of worldliness has closed the gap between believers and nonbelievers in behaviors and habits. Divorce, depression, all manner of addictions, adultery, abuse—all these show up in Christian households to a similar degree that they do in nonreligious households.

Naturally, a growing nationwide sympathy for homosexuals as social and even religious outcasts is bound to infiltrate the Church, whose population mirrors general society more and more. The form that takes in attitudes and ministry outreach varies from church to church. Can we be "set apart" as believers, clearly distinguishable from the world, and still demonstrate mercy toward our gay brothers and sisters? What does this look like for the church that wants to reflect all of Christ? A cultural shift toward worldly mores has left many churches little with which to attract the lost (should they even care to) except for entertainment-driven services and a sense of warm and fuzzy community, with often-mushy doctrine. Many churches have become increasingly feelings-oriented. Church used to be the place to go to experience God's penetrating and convicting spirit through strong, biblically centered preaching that was meant to drive us to our knees in repentance and spiritual renewal. Today, it is more often a fraternity where more and more biblically illiterate folks go to be uplifted or to fellowship with other "good" people—like-minded folks who don't want their feelings hurt or to see the feelings of others bruised with talk of sin and repentance. Exactly where does that leave the necessary, life-changing "godly sorrow" Paul spoke of in his epistles to the early churches? What much of the Church has become is not the way Christ intended us to be. It is all right for us to be intolerant of some things. We are just not meant to see people as disposable in the process.

As a Marine veteran, I see an all-too-obvious parallel in the ways the various military services are organized and populated. The Marines recruit on the never-changing philosophy that war is going to be a reality and the toughest of training is the only way to prepare. "Semper Fidelis"—always faithful—is the Corps' motto. Every Marine is a rifleman first. Their ranks are small in comparison to the other services, which have struggled with various recruiting philosophies, all meant to emphasize equal opportunity or adventure. History speaks for itself. As the military is a closed society of necessity, the Church is to be set apart. This poignant truth was never clearer than in World War II Germany, where Dietrich Bonhoeffer and other like-minded pastors inspired a Christian movement called the Confessing Church to stand up to Hitler and the Nazis and preach truth while the religious establishment cowered and became a puppet of the Third Reich.

Playing Tug-of-War with Jesus

The word "compassion" is appropriated by both sides in the Christian version of the gay culture tug-of-war, as each tries to pull supporters over to its turf by casting itself as the only real purveyor of compassion. Liberal theologians and Christian gays claim Jesus would not condemn homosexual behavior as sinful and that

God mysteriously created some people with the inclination to be attracted to the same sex. One gay activist, who is particularly wary of the ex-gay movement, told me in an e-mail exchange:

> Christ's definition (of love) was about treating others the way you want to be treated. Christ always described love for others in a very physical way—not a reproaching-sin-and-protecting-traditions kind of way. He thinks love is feeding the hungry, visiting the sick, and clothing the naked. His idea of neighbor is the Samaritan—the social outcast whose version of religion was in direct conflict with the Jews. His definition of outreach was socializing with those that the religious leaders considered sinners—not preaching, not condemning, but socializing.

Of course, that is only a partial theological and sociological assessment. It implies a moral high ground that only the liberally minded possess with regard to Christian ethics. It is a one-dimensional view of Christ—the touchy feely side with which progressives easily identify. The moral and intellectual superiority that certain gay activists project is an affront to thinking people of faith, just as Christian hypocrisy is an affront to gays. Elizabeth Birch, past executive director of the Human Rights Campaign (HRC), a gay political organization with some clout, has asserted: "[Homosexuals] hold sacred seeds. ...[T]o be gay, lesbian, bisexual, or struggle around gender is literally a gift from God and we have an enormous amount to teach this nation"[5]

Actually, I may shock Birch by agreeing with her that the struggle faced by those experiencing same-sex attraction can, indeed, be viewed as a gift from God. However, she misses the point of the struggle. It is an opportunity for us to allow God to demonstrate his love and sovereign will in and through us by helping us to grow in our faith as we overcome rather than acquiesce to the problem and redefine that rebellion as God's will.

Traditionally, most theologians and rank-and-file Christians understood that Jesus didn't come to the earth merely to "socialize" with sinners and outcasts and people who were sick or oppressed. He came to seal a covenant between God and man, to restore the fellowship that was broken with our Creator when sin came into the world. He came to be the propitiation, the perfect sacrificial lamb, the only way out of the bondage of sin. He came to heal, but he also came with a laser-like truth that would sunder earthly allegiances and divide families. He came to "fulfill" the law, not "abolish" it. Yes, Jesus did reproach sin. He hated it, as well as its author. Yet, he loved sinners. That's all of us. He understood that "the spirit is willing, but the body is weak" (Matthew 26:41). He warned against hypocrisy, and his words cut to the quick those who would call themselves spiritual leaders.

It is true that Jesus nowhere in recorded Scripture specifically condemns the practice of homosexuality, but absence of proof is not proof of absence, as the adage goes. The gospel record does not show Jesus condemning every specific sinful, unwholesome practice known to man. Many things he did and said were not recorded, according to John's gospel. It is logical to conclude that he never bothered to deal with every individual sin because he did not need to. The Old Testament had already condemned them, either explicitly or by implication. The Jewish culture of that day would have had an acute knowledge of the sinfulness of homosexual practices. In fact, Jesus clearly makes this point in the Sermon on the Mount (Matthew 5:17-20, specifically). Matthew 5:19 is a particularly strong injunction against anyone who "breaks one of the least of these commandments and teaches others to do the same." In Matthew 19:3-9, Jesus said, "Haven't you read that at the beginning the Creator 'made them male and female,' and said, 'For this reason a man will leave his father and mother and be united to his wife, and the two will become one flesh'? So they are no longer two, but one. Therefore what God has joined together, let man not separate."

We cannot know how those who were inclined toward homosexuality in Jesus' day compare with those who struggle with it or fully accept it in themselves today. Do we view it largely the same in both cultural periods? Solomon told us there is "nothing new under the sun." Human desires and sin cannot have changed much from then to now. Culture has, of course.

A marvelous expression of Christ-like compassion—with a good dose of biblical truth—toward the homosexual mindset comes from Dr. Gordon Hugenberger, pastor of Park Street Church in Boston:

> ... God made us, and Christ redeemed us and now we belong to Him twice over. So He has every right to tell me that even things that might feel very natural and pleasurable to me (like pride and selfishness) in fact displease Him. If God's Word seems to suggest this with respect to homosexual acts, while we need to go the extra mile to stress our love and respect for our homosexual brothers and sisters (and go the extra mile in protecting them from harassment, prejudice, discrimination in public housing, education, and employment, etc.), we need to be equally careful not to do them the unkindness of implying that the Bible is less clear than it is.[6]

When gay Christian leaders hijack biblical truth for their own humanistic designs, they are rightly opposed by those within the Church who know better, even if they articulate it poorly in many instances. This opposition never ought to condemn our gay brothers and sisters, but rather seek to illuminate their path—the path of truth and life found in God's Word. How could we love them and not do this? How could we love the rest of the Body and not instruct it and safeguard it by rebuking what is wrong, to include hypocritical, singling-out "truth-attacks" on gays and lesbians? It is a fact that significant numbers of men and women who struggle with their homosexual desires want to change. Ironically, they have had to leave certain churches and attend others because their former churches seemed to welcome them when they identified themselves as homosexual, but as soon as they wanted God's help to change, they felt rejected and isolated. That should no more be the case than gay-identified people facing hateful persecution from within the Church. No one is excluded from being our "neighbor," regardless of his or her beliefs or behaviors.

Even though the gay (and generally postmodern) revolution now extends to the Church, Jesus said the "gates of hell" would not prevail against his Bride, so those who try to pervert the Church in any way cannot fully succeed. They will cull out those who were already sliding toward apostasy. Sadly, they also will take with them untold numbers of vulnerable, confused people who have no clear understanding of Christian doctrines and godly truth. The faithful remnant will remain. How many will be in that remnant and how affective will it be in the prophetic "last days"? Only God knows. The curse from man's original fall consigned the future Church to being a narrow but still-powerful force. The farther we go from the garden, the more self-centered and godless we become unless we accept the simple truth of Jesus' redemption. Christ fully expects his Church to engage in this war, to defend the faith and stand in every gap in the battle lines.

What is the high ground every Christian must seek to occupy? The mighty fortress built on the two foundational God-given laws of old, reiterated by Christ in the New Testament: to "love the Lord your God "with all your heart ... soul ... and mind ... and "your neighbor as yourself" (Matthew 22:37-40). No one who carries out the first commandment can fail in the second. Jesus takes it a step further, however, and tells us that our "enemy" is also our neighbor: "[L]ove your enemies and pray for those who persecute you ... (Matthew 5:44)." This kind of love is a powerful tool for reconciliation, which is preceded by conviction in one's spirit.

Religious Liberties Under Fire

The cultural/spiritual war, a large front of which is related to gay rights, extends the globe over. One example is in Great Britain, where a push for liberal gay rights laws has had many people up in arms. A November 2006 poll showed 72 percent of Brits believe gay rights laws "should be applied selectively so as to ensure that people with strong religious beliefs are not forced to act against their conscience." According to Thomas Cordrey of the Lawyers' Christian Fellowship, the organization that conducted the poll, "The proposed Sexual Orientation Regulations display a startling contradiction. They are introduced under the Equality Act and yet with the same sweep of the brush that creates a right to non-discrimination on the grounds of sexual orientation, they discriminate heavily against Christians by forcing them to promote and assist homosexual practice contrary to the clear teaching of the Bible. It is hard to avoid the conclusion that the Government believes the right to equality is somehow weaker for someone who holds a religious belief."[7]

Canada also has seen its share of oppression of Christians who profess a biblical belief in homosexual behavior as sinful. Two conservative North American Christian news websites,

Canada's LifeSiteNews and America's OneNewsNow, have reported extensively on threats against religious liberty by activist gays and attorneys against Christians in Canada and other parts of the international community. "By redefining traditional sexual morality as bigotry, the sexual revolutionaries are using the law to assail the rights of speech, association, and religion of anyone who disagrees with them," said the Media Research Center's senior editor, Brian Fitzpatrick, in an op-ed piece after investigating this troublesome trend. "Using 'sexual orientation' statutes and hate crimes laws, they are attempting to silence anybody who believes that homosexuality is a sin, not an acceptable alternative 'lifestyle,'" Fitzpatrick wrote.[8] What galled him almost as much as the affronts to religious liberty was the giant void in mainstream news coverage of these events, which also include one infamous case prosecuted against an American political journalist over an excerpt from a book on Islamic affairs published in *Maclean's* magazine. An investigator for Canada's national commission starkly summed it up: "Freedom of speech is an American concept, so I don't give it any value."[9] If American values can be so easily dismissed in North America, how soon might biblical Christian values go the same way? It already may be happening.

The Canadian Human Rights Commission, with various regional tribunals, has won most if not all cases it has brought against defendants accused of violating its code. Quoting Scripture citing homosexuality as a sin can be a hate crime in Canada, even for preachers of the gospel. Just ask Father Alphonse de Valk, whose case came before Canada's HRC. "Father defended the [Catholic] Church's teaching on marriage during Canada's same-sex 'marriage' debate, quoting extensively from the Bible, the Catechism of the Catholic Church, and Pope John Paul II's encyclicals," according to canon lawyer and Catholic journalist Peter Vere.[10] A similar case against Canadian evangelical pastor

Stephen Boissoin, who wrote a letter to the editor of an Alberta newspaper in defense of traditional marriage, resulted in a $5,000 fine. That ruling was later overturned. The Church is facing attacks of conscience here in the U.S., as well. Massachusetts compelled the Catholic Church to end its adoption program when it demanded that a Catholic agency allow same-sex couples to adopt children under the care of the church. The Lutheran Church-Missouri Synod is under similar fire in Illinois.

Here in the freedom-loving U.S., we are far from immune to the trend toward religious freedom or free-speech violations in dust-ups between gay rights activists and Christians. During the Proposition 8 campaign in California that asked voters to restore the traditional definition of marriage in the state, many witnessed on TV some horrific behavior by protesting gays, with angry outbursts and physical attacks directed at Christians gathered at rallies staged by both sides in the marriage debate. Reports of public harassment or intimidation aimed at supporters of Proposition 8 surfaced after voters passed it.

Perhaps the most infamous discrimination dispute between Christians and gay activists to date was the case of "the Philadelphia eleven" from Repent America, who were arrested and jailed for 21 hours in 2004 for street-preaching and alleged agitation at Outfest, a gay pride celebration in Philadelphia. The group was charged with three felonies and five misdemeanors. All the charges were eventually dismissed, as was a lawsuit Repent America later brought against the Outfest organizers and the Philadelphia police. Both sides appeared to have been confrontational, but a judge ruled that those organizing such events have the right to exclude outsiders. Is the First Amendment right to freedom of assembly in danger of being discarded, however? The judge in this case ruled from a precedent that was intended to address freedom of association, an altogether different dispute, and does not involve a constitutional right. Of course, one can dispute the effectiveness of Christian street-witnessing tactics at gay events. "Homosexual sinners repent" messages are like rubbing salt in a wound to most gays.

Martyrdom for the Gay Cause

While the news of the 1969 Stonewall riots took a while to filter outside the gay community and to this day is not common public knowledge, a much later event that propelled the gay cause onto the world stage was the 1998 beating death of Matthew Shepard, a 21-year-old gay student at the University of Wyoming. The brutal assault of Shepard by two men he met in a bar, which led to his death several days later, was initially deemed a "hate crime." Unsubstantiated rumors and pro-gay sentiment fanned the flames of anger against anyone and everyone who was not on the gay rights bandwagon at the time. While gay men and women long had been the occasional victims of violent crimes because someone disliked their sexual orientation, this crime galvanized the gay community as never before. It was exploited to the point of gay activists finally seeing passed in late 2009 hate-crimes legislation that included sexual orientation—named after Shepard—even though the anti-gay motive was later found to be highly suspect, and the media minimized facts pointing to Shepard's own questionable character and actions.

It was easy to sympathize with Shepard and his family, regardless of one's beliefs about homosexuality. His death was senseless and tragic, and was rightly condemned by many people not connected with the gay rights movement. Nevertheless, it now appeared as if no other legitimate hate-motivated crimes committed against legally recognized minorities or other vulnerable people mattered. Even though statistics show hate crimes against African-Americans are twice as prevalent as anti-gay crimes (though, arguably, hate crimes may impact gays more disproportionately), homosexuals were elevated to ultimate victim status, thanks to the media's treatment of the Shepard incident. He became a martyred icon for the gay rights movement, which began to be equated more and more with the black civil-rights struggle, to the chagrin of many blacks, following this event.

Bringing the Camel into the Tent

Tragic as it was, Matthew Shepard's death may have been viewed as a godsend for gay rights activists who had been laboring especially hard during the nineties to create a more mainstream image of homosexuals. Self-appointed gay image crafters Marshall Kirk and Hunter Madsen (*After the Ball*) were not afraid to take the gay community to task for its obvious moral and strategic shortcomings. They outlined a broad, positive-image campaign with a comprehensive media-propaganda strategy for desensitizing those who objected to the normalcy of homosexuality and for winning over the middle-of-the-roaders who were the easiest to convert to their viewpoint. Central to that strategy was a plan to "muddy the moral waters" by "raising serious theological objections to conservative biblical teachings," portraying conservative churches as "callous ... to AIDS sufferers" (sadly, not without some truth) and "antiquated backwaters, badly out of step with the times and the latest findings of psychology." In fact, they fancied this plan a "Trojan horse" that would infiltrate and conquer the Church much the same as liberal attitudes about divorce and abortion had already done.[11]

Kirk and Madsen were, in many ways, applying the same socio-psychological principles that had proven effective in earlier mass communications manipulation strategies, institutionalized in America at Columbia University through the work of Marxist-influenced social scientists—Paul Lazarsfeld, Leo Lowenthal, and Marjorie Fiske Lowenthal being chief among them. Lazarsfeld and Lowenthal had migrated to New York from Germany and brought with them the work of the liberal Institute for Social Research during the years of Nazi European domination. Marjorie Fiske had been a communications graduate student at Columbia who later worked for the Bureau of Applied Social Research started by Lazarsfeld. She would go on to marry Lowenthal and in the fifties to become highly influential in public library "intellectual freedom" policy, beginning in California when she and Lowenthal moved to the Berkeley area.[12] Most people are clueless about this underground school of Marxist thought in the U.S.

The late Malcolm Muggeridge, a reluctant British Christian broadcast media pioneer who was a BBC personality during the earlier years of television, pointed out in a speech, also transcribed in his 1977 book, *Christ and the Media*, that "a few deft touches could undermine the faith of a lifetime, and impeccable humanistic sentiments open the way to debauching a human soul on a scale that the Prince of Darkness himself might envy."[13] Muggeridge also amusingly pointed out that William Blake had penned across his copy of Bacon's *Essays*—"one of the early scriptures of the age of science"—this phrase: "Good news for Satan's Kingdom!"[14] In fact, science—especially bad science—has become a religion for many, and no group genuflects before its sainted and increasingly politicized purveyors more than the activist gay community (unless it's the Global Warming disciples, now being marginalized themselves).

Muggeridge believed the media created a world of fantasy while purporting to reflect and report reality. This was especially true, he noted, in the broadcast media. Jerry Rubin likewise said in his 1970 revolutionary manifesto, *Do It*, "Television creates myths bigger than reality," adding:

> Whereas a demo[nstration] drags on for hours and hours, TV packs all the action into two minutes—a commercial for the revolution. On the television screen news is not so much reported as

created. An event happens when it goes on TV and becomes myth. ... Television is a nonverbal instrument, so turn off the sound, since no one ever remembers any words that they hear, the mind being a Technicolor movie of images, not words. There's no such things as bad coverage for a demo. It makes no difference what's said: the pictures are the stories."[15]

Television has grown increasingly gay-friendly in recent years, with more and more sit-coms featuring homosexual characters and reality shows centered on gay themes, such as "Boy Meets Boy" or "Queer Eye for the Straight Guy." There is an exclusively gay network, LOGOS. With large segments of the population turning to the tube for most of their news and entertainment—and professing Christians are no exception—we are left to ponder, as Muggeridge did, whether television is a "cause or consequence of growing illiteracy."[16] Either way, the news is good for the gay media age. The secular, sex-driven gospel—gay or straight—is giving the good news of Jesus Christ a run for its money. With most Christian media "preaching to the choir," the sailing is relatively smooth for the false prophets preaching gay theology to the confused and searching masses. I am waiting for some gay media visionary to come along with a gay televangelistic outreach. Why not? The gay community has its own church denomination, the United Fellowship of the Metropolitan Community Church (MCC), and is influencing more and more of mainline Christendom.

Marginalizing Christians

Talking heads on TV news programs and educational (propaganda) documentaries treat media consumers to an endless array of "studies" and "facts" from the scientific community that bolster the view of homosexuality as an (as yet unproved) inborn trait and a normal, acceptable lifestyle. An ABC five-part "Nightline" series—"A Matter of Choice?"—aired May 20-24, 2002. "Nightline" host Ted Koppel readily admitted to "... a bias of my own." *The Advocate*, the national gay and lesbian news magazine, reported that the program made the Bible-believing Christians interviewed look "bizarre" and "abnormal," adding, "... they make you shake your head and wonder." Chris Bull, writing for *The Advocate*, compared Koppel to Mr. Rogers with a "soothing Father Knows Best exterior" who "belies the heart of a subversive, fully intent on changing the way America thinks."[17] And America has changed its thinking, in large part, poll after poll shows. Three decades ago, only about 13 percent of Americans believed homosexuality was inborn. Now, anywhere from 42 to 50 percent or more believe so, depending on the survey. It is especially clear that the younger generations are moving toward a more gay-affirming stance.

For a while, it seemed as if every election media cycle subjected us to mounds of stock footage of gay "wedding" ceremonies, accompanied by yet another report on the latest volley in the marriage wars. Coverage of the headline-grabbing 2008 presidential primaries pushed those images aside for a while, but the California same-sex marriage battle brought them roaring back with a vengeance. As *After the Ball* made clear, if these images "stick around long enough, they'll seem normal."[18] Was Rubin right? The pictures are the stories? That's what gay activists are banking on. Or, as Muggeridge put it, "all the stage is a world."[19]

Unless you've been living under a rock, you have to be aware that "backwoods" conservatives, especially evangelicals, are blamed for encouraging an atmosphere of violence against gays. Some prominent media voices actually attributed Matthew Shepard's death to Christian "hate" speech, a tactic similar to the one they excoriated Jerry Falwell and Pat Robertson for after their post-9/11 comments in 2001. Isn't it interesting that virtually everyone knows who Shepard was but very few know anything about Jesse Dirkhising, who was murdered in Arkansas less than a year after Shepard's death? Dirkhising was only 13, and allegedly sexually abused for two years by at least one of the two gay men who were charged with his murder. He was bound, gagged, and repeatedly sodomized before dying of asphyxiation. His murderers and gay activists had the audacity to suggest that he was a willing participant in his abuse; therefore, his murder should not evoke the kind of outrage that Shepard's did and that the dearth of media coverage following his murder was justified. Check out what Jonathan Gregg wrote—sarcastically—in a *Time* magazine editorial that was an effete attempt to justify his news colleagues' lopsided coverage of the two cases: "Could it be because we in the media elite were unwilling to publicize crimes committed by homosexuals because it didn't suit our agenda? The next stop in that line of reasoning was clear: That news is controlled by a bunch of gay-loving liberals only too happy to wield a double standard." Gregg concluded, "The reason the Dirkhising story received so little play is because it offered no lessons. Shepard's murder touches on a host of complex and timely issues: intolerance, society's attitudes toward gays, and the pressure to conform, the use of violence as a means of confronting one's demons. Jesse Dirkhising's death gives us nothing except the depravity of two sick men."[20] Is hate-motivated murder no longer deemed a form of depravity, if, indeed, Shepard's murder was a hate crime? Tragically, the people both kinds of criminals victimize can end up equally dead. Did the depraved standard also apply to Bart Allen, a young man murdered in his sleep in 2001 by his former gay lover after he began attempting to leave his gay life? His parents, Joe and Marion Allen, began a ministry outreach in his memory called Hope for the Broken Heart.[21] You won't find much archived information about Allen, either.

Sometimes, it is actually the gay media that provide

unexpectedly honest coverage of their community and its issues, even from a Christian perspective. In September 2006, *The Advocate* included a "First Person" essay in its online edition by a 19-year-old Christian man, entitled "I Hate Being Gay."[22] While *The Advocate's* editorial motive for posting this piece may have been somewhat duplicitous ("let's all pity the poor gay Christian who is so deceived by his faith"), I credit them for at least giving this teen a voice, and for facilitating some needed soul searching. The article generated a lot of thoughtful discussion from those on both ends of the gay spectrum, Christian and secular. It played out at the *The Advocate's* site and on other blogs. Most had some valid points to make, and they illustrated perfectly the crux of this ongoing debate: Gay is really more than a social contruct and it is a hard road to travel, change or no; faith can matter a great deal; and judging another's motives without having walked in his shoes is dangerous.

Were it not for conservative and Christian media, the occasional mainstream op-ed, and legitimate citizen-journalist bloggers, these voices likely would not have their say. Regardless of where beliefs align on Christian counseling or programs designed to ameliorate suffering and disciple those struggling with unwanted same-sex attraction toward wholeness and a more godly life, we cannot dismiss the gut-knowledge that desiring to move away from homosexuality is as valid as the desire to overcome any unwanted, unhealthy, or sinful existence. In a relationship that focuses on long-term discipleship for the sexual sin struggler (even if it is only in thought life), the main goal is to grow closer to God while seeking to remain sexually pure, regardless of how much change one sees in misplaced sexual desires. Few folks point this out more succinctly than does Alan Chambers, president of Exodus International. Chambers' story of wrestling with same-sex attraction and finally recognizing the regenerating power of Christ in his own life gives hope to many others on a similar journey. His most recent book, *Leaving Homosexuality: A Practical Guide for Men and Women Looking for a Way Out*, contains his poignant testimony of real and lasting transformation that holds him steady, even when an occasional temptation may arise. Chambers began his journey out of homosexuality at about age 20. He is now married with two children, and oversees the worldwide outreach of Exodus. Folks like Chambers and me have come to reject the false gay mantra that same-sex sexual gratification is necessary for wholeness. All sexuality is secondary to the fulfillment that comes from a personal relationship with a loving God. In that regard, I believe many ex-gays or post-gays are more integrated and whole than a great many lifelong heterosexuals who perceive themselves as normal and healthy in their sexuality. Only those who recognize their utter depravity apart from Christ can be fully open to his healing grace. Who recognizes this more than the homosexual struggler, often viewed as some kind of latter-day leper?

The Great Divide

Finding biblical middle ground in the gay culture debate can be an exercise in futility. How do concerned evangelicals or ex/post-gays compassionately interact with gay-identified Christians or the gay community, in general, when so great a chasm exists? Should we interact at all beyond offering help to those who truly want to change, many wonder? Many in the Church believe "out and proud" gay Christians should be subject to "church discipline" as outlined in the New Testament. Of course, if the Church disciplined every person guilty of sexual sin, we would empty many pews. Are all worshipers to observe a "don't ask, don't tell" policy when it comes to sexual sins of all kinds? Where do discipleship and loving rebuke fit into the picture? This all remains an ongoing debate within many churches. Since no other sinful acts that I know of are being touted as God's gift within some church bodies, the answer should be obvious. First, the Church has an obligation to protect its members from the ravages of all known sin. That means giving no official quarter to non-celibate, unrepentant homosexuals or others known to be engaging in sexual sin. The shepherd guards the sheep from the wolves. This is where the truth has to be tough and biblically solid. We cannot confuse offering the homosexual sinner God's living water with condoning the sin. Judge not, our gay brethren will tell us. Our response should be that we will let the two-edged sword of God's word do the penetrating, dividing, and judging, as Hebrews 4:12 tells us it will. Jesus did not permit the adulterous woman to be stoned by other sinners, but he also told her, "Go now and leave your life of sin." Further, Jesus said we may not judge the acts of others—attempt to remove the "specks" from their eyes—until we have first removed the "planks" from our own so that we may "see clearly" (Matthew 7:1-5). Note the implicit command there. The trouble is much of the judging comes from hypocrites who cannot see past their noses. And removing our own planks can be all but impossible. That leaves little room for judgment. Gays shrewdly condemn this self-righteousness. Still, we must be discerning.

There has to be a purposeful pointing of the sinful to another way, otherwise, what's the gospel for? R. Albert Mohler Jr., president of Southern Baptist Theological Seminary in Louisville, Kentucky, articulated the genuine evangelical viewpoint when he said in June 2006 on CNN's "Larry King Live" show, "The Scripture very clearly tells us that our Creator has a purpose for our sexuality and that homosexuality, among other sins, is a violation of that purpose." But he went farther: "Love compels us to tell people the truth and also, as we understand the depth of their struggle with this, to tell them that there is a way out."[23] The compassionate church shows them the way out, and is willing to walk it with them. It does not force them to go there.

It is not an easy journey, to be sure. The road is bumpy and long. Many will reject it—that is no mystery. Today, many will never even come to the well for a drink because so many cultural influences have convinced them homosexuality represents a valid way of living. "The issue isn't whether or not someone in recovery ever falls or feels tempted to fall," said Daryl Pitts, D.Min., licensed counseling pastor at Thomas Road Baptist Church for a decade and founder of Freedom Ministry, the church's small-group recovery program. "It's a question of whether or not change is possible and maintainable."[24] Obviously, Pitts, a former drug addict and onetime member of an abusive Christian cult, believed change was possible or he wouldn't have invested his life in recovery ministry work. And I wouldn't have worked alongside him if I didn't believe in Christ's power to transform lives. I am a product of such change, and I see it happening for others.

To many other counseling professionals and laypeople, homosexuality is a complex form of emotional and spiritual brokenness, with possible biological precursors, that can give way to growth and healing in the same kind of Christ-centered support system as other self-medicating or unwholesome behaviors that may or may not have some biological roots. A major sticking point comes in the form of the worldview clash between "formers" and those who want to be affirmed in their gayness. Speaking of sexually active gays as living an unwholesome or broken life, or stepping forward as an example of a formerly gay but now-regenerated person generally constitutes fighting words. The world encourages this divide and the confusion it engenders. Healing and spiritual growth are an ongoing process for those who seek help. Despite those who may fall (and that is not a permanent state) on the road to whatever freedom awaits them, there are enough examples of success and hope to keep the homosexual regeneration movement going and growing. There is a hunger for it, in fact.

Many Christians appear to view some concessions to gays as inevitable. Should they insist on keeping marriage as a sacred union only between a man and a woman, as the Bible clearly tells them it is, but consent to civil unions or domestic partnerships in a live-and-let-live compromise that might defray some of the anger and perceived injustice in this war? Perhaps that is the kind of tough choice gay rights activists have maneuvered us into believing we have to make. Yet, a thief can steal just as much through the back door as through the front—maybe even more. New Jersey, which opted for civil unions over marriage, is now forcing one church denomination to forfeit the tax-exempt status of one of its properties since church officials refused to allow a lesbian couple to hold their civil union ceremony there. Is this only the tip of a growing iceberg? Regardless of what the Church says, gay activists will continue to use liberal courts to circumvent state legislatures and overturn the will of the people, placing God's law on the chopping block to be further whittled away. This battle is far from over, however, as the 2010 mid-term elections proved. Even if the world settles into an uneasy truce and gay or lesbian couples are accorded more rights on par with their straight counterparts, the Church's mission will not have changed. The unhappiness we see all around us will not have dissipated.

Confused by a dizzying array of news stories, sermons, and "expert" medical or scientific opinions rendered over the years, many people struggle to understand homosexuality. While no research has established clear genetic or biological origins for sexual orientation, even we "formers" know that homosexual thoughts and feelings are not merely a choice in the sense that many Christians want to believe they are. We can choose between capitulating to inevitable temptations or walking yoked with Christ as the burden-sharer. The twenty-first-century Church clearly has much soul-searching to do. One question we must not be afraid to ask ourselves is: To what extent has our broad-stroke rejection of those who have wrestled with homosexuality engendered much of the anger and retribution the gay community feels toward us?

Three

Mental Health Wars:
Defining Sexual Identity

In early 2004, psychologist Warren Throckmorton interviewed psychiatrist Robert Spitzer for his ex-gay ("sexual identity formation") documentary, "I Do Exist," meant to show that change is possible for those struggling with unwanted same-sex attraction. Both men have academic and clinical credentials and both have worked with clients seeking help for their same-sex attractions. Spitzer is a professor of psychiatry at Columbia University while Throckmorton, in addition to being an associate professor of psychology at Grove City College, is a fellow for psychology and public policy at the Christian school's Center for Vision and Values. The interview, part of which appears in the film, covers Spitzer's controversial 2001 study of men and women claiming to have changed their homosexual orientation through reorientation therapy. A significant number of the subjects reported they had been able to "achieve good heterosexual functioning," to varying degrees, lasting five years or more, as of the date of the study. As many as 11 percent of the men and 37 percent of the women reported complete or significant change, while a good deal more were on a continuum of change. The subjects' primary orientation had been a homosexual one for a good number of years and the vast majority of them identified as Christians or people of faith.[1]

Spitzer wrote in the conclusion to his study, "The mental health professionals should stop moving in the direction of banning therapy that has, as a goal, a change in sexual orientation. Many patients, provided with informed consent about the possibility that they will be disappointed if the therapy does not succeed, can make a rational choice to work toward developing their heterosexual potential and minimizing their unwanted homosexual attractions."[2] He further stated, "The American Psychiatric Association should stop applying a double standard in its discouragement of reorientation therapy, while actively encouraging gay-affirmative therapy to confirm and solidify a gay identity."[3]

Even though Spitzer said he believed total, sustainable change was uncommon, his study and comments still sent shockwaves through the gay community as activists, along with the usual array of liberal medical and mental health guild organizations, lined up to demean and refute his conclusions. They were not about to admit that gays—men, especially—could truly shed their gayness. Conservative Christians and those identifying as former gays or lesbians, on the other hand, were delighted and began citing the study as scientific proof for their long-held claims that homosexuality was not inborn and immutable. If even a few people can successfully change (and the study showed that significantly more than a few could change to varying degrees), then we must agree that change is possible, they said. Each side has continued to take potshots at the other whenever the study has been cited.

Throckmorton later amended his views about "I Do Exist," and now states at drthrockmorton.com, "I reported the narratives as presented and chronicled what I believed at the time to be an accurate reflection of evidence regarding sexual orientation. Current research and experience lead me to take a much more cautious view of the potential for changes in sexual attractions." Throckmorton is, in fact, an astute observer of all things related to sexual identity and is not averse to calling out his more conservatives colleagues when they make claims that he believes are even partially refuted or are not clearly supported by science. He and Dr. Mark Yarhouse, a fellow Christian psychologist who hangs his hat at Regent University, co-developed an approach to helping clients find "congruence" between their sexuality and their faith or worldview, known as Sexual Identity Therapy (SIT). Is the dissonance between a gay sexual identity and Christianity there for a reason, however?

Retaking the High Ground

The National Association for Research and Therapy of Homosexuality (NARTH) is a consortium of mental health professionals that formed in response to political correctness and perceived threats to take away the right of patients to choose therapy to help eliminate or lessen their same-sex attractions. The organization, co-founded by Dr. Joseph Nicolosi, is most known for advocating "reparative" therapy. It is a controversial approach that seeks to identify and repair developmental deficiencies, most frequently in gay men, that supposedly stem from earlier parent-child relationships and are believed by some practitioners to be a root cause of homosexuality. "Concerned that professional organizations and publications in the mental health field have fallen under the control of those who would use them to forward social constructionist theories, political agendas, and advocacy research, NARTH has fought for a return to established theoretical approaches, solid research, therapy that puts the patient first, and freedom to discuss, debate, and disagree."[4] So says Dr. Benjamin

Kaufman, former clinical professor of psychiatry at the UC Davis School of Medicine. Kaufman, along with Nicolosi and the late Dr. Charles Socarides, helped birth the organization in 1992. Nicolosi and Socarides had been actively treating homosexual patients seeking change and Kaufman had become concerned with the politicization of the mental health professions during his tenure on a local AIDS policy task force. "I watched in dismay as sensible, proven public health policy was discarded because unorganized professionals, although concerned, were no match against organized political activists," notes Kaufman. "The debate between NARTH and gay activists within mental health professional organizations ... constitutes a struggle for the conscience of the mental health profession: a battle between two radically opposed paradigms."[5]

Sparks tend to fly quickly when discussions about NARTH's role ensue, either in the therapeutic community or among those with a gay activist mindset. NARTH has pulled some articles from its website after attacks on the credibility or viewpoint of an author or the NARTH philosophy, in general, have arisen. While the organization has a valid role to play and the political agenda of sexual identity research is in evidence, it has come under close scrutiny for making some inconsistent and misleading statements in its zeal and legitimate desire to have a place at the table. Some criticize the one-note approach they say reparative therapy represents ("when you only have a hammer, everything looks like a nail"), while others simply dislike NARTH's divergence from the directives handed down by both APAs (the psychological and psychiatric guild associations). It seems NARTH has been the favorite whipping boy of the gay community, along with Exodus, which refers struggling gays and their families to both counselors and church-based small groups or local ministries and also has been closely scrutinized for its alliances and philosophies, past and present.

Is NARTH being unfairly singled out? Yes and no. Therapists who have worked to any extent with SSA clients have observed that a reparative drive approach pointing to a history of parent-child disconnectedness or alleging early trauma of some kind can damage current familial relationships when parent and child disagree or are angry about what did or didn't happen. These may be temporary rifts that some see as a necessary part of the process, but some real harm also appears to exist in some of these cases. Some clients undergoing reparative therapy may experience marked depression or anxiety, which is a health risk therapists want to avoid if possible. Where something has been amiss and families are open to examining its possible impact on sexual identity development, reparative therapy may be valid and effective. It's up to a reputable therapist and the client to make that call. Of course, there are other kinds of therapy available to those struggling with homosexuality or wanting to moderate behaviors that are incompatible with their faith or worldview.

There is no more controversial substratum within the mental health disciplines than that concerning homosexuality. No one truly understands its multi-faceted intricacies, but that does not stop those from either camp bent on forwarding their agenda from making "factual" assertions that are not. Indeed, most practitioners are now hesitant to even classify the pathologies that clearly stem from sexual identity confusion. Declared no longer a mental illness under the criteria of the DSM (*Diagnostic and Statistical Manual of Mental Disorders*, still in its fourth edition with the fifth edition under study) back in the seventies, homosexuality has broken out of the mold to stand alone as the chief social cause célèbre. There appears to be no end in sight for the scientific and theological debates it engenders. Both sides interpret the same data through different lenses and come to opposite conclusions. Likewise, Christians view the same scriptural injunctions and interpret them differently. Gay activists insist that studies purporting to show that change in sexual orientation is possible are flawed and unscientifically tainted by religious—namely Christian—zealotry. That can't be true in Spitzer's case, of course, as he claims no faith. Who is doing harm—the therapists who tell their gay clients they cannot change or those who allow them the freedom to seek the change they desire? Any dogmatic or coercive approach can be harmful, of course, and that applies to extremist views on both sides of the equation.

One of the typical firefights over gay mental health issues erupted in the summer of 2006 when then-president of the American Psychological Association, Gerald Koocher, stated in the wake of an ex-gay protest at the APA's annual convention, "APA has no conflict with psychologists who help those distressed by unwanted homosexual attraction." He was pressured by gay activists into adding later that such therapies lack "a validated scientific foundation and [could] prove psychologically harmful," adding to it this highly suspect statement: "In fact, the data show that gay and lesbian people do not differ from heterosexuals in their psychological health. By that I mean that they have no greater instance of mental disorders than do heterosexuals.[6] That claim does not quite stand up to scrutiny, as a wide swath of practitioners and social scientists understand just the opposite to be valid. What remains debatable is why the gay population experiences more mental and even physical maladies than the general population. Medical science knows that anal intercourse among men, for example, is inherently unhealthy and greatly increases the risk for HIV infections and other diseases.

One of Koocher's equally liberal predecessors, Dr. Judd Marmor, who served as APA president from 1975-76, once said, "The myth that homosexuality is untreatable still has wide currency among the public at large and among homosexuals themselves. ..." Many scienteist today disagree with Marmor's assessment that "a powerful motivation to achieve such a change" can be effective to any substantial degree.[7] Nevertheless, the mental health establishment has traveled far to arrive at where it is currently in its veiws on homosexuality.

Despite the evidence undermining the belief that homosexuality is innate and immutable, and even with occasional statements begrudgingly acknowledging some meaningful change is possible and not always a harmful process, public sentiment continues to be incorrectly swayed by the liberal mental health establishment, in cahoots with gay rights activists and the mainstream media. Confusion is still the order of the day for the average Joe and for plenty of counselors. In fact, a prominent Christian counselor recently told me he is uncomfortable with the "delicate dance" required of him and his colleagues in the realm of homosexual issues. He freely admits he does not yet know how to address it with his constituents. Indeed, ideologues on both sides blindly go on making statements of absolute certainty about various aspects of homosexuality when, in fact, there are many gray areas still needing to be cleared up. Both sides say the lack of an authoritative study, acceptable from both viewpoints, comparing the effectiveness with the possible ill effects of reorientation therapies, is a major problem. Such a study would be a mammoth undertaking, with the biggest challenge being agreement on how the subjects ought to be selected. It would seem the desirable goal in the meantime is an agree-to-disagree impasse without the ugly retribution we have seen so much of. The lack of an overwhelming consensus should trump the judicial tendency to side with either ideology, but it doesn't. And that is a major sticking point in this culture war.

An engineer familiar with scientific methods made some cogent observations about research in an online conversation in which I also participated. "Anyone who is into research knows it is not too difficult for people to manipulate data to fit into a theory they are desperately trying to justify," he said. Speaking then to the topic of homosexuality, he added, "[A] scientist working from the question to the answer is under pressure to self-censor if research results go contrary to the 'received wisdom' of the gay lobby. ... [E]ven if such a researcher is brave enough to seek publication of his/her work in a journal, the peer-review team may be too scared to allow such work through, even if it meets all required standards for publication."

What the Evidence Says and Doesn't Say

An interesting study by Mark Yarhouse and Stanton Jones, in their book, *Ex-Gays?: A Longitudinal Study of Religiously Mediated Change in Sexual Orientation*, was published in mid-2007. This was the first longitudinal study (repeated observations over a significant period of time) to track results of same-sex-attracted individuals involved in various Exodus-sanctioned ministry programs and not professional therapy. It was meant to identify the degrees of success of such programs and whether or not this kind of help was emotionally harmful, as gay activists, ex-ex-gays and the APA had been claiming it was. Throckmorton called the book "a rare, research-based look into religiously motivated attempts to change homosexual orientation. ..."[8] He further stated:

If massive harm was being done on a wide-scale basis, this design would have found it. The results are actually modest but reflect what I have been seeing clinically for years. There is a variation in how people experience attractions to the same sex and there are variations in how flexible sexuality is for different people. This is essentially what they found. They also found that Exodus programs offer benefit to some who don't change much at all. I think as a ministry, the next step would be for Exodus to take a consumer approach and survey those who have expressed dissatisfaction and see if there are any practices that associate with those who don't do well.[9]

One of the key findings of the Yarhouse/Jones study is that many of the participants felt their recovery experience was beneficial, even when they realized only small changes in same-sex attractions. Only 15 percent reported a substantial reduction in homosexual desires or any inclination toward a heterosexual orientation. Another 23 percent claimed reductions in same-sex attractions and were choosing to remain celibate, while 29 percent experienced little change. Initial reports said as many as two-thirds of participants were satisfied with their experience and remained committed to staying the course. "To me, this point may be the biggest story," Throckmorton concluded.[10] The latest ("Time 6") follow-up to the study by Jones and Yarhouse, presented at the American Psychological Association's 2009 annual convention, showed that figure to be more around 53 percent, which Throckmorton still feels is "an important finding," according to comments he made on his blog.

For 20 months, I facilitated a weekly, faith-based group for women desiring to move beyond their struggles with same-sex attraction (SSA). We met under the auspices of Freedom Ministry at my church. For my first five years in this ministry, I worked with both men and women suffering mostly from depression and anxiety, a few of whom also had same-sex attractions they had not previously felt comfortable discussing. Two-thirds of the SSA women who were a part of my latter group took the work seriously and truly moved forward. Several others got hung up in "negotiating" the price or bailed out.

Professor, Teach Thyself

While I was researching a book I was writing about depression a few years ago, I ran across what I thought was a very good analysis of a central problem in the mental health professions. It came from a person who is now a licensed marriage and family therapist, but who had observed some disturbing trends while still in school. Declaring psychopathology to be one of the most "depressing and dehumanizing courses" he'd taken, he said he came to realize that therapy was more art than science. How could the scientific method even be applied to human beings, he wondered? Can people be "reduced to variables" in some laboratory setting? Isn't all assessment subjective? Surely people are unknown variables who regularly defy the paradigms that have been assigned to them. I jumped the bell curve not once but twice in my own life. This is a therapist who truly understands the limitations of his practice.

The DSM is known as "the psychiatrist's bible." It is how diagnoses are assigned to mental disorders and how doctors receive payment from their patients' insurance companies in accordance with their diagnostic codes. I have come to learn over the years, both as a onetime mental health "consumer" with a DSM diagnosis of major depressive disorder and as an advocate for those mercilessly trapped in an inadequate system of endless mental health treatments, that therapy is more art than science. There is little consensus among therapists and doctors as to how it is best applied. The mental health literature is virtually impossible to follow. Medical or scientific journals that publish research relative to homosexuality or gender issues are legion.

What the Doctor Meant To Say

The controversy about Dr. Spitzer's study is a perfect illustration of why the gay culture clash has no clear end in sight. Not only did Spitzer's subjects attest to having unwanted same-sex attractions, but, as Throckmorton said, "It appears that some of the subjects did in fact feel depressed as the result of being told by therapists that they couldn't change."[11] Here is the pertinent exchange from Throckmorton's 2004 interview with Spitzer:

> THROCKMORTON: Were there any mental health consequences of attempting to change?
>
> SPITZER: The majority of subjects reported moderate to severe depression before they went into therapy. And—a marked change—very few were depressed after therapy. So that was an important finding, I think, that ... there was a tremendous conflict over homosexuality, and many were very depressed that they had made previous efforts. That was another interesting thing, [that] many of the subjects reported that they had gone to mental health professionals and were told just, you know, accept it, that there's no way to change. And they were not satisfied with that, and were very depressed thinking that they could not, you know, change.[12]

Spitzer has expressed concern about the way various ideologues have hijacked his study and his statements for their own designs, but it is hard to misinterpret his last statement.

It appears every piece of propaganda provided by gay rights organizations, much of it aimed at confused and immature adolescents, is saying that those conflicted about their sexual orientation or identity must embrace the gay identity. But what if some of those kids are not really gay? The Human Rights Campaign's *Coming Out Project Resource Guide* says (under "Myths & Facts About GLBT People), "No scientifically valid evidence exists that shows that people can change their sexual orientation, although some people do repress it. The most reputable medical and psychotherapeutic groups say you should not try to change your sexual orientation as the process can actually be damaging."[13] Of course, HRC and other pro-gay organizations know full well that many people do desire to come out of homosexuality or ameliorate it in some way that is consistent with their personal beliefs. And studies have confirmed that more than a few have succeeded at it to satisfactory, life-changing degrees. Yet, HRC and other activist organizations unequivocally reject one's ability to do so.

I only recently seemed to convince some diehard gays that I no longer experience same-sex attractions—a gratifying achievement, if they truly accept it. Rare are the memories of past struggles that come to me, and when they do, they most often generate a sense of great relief. I recall my depressive episodes much more readily. But it is also clear that most gays consider me an exception to the rule or simply a former bisexual who had the battle already half-won. Moreover, there is an obvious line of demarcation for them between female and male homosexuality. Of course, men and women are "wired" differently, emotionally and in other ways continually being studied. It stands to reason that the male psyche and sexual makeup would translate to greater difficulty for men who experience same-sex attractions exclusively or predominantly. Men are not inherently relationship-driven and tend, at least mentally, to swim against the tide of monogamy. Still, it is certainly not impossible for a man who, for whatever reasons, grows up strongly attracted to other males to move significantly in the other direction with valid guidance and support, as both anecdotal and scientific evidence have demonstrated.

Many gays are still bent on erasing the footprints of all those who claim to be former gays. Only a small percentage of therapists specialize in helping unhappy same-sex-attracted people seeking change. Some do the "delicate dance," and others either shun them out of fear of being shunned by their colleagues or censured by their respective guilds, or truly feel they are unqualified to conduct such therapy. In some cases, these therapists experience "ex-homophobia." Who is coercing whom? Since 1973, when Spitzer led the charge within the American Psychiatric Association to have homosexuality removed from the DSM under political pressure from militant gays, psychiatrists and psychologists have proved to be some of the best advocates the gay rights movement could have hoped for. Regardless of whether or not homosexuality ought to have been removed from the DSM, the still-prevalent intellectual dishonesty and extreme political correctness accompanying that decision should not be tolerated within the mental health community.

Burying Science

It has been alleged that the primary study cited by the APA when the decision was made to alter the DSM was a now 50-year-old study by radical left activist and psychologist Evelyn Hooker, "The Adjustment of the Overt Male Homosexual."[14] Hooker's study was problematic from the outset. Other studies contradicted it in dramatic ways. A most intriguing landmark study, virtually buried by the guild organizations and the media, is *The Social Organization of Sexuality: Sexual Practices in the United States* (1994), whose chief author was Edward O. Laumann. The study, conducted by the National Opinion Research Center and published by the University of Chicago Press, supposedly was based on a statistically representative survey (unlike the Hooker study) of American adults between the ages of 18 and 60. Other large-scale studies seemed to confirmed its conclusions.[15]

We are left to wonder, as always, how much politicking is

involved in this analysis. The most interesting conclusion drawn by the Laumann study was that homosexuality was not a "stable trait." Most surprising of all, the study found that homosexuality has a marked tendency to convert over time to heterosexuality, even without conversion or reorientation therapy.[16] "Sexual identity" is too unstable to be labeled an identity at all, according to Laumann. In other words, gayness as an identity is a social and political construct, if Laumann is to be believed. Clearly, many pooh-pooh that edgy idea. Statistically, there appears to be a greater tendency to identify as gay between the ages of 21 and 26. It happens predominantly among college-educated men and women. Exposure to liberal social thought tends to peak during the college years and immediately following.[17] So, is there a connection? Does liberal funding for most scientific studies skew them in a gay-friendly direction, burying competing conclusions? These are valid questions. How often is there fire where there is smoke?

In his 2003 book, *Anything But Straight: Unmasking the Scandals and Lies Behind the Ex-Gay Myth*, gay activist Wayne Besen said he and the HRC, for which he was an official spokesman at the time, contacted Spitzer prior to his study to suggest just how they thought it should be conducted, an unabashed move to stack the deck in their favor. Spitzer, to his credit, refused to follow their advice. When Besen learned that Spitzer was going ahead with his study, over his objections, he threatened him. Spitzer later said, "The intimidation was in the form of telling me that if I did such a study, I would be exposed as doing fraudulent research in front of my colleagues."[18] Some thanks for his 1973 coup. Besen insists that the 200 subjects for Spitzer's study were "the religious right's handpicked sample," many of whom were "professional anti-gay lobbyists."[19] Some 19 percent of the subjects were "mental health professionals or directors of ex-gay ministries."[20] It is growing more apparent that real, significant change for those at odds with their homosexual desires comes primarily through religiously mediated intervention. That truth drives secularists nuts, but it cannot be overlooked.

Homosexuality is widely linked in the more conservative-to-moderate psychotherapy community to early childhood development, parental authority, personality, and environmental issues (including childhood sexual abuse), any or all of which constitute what may appear to be a predisposition to it in some children. That makes it feel like something inborn, one could surmise. Some children are gender-nonconforming at an early age (I confess I was one of them), leading some to espouse that possible biological influences, such as prenatal hormones, could be at play. Some in the Christian community have decided that, even if genetic predisposition or other biological factors are ever convincingly shown to have a bearing on some cases of homosexuality, they will accept this news as further evidence of man's fallen nature, since we already know other conditions seen as abnormal and undesired have had such links established. Do we really need to be told that sexual drives are acutely strong and sexual sin of all kinds is rampant within society, even in faith communities? The media messages that glorify sex only serve to worsen an already difficult problem. To the extent that the Church ignores this fact, it only exacerbates the issue.

Tough Questions Needing Answers

Men and women may experience some similar developmental (that could even include the prenatal stage) prerequisites to homosexuality, but women present a far more complex picture of sexual or gender confusion. Female same-sex relationships are known to be emotionally enmeshing or dependent to a degree not generally seen in male homosexual relationships, which tend to be more physical in nature, but which uncover real emotional needs, nevertheless. Connecting emotionally and erotically with another woman for me felt almost as necessary as the next breath of air during the "acting-out" phase of my life. It went way beyond simple adolescent-like infatuation. No healthy adult relationship should be like that. Certainly for teens, already facing enough confusion in their emotional and sexual development, anxiety-fraught homosexual or bisexual relationships can be particularly risky.

Then, there is the suicide question. Dr. Elizabeth Saewyc of Canada's McCreary Institute led a long-range, student-survey-based study to assess adolescent suicide risk, examining more than 30,000 students in grades 7 through 12 in British Columbia, the Pacific Northwest, and the Midwest at various intervals from 1992 to 2003. Since 1992, teen lesbian and especially bisexual suicidal thoughts or attempts have significantly increased, according to Saewyc's research. Adolescent males identifying as bisexual also experienced a marked increase in suicide ideation or attempts. The researchers surmise that the suicide rates among bisexual, gay, and lesbian youth may be even higher, given that their study could not examine the runaway or homeless youth population. Also, they realize that "not all adolescents who will identify as gay, lesbian, or bisexual have done so in these surveys. It is possible that some of the suicidal heterosexual or mostly heterosexual teens are actually in the process of identifying as gay or bisexual but have not yet disclosed this, and so the disparity would actually be even higher."[21] Of course, it is also possible that some who are sexually confused will later identify as straight. This troubling news about bisexual- or lesbian-identified teen girls underscores the critical need to address female homosexual issues, which somehow take a back seat to male issues, and serves as a stark wake-up call. It is interesting that this study shows an increased suicide risk even among Canadian GLBT youth, even though gay marriage was legalized in 2005 in Canada and attitudes toward homosexuals are generally more tolerant than in the U.S.

Depression and suicide statistics among the gay population, along with the revised mental health guidelines from both the American Psychological and Psychiatric Associations that now more-or-less normalize homosexuality, have long been a flashpoint in the cultural debate. Why are gender-confused young people at higher risk for suicide? There is no simple answer, despite the ready explanations both sides in the cultural divide give. Counselors (and Spitzer's study) do confirm that many people who have been raised in an environment of deeply held religious faith are prone to depression when they feel there is no way out or they cannot reconcile their same-sex attractions with their faith. The answer clearly is more complex than the usual pro-gay response that homophobia or bullying are exclusively to blame. The startling statistics beg for an explanation, but Saewyc admits she does not have the answers.[22] More research is needed before the bigger picture emerges.

Some anecdotal and scientific evidence suggests a higher degree of volatility and even domestic abuse or violence in lesbian relationships than in the general population, but this may be overstated. Highly charged emotions may contribute to suicidal depression when lesbian relationships run aground. I've seen it in the lives of women I have sought to support through the recovery process. "Female homosexuality is a complex issue. It's definitely multi-faceted and there are a number of possible contributing factors," Melissa Fryrear, then-director of gender issues for Focus on the Family's Government and Public Policy division, told me several years ago. That "multi-faceted" assessment is considered axiomatic in the female gender identity "school." Fryrear and I both lived through our own years of gender confusion and had some similar psychodynamic influences in our lives. We know our respective journeys. They count. We are real, as are our many fellow "formers," despite claims by those on the other side who are not seeking or finding meaningful change that we don't matter.

Many experts do agree that several issues surrounding female homosexuality need to be explored more fully. One is the absence of fathers in many homes that impacts the vital gender affirmation for girls that fathers provide in critical stages of development. Also coming into play is a growing media and cultural fascination with bisexual experimentation, especially among girls. A (gay) psychiatrist, quoted by *The New York Times* in a story about parental fears over such experimentation in an elite school, said students often tell him "bisexuality is in vogue."[23] I daresay many people have made the same observation. I was familiar with the bisexual subculture in Southern California for a while back in the nineties. Bisexual and "bi-curious" women were and still are in great demand among "swinging" couples. Even the feminist movement may be partly to blame as lesbianism tends to be somewhat fluid in nature and can be seen as a statement of solidarity or protest against male supremacy. A perfect illustration of our cultural identity confusion is the 2008 number-one pop song by Katy Perry (formerly a Christian artist), "I Kissed a Girl." Subtle? Hardly.

A much darker piece of the puzzle may be evident in the disproportionate numbers—though this is debatable among researchers—of lesbian and bisexual girls who have experienced past sexual abuse. Both mental health professionals and survivors point to a pervasive wall of fear and silence surrounding victims of childhood sexual abuse. As many as one in three girls experience some kind of sexual abuse before age 18, according to the U.S. Department of Justice, as compared to about one in five or six boys. It is difficult to quantify the numbers of victims because many such crimes are not reported out of fear or even, tragically, family denial. What is known is the effects of childhood sexual abuse, whether it is kept secret or not, are severe and varied and often take the form of sexual brokenness of some kind. It matters little whether the abuse is homosexual or heterosexual.

Repentance and Healing, Up Close and Personal

It took me 24 years to work up the courage to admit to anyone that I had been molested as an 8-year-old child. It was a pastor who gently led me to confront it while we were working through some of the issues that led to my depression. In fact, I was reluctant to even call it abuse for a very long time. Today I realize what I experienced was far less painful than what many abused children do. Innocent as it seemed when I looked back on it (my childish crush on the 16-year-old perpetrator left me more vulnerable), my shame and even fear of punishment still had kept me from telling anyone. Like most children, I had assumed the guilt for my abuse. That fear is not totally irrational, by the way, as sometimes children are not believed or are blamed somehow for their abuse. It wasn't until after I had overcome my long battle with depression that my ultimate same-sex-attraction crisis came. Before that, I'd had periodic mini-crises in my thought life and one serious secret attraction I'd carried for quite a few years. I believe being molested did have some bearing on that whole struggle, though it does not tell the whole story.

No less than two women therapists I briefly saw had affirmed my desires to explore my "other side" as being perfectly acceptable. My walk down that dark path turned out to be the worst nightmare of my life. In desperation and seeing my marriage on the verge of crumbling, I called a local ex-gay ministry and was referred to a counselor two counties away. She was the best, they said. I wanted the best. My husband and I went together, initially. I stayed with it on my own for the rest of that year. What a wonderful breath of fresh air this counselor was after the long succession of liberal, secular "shrinks"and therapists masquerading as Christians I had seen, going back to my earliest days of depression. With her help, I got through the worst of my crisis. As long as I could remember, I had been conflicted about my sexual identity, although I had never felt exclusively homosexual. I had grown up a typical, pigtailed tomboy who still enjoyed aspects of being a girl. Yet I remember deep longings to be a boy. The girl part did not always feel natural to me. It waxed and waned over the years. My shyness may have been my savior, to some degree. My college years could well have been my downfall had I been more assertive and let my curiosity get the better of me. When I eventually fell in love with Russ and we married—after my first failed marriage and a tortuous road of guilt and anguish—I began to see the self that I wanted to hold onto emerging. Motherhood was for me a very strong affirmation of my femininity. I loved it. Nevertheless, my long battle with depression had unearthed an old demon-monster that needed to be put to death, not just shut up in a cave. My same-sex desires had an intoxicating effect on me. As I look back on it, I am actually thankful I endured this struggle. The crisis forced me to grow up.

Some time after my husband found out about my double life and I was already in counseling, I confessed my struggle to a trusted Christian friend and asked for her prayers and support. Thankfully, she did not see me as a three-eyed monster. I continued to find strength in my church family, although I only felt comfortable sharing my struggle with my pastor. Otherwise, I'd feared that no one would understand or folks would ostracize me. Sadly, that is a valid fear within many of our churches. Were that not the case, we would not need so many surrogate friends and confidants in the form of professional counselors. As I served in various ministry roles within my church and even assumed a leadership position in women's ministry, I felt myself moving farther and farther away from the old, conflicted me. I also volunteered in various capacities in my daughters' school and focused on healthy living. It was during these years that I began writing newspaper commentaries. I also found this to be a satisfying outlet, helping me to articulate my deepest-held beliefs and impact the culture in some small way.

Our marriage began to grow stronger as Russ and I not only saw our relationship being regenerated, but actually discovered a more meaningful love, one that was able to withstand any outside force. A healed marriage in which trust has been breeched never can be the same as it originally was. Scars remain. Russ and I can say we have "grown up" together in many respects. We know God specializes in second chances. Last year we celebrated our 29th anniversary. Our two grown daughters, now happily married, have remained the apples of our eyes, and we dearly love our wonderful sons-in-law. Our rebuilt marriage gives us all the more reason to reach out to lovingly establish closer relationships with Russ' adult children from his first marriage, as well. All our children, and one teenage granddaughter, are inestimable blessings. We are nothing if not the picture of hope for them in any struggles they may face. I shudder to think how close I came to throwing the precious gift of my family away. I don't think I could have lived through the pain of losing them. God used them as an anchor to hold me firm, both in my struggle with depression and during my later rebellion.

Of course, my healing had to come in stages. It took years of learning how to let the waves of confusion and old destructive desires crash over me as I swam beneath them into the deep, calm waters of wholeness. It was a journey I only could have made with God's help and the loving support of others. I have no fear of falling back. Of course I am human, and those memories will never be eradicated. But I know how to render impotent those old impulses should they ever raise their heads, even for a moment. For me, a greater concern than that of succumbing to any homosexual temptation is having to deal with an occasional shame attack from the Enemy when I am reminded of the sheer insolence of my former rebellion. "How could your husband really have forgiven you?" hisses that snide, little voice. But no sooner than that old fear arises within me, it is quelled by an attitude of amazing thankfulness for all God has wrought in my life. I am his, and no power in hell or on earth can shake that certainty.

As much compassion as I have for those still living as homosexuals, I know I cannot sit idly by and watch the destructive lies that have taken over our culture draw others struggling like I was into a web of deceit and confusion. When we speak of hope, it must be real hope in a real future and not false or inflated hope in a one-size-fits-all "change" program. But don't tell me, and all the others like me, there is no hope. No mental health system is worth existing if it denies the transforming power of a loving and powerful God, considering how many look to him. We don't have to look far to see the results of God's loving, miraculous touch. Nonbelievers cannot just slough off these miracles.

I chose to allow our daughters to get through some vulnerable times of their own and to approach young adulthood before I revealed my hidden past to them. They didn't need that burden when they were younger. They support me today wholeheartedly and are thankful for my healing journey. It is no mystery at all to me why many ex/post-gays or formers, as I prefer to call them, decline to reveal their past struggles. Their motives aren't that different from those of closeted gays. They just want to live their lives as normally and quietly as possible, and they should be entitled to do so. They know that persecuting intimidation likely awaits them if they go public. The assertion that "so many" (and those numbers are never really quantified, either) fail at attempts to find meaningful change in no way establishes that former gays or those in the process of recovering are minuscule in number. That is crab-bucket mentality. When one crab in a bucketful tries to escape, the others almost always pull it back down. It's a picture of what it can be like to leave a life of GLBT identity or struggle.

My story stands in stark contrast to that of the people once in heterosexual marriages who went on to acquiesce to a gay life. Some have virtually lost their families and others have somehow found a way to hold onto some vestige of a relationship, though frequently a damaged one, with their children. Still others appear to have intact, loving relationships with ex-spouses and chidlren. I am thankful beyond words to have lived the life of grace I have, regardless of how many others like me there are. Radical gays cannot simply "poof" us away. Regardless of what you may call me, the fact remains that I underwent a genuine and lasting change, from experiencing strong same-sex attractions to having none at all. I understand why some of the gay people I talk to believe I ought to be in a separate category from those who are exclusively same-sex oriented. I do believe it is a much harder road for those folks. But with God, "all things are possible." I know he is transforming the lives of those people who are willing to submit to him fully and find their self-worth in Jesus Christ, as it is meant to be.

I submit my own testimony here because it is important to explain that there are alternatives to what passes for authentic help within the mental health system. Diehard gay activists tout the flawed, humanistic methodology of the guild organizations they have swayed through political strong-arming. The mental health establishment capitulated far too easily to their demands. They essentially threw the baby out with the bath water. The evidence is not exactly what they tell us it is. Political correctness, greed, and power stand in the way of getting all the facts out.

Outrageous Intolerance

A prime example of a gay-advocacy drive-by "shooting" is the political uproar that torpedoed President Bush's appointment of Dr. James Holsinger as the 18th U.S. Surgeon General during the summer of 2007. Holsinger, former chancellor of the University of

Kentucky's Chandler Medical Center and Kentucky's Secretary of Health and Family Services from 2003-2005, wrote a scholarly article for the United Methodist Church in 1991, "The Pathophysiology of Male Homosexuality." Holsinger pointed out with medical clarity that an unhealthy risk of sexually transmitted diseases follows when "the complementarity of the sexes is breached."[24] That is particularly true for MSM (male-to-male) intercourse, and myriad statistics back it up. The CDC has reported a significant increase in male homosexual syphilis rates since 1999, up from 5 percent to 64 percent of all male cases. An 81-percent increase was recorded from 2000 to 2004 alone.[25] Of course, such "homophobia" could not be tolerated by radical gays. Try as they may, many gay activists, even those who are Christians, cannot separate their hatred for all things deemed "fundamental" or evangelical from the positive aspects of the Christian community's work in the ex-gay movement—or anywhere else, for that matter. Where else was it going to come from? Certainly not the secular, humanistic fields of psychology and psychiatry, with a presumed motto of "if it feels right, do it." Spiritual regeneration and loving support to disciple fellow believers toward significant life changes is the Church's job. More specifically, it is the work of the Holy Spirit. Feelings don't fix us; they deceive us.

Broken System

The mental health establishment has been under fire from without and within for years. Sadly, the Church has become complicit in the push to over-medicalize emotional problems as "brain diseases," accepting that secular therapies and antidepressants often hold the answer for troubled Christians who, in many cases, are experiencing life's normal sorrows. If we have so readily accepted what the mental health professions call help in this area, naturally, we will be only too willing and gullible to accept anything else they say that passes for scientific "proof." That means gay activists can have a field day with all the studies they cite and the pronouncements among psychiatrists and psychologists that homosexuality cannot and should not be changed on peril of "doing harm." I submit that these very professionals do damage and violate their Hippocratic Oath every day in the guise of progressive "help" for struggling gays. At least two counselors did me harm. Who would ever advocate bullying troubled gay people into attempting to change their sexual orientation? That's a ridiculous notion, and over-sold charge against Christian therapists and ministries. Neither should gay rights activists and their mental health partners seduce all strugglers into fully embracing a gay identity.

Caring for the Vulnerable

The health problems and risky behaviors among gay teens, a particularly vulnerable population, are something we should all be concerned about. Will gay rights activists (and proponents of liberal sex education programs, for that matter) ignore obvious public health concerns in favor of their selfishly motivated political power-mongering? Where are the mental health "experts" that are standing up to advocate for America's youth, who are exposed to an increasing number of media messages affirming their right to express themselves sexually, even if that means experimenting with homosexuality or bisexuality? Any kind of sexual activity at such young ages is akin to playing Russian Roulette. The so-called experts' silent duplicity is appalling. They appear to be too busy making sure that kids are being prepared at ever-younger ages to experiment or come out of the closet and embrace a gay lifestyle, with all its emotional and physical health risks.

The damage that allegedly comes from helping a questioning same-sex-attracted person to change is more myth than fact, as Yarhouse and Jones' *Ex-Gays?* confirmed. It stands to reason that some will be harmed by illegitimate practitioners, but we know quacks exist in all fields. Coercing an ambivalent person into a change program or making wildly unsubstantiated claims along with touting unrealistic goals can cause emotional harm and set people up for failure. Saddling those who want to change, especially people of faith, with the burden that they can't clearly also does much harm. How many teens teetering on the brink of realizing their true, healthy identities as heterosexuals are pushed over the edge and convinced that they are homosexual during their vulnerable years? Such a push is every bit as unconscionable as forced change therapy would be.

At the 2004 NARTH Annual Conference, Dr. Spitzer made the observation, "There is a gay activist group that's very strong and very vocal and recognized officially by the American Psychiatric Association. There's nobody to give the other viewpoint. There may be a few people who believe it, but they don't talk."[26]

Perhaps they talk, but are simply talked over or are ignored. Respectful dialogue can far better serve the needs of the mental health community. Of course, those seeking human answers when only the divine will do will either have their come-to-Jesus meeting or they won't. It is not the responsibility of any Christian to make them understand in any other way. Indeed, trying to do so is an exercise in futility.

Four

All the News that Fits:
Media Pandering to Gay Politics

The examples of mainstream media pro-gay bias are legion. Media pundits on both sides of the issues have been weighing in with increasing frequency and intensity in recent years. Media firestorms such as the Proposition 8 backlash in California, former Miss California Carrie Prejean's affirmation of traditional marriage during the Miss USA pageant, ill will from President Obama's erstwhile gay supporters, and controversy over a few of his administration's openly gay appointees, as well as the DADT repeal push, have made headline-grabbing news. Throw in the occasional conservative or Christian gay-sex scandal (Ted Haggard, George Rekers, etc.) or gay pastor self-outings (Jim Swilley) and the MSM can have a field day. The gay-related blogosphere rates a category of its own, as para-media.

Going back to the fall of 2005, Fox News' Bill O'Reilly, who has treaded rather lightly in the territory of gay issues until more recently, took the author of a *Time* magazine article focusing on gay teens to task on his top-rated TV talk show, "The O'Reilly Factor."

The article had stated that boys were identifying as gay as early as 10 years of age while girls were claiming to be lesbians at 12, on average. Supposedly in the 1960s, they were waiting until 14 and 17, respectively, to declare their sexual orientation, which in those days was rarely done publicly. O'Reilly argued, "But there's a problem here. Number one, I think almost every teenager gets confused about sexual identity at some time, okay? So, you know, rushing out to declare yourself one thing or another, I think, is foolish."[1]

In a commentary about this controversy, Warren Throckmorton, had this to say:

> Although the ages of coming out are dropping, when to have sex and with whom are generally considered to be decisions requiring an adult level of maturity. Declaring a gay identity long before reaching the necessary level of maturation to engage in adult sexuality requires the teen to either experiment sexually or predict what his sexual attractions will be in the distant future or both. Instead of expanding their possibilities, teens can feel cast into a social role. A case can be made that teens are less likely to explore their options if such a role is adopted and lived out in an environment that encourages solidarity to a political cause.[2]

Interestingly, of the highly visual media coveted by gay rights propagandists, it is in Hollywood's feature films where one is still more likely to see gay stereotypes. For example, the controversial "Brokeback Mountain," the 2005 gay-themed movie that stirred up its share of media hyperbole on both sides of the PR street, followed a much-used plot line. "Both narratively and visually, 'Brokeback Mountain' is a tragedy about the specifically gay phenomenon of the 'closet,'" said *New York Times* columnist Daniel Mendelsohn.[3] Many critics wanted us to see the film as a universal love story whose main characters just happened to be gay men. Far from bolstering the message that gay is normal, the film instead reinforces the tragic guilt and self-loathing that has led many homosexual men and women to seek unhappy marriages, either as cover or as a hopeful cure for their same-sex attractions. Just like other classic films before it—"The Boys in the Band," "Ode to Billy Joe," or "That Certain Summer," to name a few—"Brokeback Mountain" makes painfully and poignantly clear what a tragically unhappy life homosexuality can be for some. That misery is not all caused by social ostracizing. Despite their more subdued character portrayals, the two wives emotionally abandoned by their gay husbands in the film represent another tragedy in gay culture.

The Tortured "Gay American"?

Disgraced New Jersey Gov. James McGreevey embarked in 2006 on his Oprah-launched book tour for *The Confession*, his much-anticipated tell-all about his closeted gay life as a husband, father, and career politician with White House aspirations. McGreevey came out as a "gay American" in a 2004 press conference, his long-suffering wife at his side. His term as governor was rife with scandal allegations and he resigned his office at the same time he made his public confession. He left his wife and young daughter—it was his second marital break-up, and he has another daughter—and eventually moved in with a male lover. During the first week of promoting his book, McGreevey appeared contrite and kept referring to his need to live a "healthy and integrated life." Never mind that his devastated wife was tossed aside like yesterday's newspaper. To his credit, he did acknowledge in an appearance on Fox News' "Hannity & Colmes" show on September 20, 2006 that he had betrayed his wife and was willing to be held accountable for it.

McGreevey's wife, Dina Matos McGreevey, decided to pen her own book, *Silent Partner: A Memoir of My Marriage.* She says she never would have married her now ex-husband if she'd known about his sexual identity confusion. To add to the bizarre news surrounding the McGreevey scandal, media reports began circulating in early May 2007 that the former governor had enrolled in an Episcopal seminary to allegedly prepare for the priesthood. Matos McGreevey issued a press statement through WABC/CH-7 in New York, a sister company to her publisher, Hyperion, in response to these reports that said, "He needs to be in the spotlight. I am astounded by his arrogance." Despite McGreevey's apparent contrition in his own media appearances, his former wife, appearing on ABC's "Good Morning America" May 2, 2007, told Diane Sawyer, "I don't think he's still acknowledged the damage that he's done to me and to my family and that's very difficult to accept." The former governor appears to have taken narcissism to new heights. The custody battle in the McGreevey divorce was an ugly, media-driven event.

Holding The Media Accountable

Perhaps McGreevey is better suited for a media role. How is it that liberal media pundits, disguised as objective reporters, can make brazen statements that run counter to the truth and common sense with impunity? This assessment of a CNN commentary by James Dobson appeared at mediamatters.org: "In a June 28 (2007) guest commentary posted on CNN.com, Focus on the Family founder and chairman James C. Dobson mischaracterized the same-sex marriage debate to baselessly suggest that there is strong public support for a constitutional amendment to ban gay marriage."[4] Dobson's crime was insinuating there was "strong public support" for constitutionally limiting marriage to that between one man and one woman, as it had been for millennia, because 19 states by then (now 31) had passed their own marriage amendment initiatives by a resounding 70-percent average voter majority. The Dobson character assassination piece cited a number of polls that indicated precisely the opposite of what Dobson knew to be the truth. Of course, it neglected to mention the voting referenda "polls" that really counted. It was rather reminiscent of those infamous media exit polls during the 2004 presidential election that showed John Kerry was winning. The proposed federal marriage amendment, as Dobson knows well, has had a tough row to hoe in Congress, but that is more because of politics as usual rather than the prevailing sentiment of constituents.

Various media critics have noted the obvious bias in reporting the ongoing same-sex marriage debate, particularly in the media blitz that followed the Massachusetts Supreme Judicial Court's 2003 decision to legalize gay marriage. Here's a sampling:

- *Washington Post* media critic Howard Kurtz said in July 2004, "ALL of the press was being way too sympathetic to the gay marriage side, given that there are many, many Americans who don't support that issue."[5]

- Fox News Watch panelist James Pinkerton (February 28, 2004) observed, "[I]n the media's mind it is just a given that gay marriage is both inevitable and desirable."[6]

- *Washington Post* ombudsman Michael Getler (March 21, 2004) characterized *The Post's* news reports as "excellent" and "from all sides," but also said "critics who say the paper has had few, if any, features portraying opponents of this social change in a positive or even neutral light have a point. The overall picture, it seems to me, could use more balance."[7]

- *Chicago Tribune* ombudsman Donald Wycliff (July 8, 2004) also cited journalists' pro-gay bias, referring to a 2002 Pew study that found 88 percent of national journalists want gay marriage to be accepted by society. They have an "inability to see from other perspectives," he said.[8]

The media coverage that followed California's affirmative ruling on gay marriage was a repeat performance.

A similar media bias was showing in June 2007 when the Massachusetts Legislature, in its Constitutional Convention meeting, refused to allow debate and then quickly voted to deny the people the right to decide whether same-sex couples should be allowed to marry in the state. Robert Knight, formerly of the Culture and Media Institute, said on June 15, "What should have been a national news story was ignored last night by CBS Evening News and NBC Nightly News, and this morning by Good Morning America, the Early Show, and the Today Show. Only ABC World News Tonight (25 seconds) covered this story." Their headline audaciously stated, "Gay Marriage Safe in Massachusetts: Vote to *Redefine* (emphasis mine) Marriage as a Union Between a Man and a Woman Was Defeated." The cable news coverage was slightly better, with Fox News and CNN both reporting the story (CNN on three programs). Print coverage, ranging from left-leaning to fairly balanced, appeared in several major newspapers, Knight reported.[9] As to fair coverage, said Knight, "The quotes fit an ongoing pattern of media coverage, in which liberal, pro-homosexual activists often are allowed to express heartfelt sentiments while conservative spokespeople get to comment only on strategy or technical details."

On the plus side of media coverage more favorable to the conservative view, several talk show hosts opined that the Federal Marriage Amendment might be a necessary safeguard against activist judges who could override the will of the people. Even Chris Matthews, host of MSNBC's "Hardball," said gay marriage "should be a popular decision. ... I don't think it's a rights question, I think it's a cultural question; it's up to everybody to participate."[10] Fox News' Bill O'Reilly asserted in an exchange on "The O'Reilly Factor" with Massachusetts attorney Wendy Murphy that the courts had "found a way to get around [the Constitution] against the will of the people. ... The polls show that."[11] California and Maine voters' overturning of their state legislatures or courts affirmation of gay marriage shouted that message loud and clear, though California has been all over the map. Now, an appeal is pending to a federal court ruling ultimately upholding gay marriage there.

The Gay Media Coup

Gay or gay-sympathizing media executives are growing bolder as they seek more and more influence. Consider these comments made by *The New York Times'* Richard Berke while appearing on behalf of the National Lesbian and Gay Journalists Association (NLGJA):

> [W]hen I started there [*The Times*] 15 years ago ... the department heads were asking for lists of the gay reporters on different sections so they could be punished in different ways. ... Since I've been there, there's been a dramatic shift: I remember coming and wondering if there were ... any gay reporters there. ... Now ... literally three-quarters

of the people deciding what's on the front page are
not-so-closeted homosexuals. ... a real far cry from
what it was like not so long ago. ...[12]

A fair number of well-known gay and lesbian media moguls
in America are "out and about." Many others likely are still in
the closet. Infamous gay-outing journalist Michelangelo Signorile
named names in an article he wrote for *New York* magazine in 2001.[13]
Out Magazine did the same in 2007, citing a group of seven men
referred to as *The New York Times* "Gay Mafia" as number seven
on its infamous Top 50 Gay Men and Women in America list.
The entire list—whether accurate or urban legend—can be viewed
at *Out's* website (Out.com).

The NLGJA formed in 1990. According to its website, the
organization "works within newsrooms to foster fair and accurate
coverage of lesbian and gay issues ..." and has more than 1,300
members and 25 chapters in the United States and Canada.
National directors currently include *The San Francisco Chronicle's*
David Steinberg (president), NPR's Trey Graham (treasurer), and
CNN's Jen Christensen, broadcast vice president. Fox News has
had a past board member and several large-market newspapers,
along with several college papers, are represented. Interestingly, "fair
and balanced" Fox News' Roger Ailes allegedly made a $10,000
contribution to the NLGJA to sponsor the group's August 2006
conference. Peter LaBarbera, of the much-hated-by-gays Americans
for Truth, asked Ailes to make a matching contribution to a pro-
family group. "You can't just give to the homosexual activists when
the country is divided over the question of gay rights," LaBarbera
said.[14] Obviously, Fox/Ailes can and did.

Even some respected Christian media giants have allowed
surprising editorial positions to surface in coverage of gay issues.
A 2006 *Christianity Today* blog report, compiled by Rob Moll and

entitled "Against the Ex-Gays," was ostensibly written as an analysis about Salon.com and *New York Times* articles covering the ex-gay movement. The writer got a bit caught up in political correctness, however, stating, "Both articles focus on the difficulties of changing sexual orientation, saying that mainstream psychiatric organizations don't support such therapy, that success rates are usually low, if counted, and for participants who don't change their orientation can result in simply feeling more guilty." The writer made no attempt to counterbalance those claims with a statement from a healthy, formerly gay representative, however, no doubt leading readers to wonder if such folks are merely a figment of evangelical imaginative zeal. The piece ended with the syrupy statement: "We're all abnormal, we all have wounds. We all have sinned, and we all need a Savior." Rather obvious, if mushy. A nice try, but *CT* missed the mark on this one.[15]

Conservative Media Powerhouse

Traditional media outlets have seen their influence as cultural gatekeepers wane, thanks to the alternative press and the Internet. According to a 2009 *Wall Street Journal* article, there are more than 22 million bloggers in the U.S., 1.7 million of whom do it for pay.[16] These citizen-journalists have created a tsunami in mass communications, to the great consternation of the old ivory-towered media elites. Paul Greenberg, editorial pages editor of *The Arkansas Democrat-Gazette* and syndicated columnist, is one of the few old-timers (and likable curmudgeons) who rails against his elite colleagues in his decidedly traditional forum. He has observed, "The proliferation of blogs may be much closer than oh-so-respectable journalism to the freedom of the press envisioned by the authors of the First Amendment. They lived in a world of pamphleteers in which the readers were the judge of quality, not some distant authority cloaked in a Ph.D. with a magisterial column in the New York Almighty *Times*."[17]

The modern conservative media revolution began with the rise of direct mail newsletters, which originated in the 1960s with the Goldwater presidential campaign, but really took off in the hands of Jerry Falwell as a Christian call to activate the too-long-silent bloc of voters he called the Moral Majority in the 1970s. This movement helped propel Ronald Reagan into the White House in 1980. Until then, Christian activism had been more of a liberal exercise. Mainstream liberal churches commonly advanced liberal political and social causes without cries of separation of church and state being raised. Falwell's activist persona, along with those of conservative forces Paul Weyrich and Ralph Reed, helped give rise to James Dobson's influence. Dobson—now semi-retired but very much alive and well—was characterized in his heyday as "the Big Enchilada" of the conservative Christian community by Richard A. Viguerie and David Franke, authors of *America's Right Turn: How Conservatives Used New and Alternative Media to Take Power*. Dan Gilgoff, keeper of *US News & World Report's* "God and Country" blog, also penned a book about Dobson's and the Christian Right's rise to influence, *The Jesus Machine: How James Dobson, Focus on the Family, and Evangelical America Are Winning the Culture War*. Dobson's many books have sold millions of copies and his Focus on the Family newsletter subscribers peaked at more than three million—as many as *Newsweek* could boast in recent years.[18] Those numbers have tapered off in recent years, and with Dobson now pulling back to be more of a behind-the-scenes elder statesman, his continued influence will be measured with great interest.

Of course, mainstream news magazines, as well as many newspapers—those that haven't folded altogether, that is—have seen their own circulation drop dramatically. In November 2009, Window Media, publishers of *The Washington Blade*, the gay newspaper of record, and other gay papers, suddenly closed it doors and filed for Chapter 7 bankruptcy. *The Blade* later came back under a new flag. The sagging economy has been no respecter of ideologies. Dobson and Focus on the Family have been alternately victimized by liberal angst and a growing wave of moderate posturing that extends from the political arena to the Church. As Peter Wehner, senior fellow at the Ethics and Public Policy Center, opined, there is a growing tendency "to take conservative principles, which are enduring, and apply them to issues and circumstances that are different than they were a quarter of a century ago."[19]

Are conservatism and evangelicalism taking a progressive turn? Time will tell. As Jerry Falwell and the Moral Majority earlier rallied Christians around abortion and gay issues—an effort that was later taken up and made more politicized by the Christian Coalition—Dobson and Focus on the Family have led the charge in marriage and family preservation and the gay culture war, in concert with other like-minded organizations. Dobson has been both feared and reviled by radical gay rights activists. They could not accept that the FOTF message attempted to reflect biblical truth softened by grace during its eleven years of Love Won Out conferences. Naysayers honed in on the few ill-considered claims of conference speakers to the general exclusion of all else. The one side of Dobson they acknowledge, as was the case for Falwell, is the tough-love side, which they cast as hateful.

According to a January 2008 *Time* magazine article that ruminated about the extent of Dobson's political clout, one number that has remained consistent for some time is the worldwide audience of 220 million who listen to his radio broadcasts (which began airing in March 2010 without Dobson at the microphone except for an occasional guest appearance). Those broadcasts generally have broken down to eight percent dealing with public policy issues with the remainder focusing on issues common to all families (ostensibly, some even to gay families). It is the latter focus that propelled the program into the National Radio Hall of Fame in 2008. Gay activists were unhinged over FOTF receiving this honor and ranted for weeks about it, given their hatred of the 8 percent of FOTF's mission. It is interesting to note that in an October 26, 1988 letter, Dobson wrote to a friend concerned about Focus on the Family's increasing involvement in politics and policy: "Our movement into the arena of public policy is unsettling to me. It is so easy to make a mistake in that dimension, and if I had my way, we would stay out of it. On the other hand, I feel that God has put us in a position of leadership there, and we would displease Him if we refused to accept the challenge. Thus, we proceed, with fear and trembling."[20]

While Dobson's folksy brand of parental advice characterizing 90-plus percent of his famed radio broadcasts has been warmly unique, his policy-driven broadcasts notwithstanding, there has been no mistaking the confrontational tone of the next rung on the conservative media ladder that came storming onto the scene in the 1980s: issues-driven talk radio. That hugely successful venture opened the door for alternative cable TV programs in the 1990s. Try as they may, liberal radio broadcasters have been unable to compete with their conservative counterparts. As Viguerie and Franke point out, and most conservatives realize because of talk radio, liberals in Congress like John Kerry and Nancy Pelosi have complained that the Fairness Doctrine ought to be brought back to ensure a "balance" in media coverage. "Somehow we doubt he was referring to NBC, ABC, CBS, or NPR—networks that come closest to providing a single (liberal) point of view, under the guise of objectivity. ..."[21] No, the First Amendment is definitely applied differently to the liberal and conservative media, depending on who's doing the analysis. Both liberals and conservatives have earned rebukes in this regard, of course.

The "Dominionists"?

What's the current en-vogue label for conservative evangelicals? "Meet the Dominionists—biblical literalists who believe God has called them to take over the U.S. government." That one comes from Bob Moser's inspired anti-evangelical rant in *Rolling Stone* (April 2005). "They want to rewrite schoolbooks to reflect a Christian version of American history, pack the nation's courts with judges who follow Old Testament law, post the Ten Commandments in every courthouse and make it a felony for gay men to have sex and women to have abortions."[22] Don't blink or you might miss this mighty army of masked marauders as they ride by. While such folks do mill about, they have not shown themselves to be an organized movement with any real power. Leftist conspiracy theorists regularly conflate them with Bible-quoting evangelicals who happen to be politically engaged.

While the framers of our Constitution understood the need to keep established religion from being imposed on the people, they never sought, as has been falsely claimed, to restrain the hand of God (as if one could actually do so) from the business of governing, or deny the need for godly wisdom and guidance in our corporate affairs. The widespread belief in a separation between church and state mandating the latter has shaped the political arena to an unfortunate degree. Complacency or confusion among growing numbers of conservative voters figured in the ideological power shift following the 2006 and 2008 elections. There is plenty of evidence that leftist forces with an ungodly bent are taking advantage of this unrest to push a divisive agenda that will usher in an era of even more radical social change that bodes ill for the health of the beleaguered family, as well as the Church. An increasingly vitriolic Congress—Democrats and Republicans alike—has grown more egocentric, "fat," lazy, and drunk on its own power. And the current White House occupant has shucked the people-imposed boundaries of logic and sensibility at every turn, enjoying unprecedented centralized power and seeking to edge us ever closer to socialism.

Gay activists know they will benefit from a sustained liberalized political climate. We have not seen that for some time, and the "hope and chance" touted by the Obama administration appears to be short-lived. Along with Democrats winning the White House and the House of Representatives in 2008 came a two-year window of opportunity to appoint activist judges and others sympathetic to the gay agenda and other liberal social/political causes, setting the stage for deeper divisions among Americans. In the tit-for-tat game of politics, the country's electorate shifted sharply back to center-right in the 2010 midterm elections. President Obama has clearly stated objectives, among them to repeal DOMA (the Defense of Marriage Act) and the "Don't Ask, Don't Tell" policy preventing gays from serving openly in the armed forces. In a bit of media theater, gays began lamenting that Obama was turning his back on them at the precise time he was overseeing the appointment of several liberal gay activists to influential posts, among them former educator Kevin Jennings, who serves as the Department of Education's School Safety "czar." Jennings is also the highly controversial founder of GLSEN—the Gay, Lesbian, and Straight Education Network. Obama added to his gay appointment or nominee list lesbian activist attorney Chai Feldblum to head the Equal Employment Opportunity Commission (EEOC). He gave the keynote address to the Human Rights Commission, sharing stage time with the infamous bad-girl entertainer Lady Gaga. Add to that a presidential proclamation of June 2009 and 2010 as LGBT Pride Month, along with the hoopla of a who's who of gay power brokers invited to the White House to revel in this unprecedented support. Obama's 2009 proclamation recited his gay rights credentials:

My Administration has partnered with the LGBT community to advance a wide range of initiatives. At the international level, I have joined efforts at the United Nations to decriminalize homosexuality around the world. Here at home, I continue to support measures to bring the full spectrum of equal rights to LGBT Americans.

These measures include enhancing hate crimes laws, supporting civil unions and Federal rights for LGBT couples, outlawing discrimination in the workplace, ensuring adoption rights, and ending the existing "Don't Ask, Don't Tell" policy in a way that strengthens our Armed Forces and our national security.[23]

Understanding the "house divided" principle themselves, liberal social activists and their media accomplices have taken to casting evangelical Christians as ideologically or theologically divided and at war among themselves. Evangelicals also are being described as having been duped by certain Republican power brokers who privately have viewed them as "nuts" while realizing how critical their votes may be. Such is the discomfiting claim of a book by David Kuo called *Tempting Faith: An Inside Story of Political Seduction*. Gilgoff's book asserts it, as well. Kuo was the number two official in the Bush administration's faith-based initiative program. Whatever truth is in his assertions may be disheartening for Christians who believe impacting the culture is best done through policy initiatives. This news should encourage Christians to think twice about being in bed with any political party, as the demise of the Christian Coalition ought to have demonstrated.

A recent book by Michael Gerson and Peter Wehner—both men also worked in the Bush White House—called *City of Man:*

Religion and Politics in a New Era, is well worth reading. The authors give what I think is a balanced picture of what it means to be Christian (a citizen of what St. Augustine called the City of God) and a citizen on earth with a vested interest in society (the City of Man). The next generation of Christian conservatives, including pastors, appears to be moving away from the perception that to be evangelical is to be, by association, Republican or even politically active. Many are no less committed to cultural change than were some of their predecessors, but they are more attuned to how their tone affects their message. Top-down policy change or power brokerage is not their focus. They are committed to their flocks first, social change second. Few media moguls can see this.

There is no denying the Church could yet become a larger battleground in the culture war's gay front. Even with evangelicalism seeking to move away from its former rigidity, it is not necessarily being taken over by moderates or liberals whose pet causes are social justice, world peace, and the environment. The Christian agenda is meant to include the entire spectrum of social and moral concerns. Progressive pastors like Jim Wallis of the Sojourners are preaching that abortion and gay rights are not still defining issues for the Church. With more reports like one aired in September 2006 on the CBS Evening News, he may succeed. "I want to announce tonight that the monologue of the religious right is finally over," Wallis said during the interview. "With 30,000 children dying every day needlessly from poverty and disease, I can't imagine Jesus thinking the top issue on our agenda ought to be gay marriage amendments in Ohio."[24] It was an unfair pot shot. Wallis was counter-positioned in the CBS report against the Family Research Council's Tony Perkins, who articulated the conservative evangelical view: "I think more and more people are standing on our side, on the side of sanctity of human life, the preservation of marriage. I don't mind having these debates because when the truth is on your side, you ultimately win."[25] I watched this news report because I'd been tipped off it was to air (by the Wallis camp, no less). Of course, CBS didn't even try to disguise its obvious liberal bias. Wallis was given considerably more air time to expound on his views while Perkins' views—defensive responses, really—were reduced to a few sound bites and wordless or unintelligible voiced-over video clips. This tactic serves the liberal media well.

What kind of voice more accurately reflects the majority of evangelicals on the issues? As many as 78 percent of white evangelicals voted for George W. Bush in 2004, with a majority 36 percent of the overall evangelical vote going to him. In 2008, a slightly greater number of evangelicals voted for John McCain: more than 38 percent, according to BeliefNet, and still the highest percentage of all groups. How many were simply voting against Obama? Perhaps, in part, because Bush turned out not to embody the great hope for social and religious conservatives that his campaign touted, the number of evangelicals voting Republican decreased in 2006 and 2008. Yet, some socially conservative religious Democrats also made it into the House of Representatives in 2008, some of them perceived as feckless being thrown right out again in 2010. Voters can be fickle, but liberal politicians have begun to figure out that faith counts, even though they can't quite get a handle on just what their faith ought to look like.

Meanwhile, gay activists are pushing for more openly gay politicians. GayPolitics.com sings the praises of The Gay & Lesbian Victory Fund: "Since 1991, the Victory Fund has helped to grow the number of openly LGBT elected officials serving in office in the U.S. from 49 to nearly 500. It's [sic] endorsement means candidates are recommended to a national network of donors, and they also receive expert campaign and technical advice from an experienced political staff." Homegrown candidates are better than working to convince those already entrenched in government that gay is good. It was an easier process with the media.

Love and Truth Win Out

One of the most interesting media brouhahas of recent memory occurred in the summer of 2006. It was touched off by a Love Won Out conference in Indian Wells, California (about 20 miles from Palm Springs), whose then-mayor, Ron Oden, is an openly gay African-American. The conference, which drew around 1,400 attendees, was reported to be the third largest in the ministry's then-eight-year history. Of course, the Palm Springs area is known for its sizable gay community. Mayor Oden had sent a welcome letter to Focus on the Family several weeks prior to the event that caused a firestorm of protest from local gays and lesbians. He even said he would attend the conference, and he kept that promise, giving a brief welcome speech. Citing his pride in Palm Springs' diversity and his disagreement with FOTF's positions on homosexuality, he nevertheless told his gay brethren, "I believe that I should show them common or Christian courtesy."[26] For that decision and his suggestion that the local gay community should reach out to the conference attendees to "show them who we are," he was blasted by his gay constituents. "I don't think it's my responsibility as a lesbian who's been in a relationship for 18 years to stand out and be a role model," City Councilwoman Ginny Foat said.[27] Her comments represented the in-your-face attitude that many have stereotyped as the face of secular gay activism.

CBS interviewed Oden, who, to his credit, continued to defend his welcoming gesture. But the report contained this misleading statement: "Focus on the Family, based in Colorado Springs, Colorado, teaches that gays and lesbians lead deviant un-Christian lifestyles and have a choice in their sexual orientation"

(I am not aware of FOTF officially calling gays and lesbians "deviant," and they maintain gays have a choice in their *behavior*).[28] The blatantly hostile phrase "teaches that gays and lesbians lead deviant un-Christian lifestyles," was repeated in other news stories, especially among the gay media. Obviously, some of the media reporting on the conference ignored former lesbian and conference speaker Melissa Fryrear's message in an earlier newswire release:

> We were invited by people in the community who want to hear our view that unwanted (emphasis mine) homosexuality can be overcome—and that it is possible to love a gay son or daughter or parent or friend without compromising your Christian faith. It's obviously a view some in the region don't think we have the right to share; but we do have the right, and those attending the conference Saturday have the right to hear it—as do the readers and viewers and listeners of area media.[29]

Evangelicals are largely misunderstood and misrepresented in the media. Not that all of us ought to get a pass, mind you. We do have our share of misguided, Pharisaic mouthpieces. "The outrageous things you see on TV are an aberration, though some people do hold those views," says Jeffrey L. Sheler, author of *Believers: A Journey into Evangelical America*.[30] "But the vast majority of evangelicals are normal, reasonable people. They are hardworking, love their families, and are not out to cram religion down your throat and turn the country into a theocracy."[31] Precisely.

A Good Journalist Is Hard to Find

Rick Warren, pastor of the mammoth Saddleback Church in Orange County, California, (an evangelical Southern Baptist church) and author of the mega-bestselling book, *The Purpose Driven Life*, has had to defend himself against a number of inane and condescending comments and misquotes made in media stories and blogging reports about him. He is not alone, of course. Many in the media are still fond of profiling some big-name evangelicals as buffoons. In this case, the "reporters" were incapable of doing even basic fact-checking and echoed each other's misinformation. "I used to think that only journalists were lazy and relied on the articles of others, but I've since learned that bloggers are lazy too. Both tend to just repeat what others have said—without checking the accuracy—instead of doing their own original research," Warren wrote in July 2006 to Simon.com, a popular blog site. Then, he proceeded to take the reporters and bloggers in question to the woodshed, responding with the accurate information to a series of inaccuracies.[32]

It takes a lot to get someone as mild-mannered as Rick Warren that worked up. I guess he had had enough drive-by media shootings. Warren had to defend himself and his church yet again in 2008 from media misreporting, which included some Soulforce media tampering via sketchy statements in a press release. In a story following the Soulforce visit to Saddleback Church, *Newsweek* reported: "... Rick Warren announced that he was welcoming a group of gay fathers to his church for Father's Day. Now, even on very conservative Christian campuses, there are gays who are 'out' and who want their authority figures to recognize them—and their sexuality—as deserving of God's love. Thanks largely to the efforts of Soul Force [sic], which encourages dialogue between gays and Christians on campus, these students are trying to get organized." The story was picked up in a blog report at GetReligion.org, which called Soulforce to accountability for misrepresenting the truth to *Newsweek*. Warren, himself, then posted a response:

(You) were correct in assuming *Newsweek* quoted
a Soul Force [sic] press release headline that was
100 percent false. We did not invite this group
and I will not be meeting with them. They invited
themselves to draw attention to their cross-country
publicity stunt. ...[33]

A few Saddleback staffers did consent to meet with the Soulforce
reps and some of the gay families that visited the church.

Unfortunately, "sketchy reporting" is business as usual for
many news organizations, especially when homosexuality is the
topic de jour. The October 2005 *Time* cover story, "The Battle
Over Gay Teens," included this blanket statement: "It's important
to note that nearly all mental-health professionals agree that trying
to reject one's homosexual impulses will usually be fruitless and
depressing—and can lead to suicide, according to Dr. Jack Drescher
of the American Psychiatric Association. ..."[34] Of course, significant
numbers of psychologists and psychiatrists do not agree with
that assessment. As many as 69 percent of American Psychiatric
Association members, when surveyed following the decision to
remove homosexuality from the DSM, said they still considered
homosexuality a "pathological adaptation." Only a third of the
membership even cast a vote on the matter in 1974.[35] Time and
continued activism have reshaped the establishment view, of course.
If you chip away at the facts long enough, you can rewrite them.

Taking it in the Chops

Does the media apologize for or correct such blunders or
inappropriate reporting? Rarely. But if a politically incorrect
comment by a conservative or a Christian that dares to point
out the inconsistencies or outright lies in the pro-gay message
makes it into print, woe be unto whomever said it! The politically

correct rabble will hound them to the ends of the earth, calling them names that are not always printable in the process. Case in point: now-retired Marine Gen. Peter Pace, former chairman of the Joint Chiefs of Staff. Pace stirred up a hornet's nest in March 2007 when he said in response to questioning about the military's "Don't Ask, Don't Tell" policy from *The Chicago Tribune* editorial board that he believed "homosexual acts are immoral." In fact, he equated such acts to heterosexual adultery and said the government should not be sanctioning either. His comments unleashed a media firestorm, largely fed by *The Washington Post's* outrageous and inaccurate editorial statements. The subhead of a *Post* editorial read, "Gen. Peter Pace Denounces Gays and Lesbians who Are Busy Defending their Country." Gay activists called for the general to apologize and even resign. To his credit, he did neither but only expressed regret that he had interjected his personal beliefs into the public policy debate. Pace did not say gay servicemen and women were not patriotic or had not served honorably, despite *The Post's* inference to the contrary. Sadly, some key conservative politicians knifed him in the back and cast a shadow over his stellar service with spineless public comments.

To his credit, Gen. Pace refused to change his stance during questioning before the Senate Appropriations Committee in September 2007, a month before his retirement. The hearing was meant to address the 2008 proposed war budget. Instead, Pace was prodded into "clarifying" his prior statements by Sen. Tom Harkin (D-Iowa), who said he'd found those remarks to be "very hurtful" and "very demoralizing" to homosexuals serving in the military. "Are there wonderful Americans who happen to be homosexual serving in the military? Yes," Pace said. He then added, "We need to be very precise then, about what I said wearing my stars and being very conscious of it. And that is, very simply, that we should respect those who want to serve the nation

but not through the law of the land, condone activity that, in my
upbringing, is counter to God's law." Pace noted that the Uniform
Code of Military Justice (UCMJ) prohibits homosexual sex acts as
well as heterosexual adultery. Harkin said, "Well, then, maybe we
should change that."[36] That's our government in action.

Moving too swiftly to change a long-held policy as touchy
as DADT has generated much debate, rightly so. Allowing gays
and lesbians to openly serve in our armed forces may be inevitable
in our open, pluralistic society. Still, it could have unforeseen
consequences on military readiness and morale, as a noteworthy
cadre of high-ranking military leaders has pointed out. Military
chaplains may have the most sensitive adjustments to make in
the face of such a change, as they represent denominations with
opposing theological viewpoints on homosexuality.

All the Propaganda that's Fit To Print

There was a time when the ranks of the Fourth Estate
overflowed with principled journalists, who took their role as
dispassionate reporters of the news seriously. As veteran journalist
Cal Thomas recalls, they believed journalism was "a calling and
a public trust."[37] That time has passed. Now, we have "opinion
journalism," an oxymoron, and compromised ethical standards.

The left-leaning *Washington Post* has been an unapologetic
financial contributor to the NLGJA. While *The Post* has an archive
full of pro-gay articles, one that was actually touching in some ways
was a February 24, 2007 editorial about "Gay Rights Pioneer"
Barbara Gittings, who had died several days earlier. Quoting
her fellow gay rights activist, Frank Kameny, the editorial called
Gittings the "Founding Mother" of the gay rights movement. She
is best known for her success in getting gay literature and other
materials into public libraries, as well as helping to lead the early
push to have homosexuality recognized as normal rather than as a

mental illness (she and fellow gay activist Frank Kameny reportedly found a closeted gay psychiatrist, John Fryer, to testify in disguise in 1972 on a panel before the APA, which in 2006 named an award after him). *The New York Times* took a full month to publish its Gittings obituary, certainly not the way the Gray Lady's "gay mafia" glowingly treated the death of Harry Hay, the far more flamboyant gay socialist who openly lobbied for pedophilia rights. Could it have been a backhanded swipe at feminists?

One almost wonders how the Church would look today if Christians had the same fervor for carrying out the Great Commission as early gays and lesbians did in seeking to be recognized as human beings. What began as a quest to overcome gay and lesbian invisibility, with events that sought an air of respectability, was hijacked along the way by radical militants, who delighted in pushing the envelope, inviting conservatives to push back. The sexual and gay revolutions have impacted both the gay and straight worlds in unfortunate ways. Evangelicals sometimes have painted the gay community with one broad brush, whipping up fears that all homosexuals are child-predatory perverts or making other extreme statements that are not entirely factual. "The Christian church has a sordid history—a history of the televangelists from the eighties who would malign homosexuals and say they're all perverts and pedophiles and going to hell—but didn't actually offer you redemption," said Chad Thompson, a young Christian formerly gay man who runs Inqueery.com, a website that seeks to help young gays or teens who may be confused about their sexuality, and takes that message into schools.[38] Thompson is also the author of *Loving Homosexuals as Jesus Would*.

Of course, gay rights advocates can legitimately say most gay folk are civilly obedient, reasonable people who contribute positively to society, just as Sheler says of evangelicals. Yes, there surely are those few conservatives or evangelicals who loathe the mere existence of gays, the same as there are gay activists who are incensed by the existence of ex-gays or who take a condescending view of evangelicals. Many others see America as a patchwork quilt of diversity that allows for those of all persuasions or faiths or no faith at all to peacefully coexist and enjoy the same basic freedoms and opportunities. Naturally, gay people are entitled to the same freedoms all Americans have, as guaranteed by our Constitution, though recognizing gay marriage as one of those rights remains on the margins and is unacceptable, period, to most Bible-believing Christians. It is the pushing of the more radical gay agenda that would place innocent children in the crosshairs of political expediency or judicial activism in ex-gay vs. gay custody battles or indoctrinate school children in one-sided gay propaganda that especially rankles many of the 95 percent or so of straight Americans. Homosexuals deserve to live safe from unlawful discrimination and violence. The rest of us deserve the freedom to teach our children our creeds or religion and to raise them in a healthy society where they can learn what it means to be created in God's image—his originally intended image of male and female with distinct and complementary gender roles. Unhappy gays deserve the right to attempt change. And we all deserve to be treated fairly by the media.

Five

Image "Gerrymandering": Redrawing and Muddling the Truth

In February 1988, a "war conference" of some 175 gay activists from across the country is said to have convened in Warrenton, Virginia to establish a "four-point agenda for the gay movement." This gathering reportedly led to the Kirk and Madsen gay image-rebuilding manifesto, which had a six-point agenda. "Dismissing the movement's outworn techniques in favor of carefully calculated public relations propaganda" was the war room theme.[1] As Paul E. Rondeau ("Selling Homosexuality," *Regent University Law Review*, Vol. 14, 2002) has pointed out, gay activists essentially were reinventing the ancient Greek and Roman ploy of sophistry, or the art of persuasion and rhetoric in the marketplace. "The main thing is to talk about gayness until the issue becomes thoroughly tiresome."[2]

Today, few social or political issues generate the raw emotion and angry jabs—and that even includes some infighting on both sides—that frequently occur in the gay culture clash. If the mainstream media's treatment of the issues signifies anything, it is that the gay revolution is succeeding and it is along the lines of Kirk and Madsen's (or whomever's) blueprint. "If history repeats itself, the point of view that holds sway in America's courts will first hold sway in the minds and hearts of individual citizens, judges, and lawmakers. And the heart and mind of society is the target market that the gay rights campaign means to capture in order to win the courts." That is the sobering assessment of Paul Rondeau.[3] Indeed, ceding even the moral high ground to gays is becoming an axiomatic proposition. "[Reality] has become nothing more than an advertising battle fought by opposing forces. The best and most constant advertising will win the day," said Stanley Crouch in his *New York Daily News* column on November 29, 2010.

Of course, this war is far from over. Lest we forget, it is not man who will end it but God. As we have seen, the most significant "poll" not among those pundits cite ad nauseam is the one represented by the 31 states that have handily voted in favor of adding traditional one man, one-woman marriage amendments to their constitutions. All the states' measures were preemptive measures to prevent similar actions. Traditional values-minded Americans are not ready to concede the fight to preserve marriage, balance classroom education, and maintain free speech for pastors and others who wish to counter what is unbiblical. They realize the gay "ghettoes" congregated mostly in urban areas, predominately on both coasts, stand in stark contrast to the more conservative, middle-American territory on the map. What they don't want to see is Bible-preaching churches relegated to their own ghettoes.

Gays as the Ultimate Victims

Gay rights activists count on their ability to convince a great many unsuspecting people that they have truth and justice cornered through manipulative tactics that give them the appearance of being victimized at every turn, despite the glowing gains in gay rights. Rondeau, a former senior sales and marketing manager with 25 years of industry experience, also observed, "The very use of the phrase 'gay rights' illustrates both the rhetorical success of pro-gay activists and the rhetorical problem facing those opposing the homosexual movement's campaign to legitimize homosexuality as a protected class status. While the origins of the term 'gay' to substitute for homosexual are debated, the term ... de-emphasizes sex and makes more palatable the basic idea of homo-*sex*-uality. Likewise, use of the term 'rights' presumes, or at least frames any discussion with, a pro-gay bias; homosexuals either are entitled to or are being deprived of something."[4] As Rondeau further states, "Hearing about the need for gay rights from a presumably neutral newscaster, educator, or clergy is far more credible and therefore persuasive. 'News' is more persuasive than 'advertising.'"[5]

Believing they have endured these manipulative techniques long enough, those advocating traditional marriage and family values often are fixated on discrediting the rhetoric of the gay movement in order to put its players on the defensive. The predictable response is rather like that of a wounded animal backed into a corner. What does not work is senseless name-calling and attempts to cast the entire gay community in the same mold, even though gay shills somehow get more leeway from the media when they resort to such tactics. A more effective message is one that points out the inconsistencies and distortions in gay propaganda and offers concern for the individuals deceived by it. How difficult is it to hold to a message of truth and compassion without appearing to attack the individual? Extremely difficult, given the defensive position "truth-in-love" Christians have been boxed up in by the gay image crafters. Yes, it ought to be an embarrassment when their spokespeople have their own duplicitous words quoted back to them, just as it should be when it happens to the other side. What ensues, however, is a loud chorus of accusations that the purveyor of such a message is a hateful, priggish, homophobic bigot. And that has effectively drowned out the worthiness of the Christian message.

Honesty and integrity are the only way to truly inhabit the moral high ground. The truth has a way of bubbling to the surface. Excessive emotion—the tool most employed by activists on both sides—is best left aside. Passion is called for, of course, but it can be portrayed with measured and dignified restraint. Paul instructed Christians in 2 Timothy 2: 23-25 to "refuse foolish and ignorant speculations" and not to be "quarrelsome," but to be "kind to all, able to teach, patient when wronged with gentleness correcting those who are in opposition. ..." What defense is there against such a strategy? While this teaching is meant more for the church body, it also applies to the larger community. God's people should confront real evil head-on, but we should not be inventing it. Nor should we be spoiling for a fight. We must carefully choose our battles and our language. "Hate the sin but love the sinner" is a cliché that needs to go. Those have become passive-aggressive fighting words, like it or not.

Successful public relations may mean eliciting the desired emotional response, but it also can backfire. Let's look at a consistent PR talking point/flashpoint repeatedly raised in the gay debate: that GLBT youth are subjected to constant harassment and violence in their schools and communities. Is this true? The *Time* magazine story previously discussed was quite revealing on the subject:

> When [Ritch] Savin-Williams surveyed 180 young men ages 14 to 25 for an earlier book, ... *And Then I Became Gay*, he found that nearly all had received positive, sometimes enthusiastic, responses when they first came out. (Many others are received with neutrality, even boredom: University of Washington

senior Aaron Schwitters, who was not interviewed by Savin-Williams, says when he came out to his fellow College Republicans at a club meeting last year, "there was five seconds of awkward silence, someone said 'OK' and we moved on"). ... In a 2002 study he quotes in the new book, gay adolescents at a Berkeley, California school said just 5 percent of their classmates had responded negatively to their sexuality. ...

[Kevin Jennings, GLSEN founder] often asserts that "4 out of 5" students have been harassed because of their sexual orientation. (He doesn't mention that GLSEN's last big survey, in 2003, found "a significant decline" since 2001 in the use of epithets like fag.)[6]

Without a doubt, bullying and harassment of gay students happens every day. Frankly, I think gay PR folks made a miscalculation in seeking to use information like that quoted above to give the appearance that gay was becoming more acceptable. Is it? Old prejudices run deep, but what does the picture really look like today? It varies greatly. Students who see themselves as gay should receive the same protection and respect as other students, whether bullied or not. Lots of kids are bullied for lots of reasons. Wise teachers and administrators will realize that adolescents have always picked on those they deem different or inferior. It's base human nature, whether we like it or not. Even students from "good" homes can get caught up in this "Lord of the Flies" pecking order, given the chance. Who of us does not have a painful memory of either being on the receiving end or, to our shame, the bullying end of such playground shenanigans? Teachers who learn how to properly shame bullies in front of their peers (reverse psychology) can gain the traction they need to maintain order. Too many school officials allow the inmates to run the asylum, however.

Bullying took center stage in the national debate during 2010 in the wake of a string of tragic adolescent suicides. Most of these victims were gay-identified and alleged to have been bullied by their peers. The sudden spike in suicides was inexplicable. Bullying for any reason, of course, is inexcusable. At issue is how to bring a balanced approach to bullying prevention and intervention without tipping the moral scales in favor of either pro-gay or anti-gay extremists. School systems—educators, parents, and students—are the chief players and should be able to determine how best to handle their own turf. Politicizing the issues is not the answer. Teaching respect for all, regardless of ideology or appearance, and consistently enforcing that policy are what is needed.

Fighting Fire with Fire

Organizations like GLSEN and the Gay Educator's Caucus of the NEA have become emboldened to the point of branching out beyond the anti-bullying mission. Unfortunately, that causes even their legitimate work to appear circumspect to the thinking of many. They are encouraging students to explore their sexuality at ever-earlier ages and to become "allies" and advocates in the gay rights movement. Johnny can't read or do math, but he is attuned to "social justice." If you look at some of GLSEN's school materials, you will find mentions of something called the Riddle Homophobia Scale. Developed in 1994 by psychologist Dorothy Riddle, it consists of eight responses to homosexuality. Of particular concern is that "revulsion, pity, tolerance, and acceptance are on the negative side of the scale. Support, admiration, appreciation, and nurturance are on the positive side. So, being tolerated or accepted is no longer good enough for gay advocates. In fact, you are now considered homophobic if you adopt these attitudes toward gays. How or why, you may ask, is a committed Christian who accepts the biblical view that homosexual behavior is sinfully disordered supposed to "admire" and "nurture" such behavior in anyone? That's just one of the "sixty-thousand-dollar" questions we are asked to wrestle with. There is no wrestling, of course, for those who have a biblical apologetic worldview. The question is settled.

The GSA school club strategy does not always work as gay propagandists think it should. Consider David Williams' story. A mid-Oklahoma representative of the Christian Educators Association International (CEAI), Williams discovered in December 2004 that GLSEN wanted to form a GSA at his son's school, Eisenhower High School in Lawton, Oklahoma. School officials told him they could not legally prevent a GSA club from forming, even though many people in the community were on Williams' side. So he decided to use the equal access law to push for an ex-gay club. "If they were going to promote one view of the gay agenda and not include the ex-gay agenda—which means that people can change their perspective—then that would be unfair," Williams said. His strategy worked. The student government voted not to have a GSA.[7]

The gay rights propaganda wall is not built with impermeable stone. And it is not all inherently evil. Please understand I am making a clear distinction here between a movement and the individuals that comprise it. If we seek to engage and befriend our gay neighbors one at a time, we will begin to see them as fellow human beings, with the same hopes, fears, and dreams that we have. The gay ideological movement reflects people of all stripes, including sympathizing straight folks. Gay rights proponents firmly believe their motives are pure. And they are to the degree that we all share the same right to self-worth and dignity. Yet, this is a movement that is still vulnerable in its "peculiarities." How are we to bring those fringe oddities into the light of day—the marketplace of ideas—and show them for what they are without deeply wounding those who are nearly as offended by them as we are? The gay community is not defined by its campy, outrageous, Folsom Street Fair image. Those who are bent on pushing that view would be well-served to step back and take a closer look at the big picture. Does that mean we pretend those things don't exist or are not harmful? Of course not. Kirk and Madsen knew they were problematic. Their game plan was: "[F]irst, you get your foot in the door, by being as similar as possible; then, and only then—when your one little difference [orientation] is finally accepted—can you start dragging in your other peculiarities, one by one. You hammer in the wedge narrow end first. As the saying goes, allow the camel's nose beneath your tent, and his whole body will soon follow."[8] *After the Ball* came across as somewhat two-faced because Kirk and Madsen, on the one hand, wanted to play down the ugly stuff while, on the other, admitting it existed and was a problem the gay community was handling poorly.

Of course, homosexual orientation is hardly a "little" difference. Those peculiarities are a troublesome penchant for unsafe sex, high rates of HIV/AIDS and associated sexually transmitted and chronic diseases (especially among younger males), closeted gay domestic violence, same-sex pedophilia, unusually high rates of substance abuse and mental illness, a near-pathological hatred of evangelical Christians and former gays, and an underground movement favoring polyamory or group "marriage." Reality check: That same laundry list impacts the straight world to more of a degree than we want to admit. Many old-guard gay activists rejected Kirk and Madsen's analysis. A 1989 *Time* magazine review of *After the Ball*, said: "While praising the book's analysis of anti-homosexual sentiment, many gays reject its arguments. Self-acceptance is still a major hurdle for gay men and women, critics insist. But they are most riled by the suggestion that gays need to tone down and blend in: that would slash at the heart of the gay rights movement, they charge."[9] That was twenty-odd years ago. Out with old, in with the new.

Of course, activists on both sides will seek to frame the national debate in a fashion that favors them. But do gay activists want Christian love and civility to guide their opponents, yet not apply to them? It frequently appears so. If a Christian believer dares to exhort or to rebuke the selfish, sinful behavior observed in the gay community, it's off with his head! Most of all, they want us to look at them through rose-colored glasses and see lovely, normal, productive (and above all, oppressed) men who just happen to love other men and women who do the same. Forget about what they do in the privacy of their bedrooms. Put that unpleasant image out of your mind. If it worked for abortion rights, it will work for gay rights, reason the pretenders. Of course, the word "choice" elicits a far different emotional response from gays than it does in the abortion camp. Who wants to think about what abortion entails? The truth about abortion and the truth about some gay (and yes, straight) sex acts are equally inconvenient, as is the truth about all sin.

The human race will default to its basest behavior, if given the opportunity. "Where there is no revelation, the people cast off restraint ..." (Proverbs 29:8). Jesus used strong and unpleasant imagery in rebuking both his Church and nonbelieving hypocrites. He gives his Church the authority to do likewise in rebuking sin and hypocrisy, as long as we remember his injunction against judging unrighteously (Matthew 7:5): "First take the plank out of your own eye and then you will see clearly to remove the speck from your brother's eye." If we can't see how depraved our sin nature is and how lost we are apart from our Savior, then we have no business calling ourselves members of Christ's true Church. Romans 1:24-28 could hardly be clearer in describing the consequences of abandoning the "incorruptible God"—unbridled sin and depravity with all its consequences. In examining the whole picture, we cannot forget that adultery, long the not-so-hidden, hypocritical sin of the self-righteous, and lusts of every kind also are being judged here. Who can argue with gay activists when they rightly point this out? We have flung the door wide open for them. The hypocrite tries to hide his private sin while the out-and-proud crowd shun the shadows and parade their sin for all to see. Both kinds of sin should elicit godly disgust.

The Ugly Side of Gay

One dark shadow over the gay community is homosexual domestic violence. This dirty little secret within the gay community is routinely covered up, but also "grossly underreported," according to the National Coalition of Anti-Violence Programs (NCAVP). A Google News search shows it also is neglected by the media. Yet, a variety of sources indicate it is a significant problem. Gay male domestic violence is secretly viewed as the third most severe health problem facing gay men today, after AIDS and substance abuse, according to some sources. An article in the *Journal of Interpersonal Violence* maintains such victims are trapped in a "conspiracy of silence" and are "double-closeted, entombed in their same-gender identity and in their personal pain of abuse."[10]

The NCAVP's annual reports are interesting because they seem to highlight a different aspect of suspected hate-motivated violence against homosexuals each year. They also focus on problems within the gay community. These reports are politically charged, to be sure, given the biased language and sketchy arguments they sometimes contain. Common sense says some circumstances are tailor-made for anger and retaliation against the "victims," especially given that alcohol and drugs often are involved. The reports do acknowledge that some crimes are "pick-up" incidents, which is a risk too many gay men, in particular, seem willing to take in their quest for anonymous sexual encounters. Others are transgender-related—again, highly charged circumstances. Think of the angry reaction many a man is likely to have when he finds out the "woman" he met or picked up at a bar or a party is really a man. This exact scenario is alleged to have fueled the murder of a gay teenager in Puerto Rico in late 2009. Macho men don't like other men flirting or even appearing to flirt with them, either. The gay community has its collective head in the sand if it denies these are contributing factors in some of the reported violence against GLBT people. They should be teaching younger gay-identified people, especially, how to avoid these situations.

While gay activists may ardently dispute this, domestic violence in the homosexual community does appear to be more prevalent, in terms of its frequency, than heterosexual domestic violence. Based on the U.S. Justice Department's massive National Criminal Victimization Survey (1993-99) and the 1996 National Household Survey on Drug Abuse (NHSDA) conducted by the CDC, males are at least 18 times more likely to suffer violence at the hands of a gay partner than their counterparts in heterosexual relationships. We would expect that, of course, as women are generally the abuse victims in heterosexual relationships. But females may be anywhere from 4 to 10 times more likely to be battered by a lesbian partner than heterosexual women are by a male partner.[11] These statistics come from official government entities, not anti-gay groups with a political agenda. Of course, Kirk and Madsen recommended playing down this kind of ugly stuff in their gay PR campaign strategy. File the growing epidemic of unprotected gay male sex and the resurgence of HIV and syphilis infections under "ugly stuff" too.

Playing up what is only advantageous to the gay rights message is also a strategy. "The literal blood of the thousands of gay people physically wounded by hate during 2004 is on the hands of Jerry Falwell, James Dobson, Tony Perkins, and so many others who spew hate for partisan gain and personal enrichment," said then-National Gay and Lesbian Task Force (NGLTF) executive director Matt Foreman.[12] Foreman shocked many on both sides of the debate when, to his credit, he admitted that AIDS was a "gay disease" as he was leaving office in 2008.[13]

Neosocialists and Anti-Evangelical Sentiment

Mel White was so obsessed with pursuing Jerry Falwell in hopes of changing his heart and mind toward gays that he and his partner, Gary Nixon (they later married in California), moved across the street from where Thomas Road Baptist Church in Lynchburg, Virginia was formerly located and attended services there from time to time. I believe Falwell did give lots of thought in his latter years to how gay cultural and spiritual issues were best addressed. He had more compassion for gay individuals than most people were ever aware of, including his old friend White. I know because he was my pastor and we had occasion to discuss this. But White's needling approach had the opposite effect of what he desired.

White continued to fan the flames of the gay culture war with his latest book, *Religion Gone Bad: The Hidden Dangers of the Christian Right*. The book's description at Amazon.com calls White "a deeply religious man who sees fundamentalism as 'evangelical Christian orthodoxy gone cultic.'" According to White, "it is not a stretch to say that the true goal of today's fundamentalists is to break down the wall that separates church and state, superimpose their 'moral values' on the U.S. Constitution, replace democracy with theocratic rule, and ultimately create a new 'Christian America' in their image. ..." "These are not just Neocons dressed in religious drag," says White. "These men see themselves as gurus called by God to rescue America from unrighteousness. They believe this is a Christian nation that must be returned forcibly to its Christian roots," he adds. Dominionism again. There's more. "*Religion Gone Bad* documents the thirty-year war that fundamentalist Christians have waged against homosexuality and gays and lesbians and offers dramatic, heartbreaking evidence that fundamentalist leaders—Protestant and Catholic alike—are waging nothing less than a 'holy war' (jihad) against sexual minorities."[14] Yes, there has been a thirty-year (or more) war, but many see it a bit differently—to wit, a defending of the family and our sacred institutions in a just war whose first shots were fired against conservatives and those dreaded Christian "fundies," who also happen to be protected by the same Constitution that protects the liberties of gay activists like White. Bruce Carroll, former Log Cabin Republican, admitted this to *The Washington Blade* in a 2004 opinion piece, "A Fine Mess We're In Now":

> [I]t wasn't the "religious right" or President Bush who started this round of the culture war. It was us. The battle was clearly started by gay activists who adopted the tactic of challenging marriage laws across the country.

I truly do not wish to appear cruel toward White or those who encamp with him in Soulforce. He is a likable guy in so many ways, and he is sincere in his beliefs. He cannot make the extreme statements he has made, however, with impunity. I realize he has plenty of justifiable anger, but so do conservative evangelicals. What on earth do we do with these emotions? Do we even need to dwell on who fired the first volley in this culture war? That blame game won't move us to where we need to be.

White parrots the party line, right from the gay playbook. Here's how the 2005 NCAVP report put it: "In fact, it is now clear to most that the social and political forces now holding power are beyond simply opposing issues supportive to GLBT people and now [have] moved to open warfare against all they hold in contempt, including and especially the GLBT community. Further, the successful integration of the concept of GLBT people as the enemy by right-wing political forces has only emboldened far-right and Christian forces who claim credit for both the re-election of President George Bush and the deepening and maintenance of Republican majorities in both houses of Congress."[15] The NCAVP also had this to say: "Now that Communism has been rendered nearly extinct, the religious right is the dreaded enemy in the next Cold War." And this: "We know from both statistics and anecdotal evidence that when attention is paid to LGBT communities, LGBT individuals and communities are targeted for violence. ..."[16] And who is drawing the most attention to the gay community? Gays! When the turkey raises its head and preens and gobbles, it tends to get shot at. Predictably, there does not appear to be any discussion in the report about the possible impact that gay activism might have had on violence or harassment. Is it possible some people may be getting a little tired of this nonsense and have chosen a vigilante approach, wrong as that is?

The great moralist "Sir" Elton John has gone so far as to suggest that all religion should be banned since, in his esteemed view, "religion has always tried to turn hatred towards gay people. ... Organised religion doesn't seem to work. It turns people into really hateful lemmings and it's not really compassionate."[17] He, on the other hand, wants to be celebrated as the "acceptable face of gayness." On Planet Elton, I'm sure he is. Actually, his feelings toward religion are not all misplaced. Christianity is based on a relationship with God through Jesus Christ and not on a set of impossible rules. And everyone, regardless of how much red-ink or "scarlet-thread" Scripture they know, has their own ideas of what Jesus would say or do in any given situation. That's part of our problem.

ABC aired a news report on September 17, 2006 that noted, in the past 15 years, "enrollment at Christian colleges is up 70 percent. Sales of Christian music are up 300 percent" and "tens of thousands of youth pastors have been trained."[18] The same report highlighted the work of Lauren Sandler, described as "a secular, liberal feminist from New York ..." who "spent months among the believers researching her new book, *Righteous*." Sandler has concluded, "the evangelical youth movement will have a negative impact on the country's future, because the most moderate young evangelicals are inflexible on issues such as abortion and gay marriage."[19] Heaven help us.

The growing fear of on-fire evangelical Christians has led to a spate of recent books on "the apocalyptic dangers of the religious right," in Feder's words. In addition to Sandler's and White's screeds, other related titles have appeared. They include *Holy Vote* by Ray Suarez; *Why The Christian Right Is Wrong* by Robin Meyers; *The Left Hand of God: Taking Back Our Country from the Religious Right* by Michael Lerner; *Theocons: Secular America Under Siege* by Damon Linker; *Crazy for God: How I Grew Up as One of the Elect, Helped Found the Religious Right, and Lived to Take All (or Almost All) of It Back* by Frank Shaeffer; and *Souled Out: Reclaiming Faith and Politics after the Religious Right* by E J. Dionne. Such books invariably take a back seat in sales to those of a conservative bent, but the authors keep trying. And they should as it makes for a more interesting checks-and-balances sociological debate.

Gay Madison Avenue

Regardless of how oppressed homosexuals really are, relentless pressure from gay rights groups has influenced American business in significant ways. This was one of Kirk and Madsen's six points, by the way: to gain support and funding from corporate America. In 2004, 36 percent of Fortune 100 companies targeted advertising to the lesbian and gay market. In fact, American corporations spend about $212 million annually in gay print media, $12 million in online gay media and more than $7 million in sponsorships in the gay community (according to the 2006 GLAAD Commercial Closet reports), for a total exceeding $231 million in annual corporate gay- and lesbian-related spending.[20] A growing number of corporations are easing traditional restrictions on domestic partnerships and granting more benefits to gay and lesbian couples. In its latest annual survey of 519 U.S. companies, the Human Rights Campaign compared benefits for GLBT employees, ranking companies on policies related to discrimination, health, and family leave. In 2008, HRC's Corporate Equality Index gave 195 companies a rating of 100 percent, compared with 101 companies in 2005. The first HRC survey in 2002 only gave 13 companies a perfect score.[21] What we don't know is how many of those same companies have been discriminating against people of faith in their employee ranks. More stories of employers harassing and even firing such employees are coming to light—hardly an equitable fix to the problem of gay discrimination. Are gay advocates standing up and speaking out against this inequity? I don't see any.

Conservative and liberal camps still spar over the demographic makeup of the gay community. Are they generally settled and more well-off than average Americans or do they tend to be sporadically employed and nomadic? Madison Avenue believes it's the former. A relatively new development is gay chambers of commerce in a number of cities, including Cleveland and Chicago. There were as many as 45, "all hoping to connect gay-friendly businesses and promote insurance coverage for domestic partners," according to a Focus on the Family *CitizenLink* article in 2006.[22] Some people see this move as a drive for homosexuals to gain minority status. "That way they can access federal funding, state funding, local funding as a behavior-based minority," said one Cleveland resident.[23]

All sensible people want to see GLBT people treated with dignity and fairness. Christians should acknowledge the past (and current) abuses of gays and lesbians within many of our churches. More and more churches are starting to wake up and get it and offer a loving, redemptive hand to their gay and lesbian brothers and sisters that has long been absent. But acknowledging their human suffering and problems without endorsing their lifestyle is not enough from the put-upon gay perspective. This growing church alliance is a budding but still-uncomfortable liaison. Who has the right to expect the other to acquiesce fully? Where is the point of meaningful and productive meeting? What *would* Jesus do?

Can we all back up, let God be God and realize none of us can take his place? Despite the clear evidence that many gay-identified people are not happy with their lives and do want to seek whatever change is possible for them, gay activists continue to rant against ex-gay ministries and therapies for these people. In so doing, they discriminate against their own, figuratively shooting their wounded, just as the Church has historically treated them. For the Church, this cannot simply be a PR war. It is not merely an image we need to change. Christians know that "man looks at the outward appearance, but the LORD looks at the heart."[24] We can pray and work toward changed hearts and attitudes—first our own, then others' through us. Many gays will never be comfortable in any church except those that fully affirm homosexuality as a God-ordained alternative to heterosexuality. Many Christians will never be accepting of unrepentant gays wanting to worship alongside them. This is an opportunity for the Church to examine the propriety of allowing any persistent sin, particularly sexual sin, tacit acceptance within the body of Christ.

Michael Glatze, former editor-in-chief of YGA (*Young, Gay America*) Magazine and a self-identified former gay man, points out, "I don't think the gay movement understands the extent to which the next generation just wants to be normal kids. The people who are getting that are the Christian right."[25] While Glatze, a relatively young Christian, has stirred up a bit of controversy with some of his extremist statements, he may be onto something here. Indeed, many younger people who attend ex-gay conferences acknowledge that they "find something empty about gay culture," as John Cloud noted in his 2005 *Time* story. I predict that the next push in gay-targeted advertising and marketing will be toward teens. It's already happening in subtle and not-so-subtle ways in TV programming. Check out MTV. How about the infamous Abercrombie and Fitch Christmas catalogs, which are little more than soft teen porn, some of it gay- or bisexual-themed?

Indefensible Vices

It may be business as usual for companies to target youth for marketing purposes, but we respond with appropriate disgust when we hear how the fringes in any segment of society, gay or straight, are targeting young people in sexualy exploitave ways. The blatant sexualizing of youth culture is more and more accepted, from Abercrombie and Fitch models to sites like chadzboyz.com, where "Gay boys can chat, vote for the Lord of the Rings character they would most like to date—Legolas is leading—learn how to have safe oral sex and ogle pictures of young men in their underwear."[26] Taking it to another level, check out the North American Man-Boy Love Association (NAMBLA), an organized group of gay pedophiles whose free speech is protected by the ACLU but who have been excluded from gay pride parades because they are too controversial and generate bad PR. Amazon.com, under considerable pressure from irate citizens, pulled in November 2010 a Kindle book on its top-100 best-seller list, *The Pedophile's Guide to Love and Pleasure.* The book's cover had an image reminiscent of a Greek urn depicting a man and a boy. What of the infamous *Little Black Book*, a near-pornographic sex guide for "queer boys" of questionable age, "mistakenly" (oops!) handed out to a good number of middle/high school students at a school-sanctioned seminar in Massachusetts.

Gay scholars, such as San Francisco State University's professor John DeCecco, who edits the *Journal of Homosexuality*, also sat on the editorial board of the pedophile "academic" journal (seriously, there was one), *Paidika*, which published from 1987-1995.[27] The journal sought "to examine the range of cultural, historical, psychological, and literary issues pertaining to consensual adult-child sexual relationships and desires." It came from—where else?—the Netherlands, home of the Paedophile Emancipation Movement and the most liberal pedophilia laws in the world. Dutch law permits sex between an adult and a child as young as 12 if the younger person "consents." The high rates of adolescent mental illness and behavioral problems in the Netherlands couldn't possibly have any correlation, could they?

Is pedophilia tacitly encouraged by some in the mainstream gay community? Steve Baldwin, executive director of the Council for National Policy in Washington, D.C., somehow had the stomach for researching this. Among his findings:

- *The Journal of Homosexuality* recently published a special double-issue entitled, "Male Intergenerational Intimacy," containing many articles portraying sex between men and minor boys as loving relationships. One article said parents should look upon the pedophile who loves their son "not as a rival or competitor, not as a theft of their property, but as a partner in the boy's upbringing, someone to be welcomed into their home."

- In 1995 the homosexual magazine *Guide* said, "We can be proud that the gay movement has been home to the few voices who have had the courage to say out loud that children are naturally sexual" and "deserve the right to sexual expression with whoever (sic) they choose. ..." The article went on to say: "Instead of fearing being labeled pedophiles, we must proudly proclaim that sex is good, including children's sexuality ... we must do it for the children's sake."

- Larry Kramer, the founder of ACT-UP, a noted homosexual activist group, wrote in his book, *Report from the Holocaust: The Making of an AIDS Activist*: "In those instances where children do have sex with their homosexual elders, be they teachers or anyone else, I submit that often, very often, the child desires the activity, and perhaps even solicits it."[28]

Clearly, one of the more maddening controversies within the gay community is that surrounding pedophilia. Gay activists contend it occurs at a rate far less than heterosexual pedophilia. They are constantly on the defensive because of conservative para-church PR that tends to blow the topic out of proportion. Some of the hotly disputed research contends that, in terms of numbers of children abused per offender, "homosexuals abuse with far greater frequency; and boys, research shows, are the much-preferred target."[29] Still not clear is just how many homosexual offenders exist and what the sheer numbers of their crimes are, as the studies appear to offer conflicting conclusions. Reason says that, given the estimated prevalence of homosexual men or women is between 2 and 5 percent of the general population (depending on which survey is being cited), there would be many more heterosexual pedophiles. What about the reporting of these crimes? Steve Baldwin asserts, "[M]any reporters will not report if a child molester is a homosexual, even if he knows that to be the case."[30] That statement is certain to be debated. Bottom line: All child sex abuse likely happens more than we tend to believe it does. Many gays contend that male-on-male offenders are not all gay while others call that hair-splitting nonsense. Neither the Christian nor the gay community has a corner on all the facts.

Media coverage of gay pedophilia is not totally forthcoming, either, as Henry Clough pointed out in his assessment of the prominent coverage of Harry Hay's death, his October 25, 2002 obituary running for 35 column inches in *The New York Times*, which also featured prominent stories about him in a later edition and in the Sunday magazine section:

> *The Times* couldn't tell us enough about Harry Hay, the founder of gay liberation, who had died at age 90. ... *The Times* even made mention of Harry's participation in the Communist Party agitation that led to a union strike that closed the Port of San Francisco in 1934. So it's mighty peculiar that the *New York Times*, the newspaper of record, the paper all the other papers and all the television networks look to for direction, somehow never got around to mentioning that Harry Hay was an enthusiastic supporter of NAMBLA, The North American Man-Boy Love Association, which advocates the abolition of all age-of-consent laws.[31]

It isn't only men who make up the ranks of homosexual or heterosexual pedophiles. Within the past few years, a movement that researcher Judith Reisman calls the "Women's Auxiliary of NAMBLA" has emerged. Counselors and law enforcement officials say that women likely account for about one in four cases of child sex abuse involving both sexes.[32] Pat Califia, a notorious lesbian feminist and pedophile advocate, said in an article appearing in *The Advocate*: "True, not all younger dykes are interested in older women. But if a woman is interested in having a cross-generational lover, I cannot think of one good reason—apart from the threat of persecution—why she should deny herself such a relationship." She continues, "Minors who are given the power to say 'no' to being sexually used by an abusive parent or relative are also going to assume the right to say 'yes' to other young people and adults whom they desire. You can't liberate children and adolescents without disrupting the entire hierarchy of adult power and coercion and challenging the hegemony of anti-sex fundamentalist religious values."[33] Califia no doubt influenced Judith Levine's infamous 2002 book, *Harmful to Minors: The Perils of Protecting Children from Sex*. Several more recent studies seem to be trying to resurrect her ridiculous arguments that pre-adolescent sex actually can be beneficial for children.

Many female advocates of pedophilia believe that children are being "oppressed by adults who have taken away their right to fully express their sexuality in any way they see fit."[34] A popular lesbian pedophile website that either disappeared or went underground via an obscure URL—it was known as "Butterfly Kisses" and I saw the site while it was active—included a section called "Rights Advocacy" featuring writings or links such as "Feminism, Pedophilia, and Children's Rights" (by Califia), "A Child's Sexual Bill of Rights," "The North American Woman-Girl Love Association," and "Sexual Revolution and the Liberation of Children," by longtime feminist Kate Millett. If you really want to read something scary, consider the similarity of Califia's rantings to those expressed by liberal social scientists who migrated to America from pre-Nazi Europe and the people they influenced both in the public education system and the American Library Association (ALA). It was this Marxist and Freudian influence that helped fuel the intellectuals' fear and hatred of conservatism and created a disdain for "authoritarian" parents. This attitude led to the addition in 1967 of the "age clause" in the Library Bill of Rights that would allow children the unrestricted freedom—the "right"—to view even pornography in public libraries without parental consent or knowledge:

> Getting down to the very basics in librarianship, librarians and library trustees ... must not try to improve or regulate the morals of today's teenager.
>
> —Eli M. Oboler
> Member of the ALA Intellectual
> Freedom Committee, 1968[35]

> [M]ost [public librarians] are frank to say that their "special responsibility" is designed not to protect children or young people but to protect themselves from parents.
>
> —Marjorie Fiske Lowenthal
> Columbia University's
> Bureau of Applied Social Research, 1959[36]

> All adolescents who do not have a gratifying sexual life ... are threatened with a future disturbance of their potency and severe psychic depression.
>
> —Wilhelm Reich
> Germany's Institute of Social Research, 1933[37]

Do not suppose these radical ideas have not been in the mainstream of American academic thought. An article entitled "Child Sexual Development" by Loretta Haroian, Ph.D. was published in 2000 by the Institute for Advanced Study of Human

Sexuality in San Francisco. The institute was founded by associates of the infamous sex researcher and pedophile Alfred Kinsey, whose discredited findings still hold sway over the body of gay research. The article maintains there is "considerable evidence" that there is no "inherent harm in sexual expression in childhood."[38] Where else have we heard assertions that intergenerational sex is harmless? From none other than the American Psychological Association, in an infamous 1998 *Psychological Bulletin* article.[39] But then, victims of gay and lesbian child sexual abuse are as much a myth to the gay community as ex-gays are. Their voices are effectively silenced. One female victim, abused by her mother, says, "[A]s a child my body belonged to someone else and I had no boundaries. I never felt safe or whole. It almost feels like you are someone else. Almost as if you are the abuser. That you and her are one person."[40] Nearly all victims of sexual abuse as children can make the same statement.

To her credit, Oprah Winfrey probably has done more to bring awareness to the horrors of child sexual abuse for both women and men than anyone in the world today, having aired repeated TV programs featuring victims and their moving stories, as well as telling parts of her own. At the same time, she has been unapologetically pro-gay, of course.

The Gay PR Gravy Train

Despite some well-concealed ulterior motives and bad news, profitable gay branding rolls on with good impetus. Advertisers looking to make a buck off the increasingly friendly media image of gays and lesbians have studied the demographics of the GLBT community and learned there is a lucrative market there. Here is a look at some of the statistics:

- 61 percent of gay men and 69 percent of lesbians own a home.

- 5 percent of gay men have children under 18 living at home, while 20 percent of lesbians do.

- 65 percent of lesbians live together as couples while 46 of gay men do.

- Median income for gay men is $83,000 and for lesbians, $80,000.

- Among gay men and lesbians, around 90 percent say they are "more likely to support companies with favorable LGBT employment practices."

- "The median U.S. gay male respondent spent $5,200 dining out in the last year, with a median of 4 times per week and a median of one of those in a fine dining establishment."

- Lesbians spend a median amount of $3,640 on dining out annually. The average American household spends $2,434 annually dining out.

(Data from Gay/Lesbian Consumer Indexes 2007, Community Marketing, Inc.)

- Alcohol is "the most developed advertising category to the gay market. ... While causing health concerns, 'sin product' marketers have long been aware of higher-than-average smoking and alcohol consumption rates among lesbians and gays. Gay men and lesbians of all ages report alcohol problems nearly twice as often as heterosexuals. ... In a household-based survey, 41 percent of gay men identified as smokers (compared to 26.6 percent of men in the general population), and twice as many lesbians smoke as heterosexual women."

("Healthy People 2010," LGBT Health, Gay and Lesbian Medical Association-GLMA, 2001)

- The American gay and lesbian community represents a $54.1 billion travel market, or an estimated 10 percent of the U.S. travel industry. In a 2001-2003 study of the gay and lesbian market, 97 percent indicated they took vacations within the previous 12 months (the national average is 64 percent), 82 percent spent five or more nights in hotels, and 20 percent took at least one cruise (the national average is about 2 percent).

  ("Gay Marketing Resources," GLAAD Commercial Closet Association)

Gays and lesbians will continue to make their mark on the socioeconomic landscape. They vote in significant numbers, and that is as it should be. To claim they are disenfranchised in ways that other minorities are or have been is disingenuous. It requires misappropriating the word "equality," a word never to be taken lightly in this country. The GLBT community has a responsibility to examine and police its improprieties, as the Church and parachurch organizations do their own. Concerned citizens need to be careful about relying on endlessly repeated sound bites that are merely propaganda in disguise for either ideological side. Few people have the patience to dig beneath the surface in search of the truth. We expect elected officials or media professionals or the medical establishment to do that for us. The problem is, fewer and fewer of those folks appear to be trustworthy anymore. It is sad that we also have to lump some "professional ministry" officials in with them. And we wonder why we have a never-ending battle of the watchdogs in this country.

Six

Education Wars: Do "Social Justice" and "Equality" Trump the Three Rs?

The mammoth and well-funded National Education Association (NEA) is a favorite playground for gay lobbyists who covet the fertile public education turf. As we have seen, liberal educators are easily influenced by pro-gay "science" and social justice ideology, and this forms the basis of their doctrinaire attitude toward curriculum and their students. The influence of GLSEN has led to 4,000 or more Gay-Straight Alliance (GSA) clubs in taxpayer-funded middle and high schools across the country. That number represents explosive growth within the past decade. Former gays are not likely to find room under their tent, however, despite government guidelines stating that all viewpoints should be represented in school groups. Conservative, dues-paying teachers have long balked at the decidedly liberal bent of the NEA and have argued for more balance in its views. The nascent Ex-Gay Educators Caucus within the NEA has hit an especially raw nerve with liberal gay educators and their cohorts. Predictably, the supposed church-state separation card is played in an attempt to keep the former gay/post-gay message that meaningful change is possible—a largely faith-based effort—out of schools. One of the problems stems from the confusion over what constitutes "change" and whether it is fair to make it a stated objective of any effort aimed at helping those with unwanted same-sex attraction. It remains a politically charged arena, with the NEA wanting the change message to go underground or disappear altogether and organizations like PFOX (Parents and Families of Ex-Gays and Gays), naturally sympathetic to the Ex-Gay Caucus, fighting the NEA in court to gain more visibility for ex-gays and their cause. Meanwhile, there are real kids in real schools to educate so they can make their way in a real world.

The American Academy of Pediatrics, American Counseling Association, American Association of School Administrators, American Federation of Teachers, American Psychological Association, American School Health Association, Interfaith Alliance Foundation, National Association of School Psychologists, National Association of Social Workers and the NEA make up the Just the Facts Coalition. In 1999, they developed and endorsed *Just the Facts About Sexual Orientation & Youth: A Primer for Principals, Educators and School Personnel.* It includes a number of statements from the aforementioned guild organizations expressing concern about the futility and possible harm in "reparative" therapy and other methods of attempting to mitigate unwanted same-sex attractions or change sexual orientation. One example comes from the American Academy of Pediatrics, which stated: "Therapy directed specifically at changing sexual orientation is contraindicated, since it can provoke guilt and anxiety while having little or no potential for achieving changes in orientation."[1]

Actually, those considered part of ex-gay culture have begun speaking out more and more against therapies or ministry programs whose chief aim is eradicating all same-sex attractions or turning gays straight. It became painfully obvious that many who had felt compelled by the political climate to call themselves completely changed did, indeed, still experience unwanted attractions. What they also have been able to make clearer, however, is that change for them still has been significant and their lives are much better, whether they have married and have families or have chosen celibacy. It is patently unfair for disgruntled gay activists to behave as if they smell blood in the water, however, and to gang up on these folks, falsely accusing them of being repressed homosexuals or hypocrites. The honest and magnanimous gesture of coming clean about the extent to which they may still struggle ought to earn these people a round of applause from the affirmed gay community. It does not negate the validity of the journey to wholeness. Exodus president Alan Chambers speaks for this group when he says, "... there was a time when I was ambiguous, even untruthful about my own story of change because I was afraid of being less than what others expected me to be. In 2006, that all changed when a young friend came to me in tears, saying that he would never be like me. I knew then that being completely honest about my struggle was the only course of action. Four years later, I am freer than ever and people who contact Exodus are not set up for a fall, due to a perception that perfection is attainable" (from the Exodus Newsletter, May 2010).

Bob Chase, former NEA president and former co-chair of the board of GLSEN, once defended the NEA's pushing of the gay agenda to students by warning: "Some critics want the public schools to be an agent of moral doctrine, condemning children and adults when they are not in accord with Biblical precepts."[2] Are public schools not already agents of "moral doctrine," edging students toward a warped morality that denies the traditional, commonsense values of their parents and grandparents? It is as if they have dared parents to challenge them. And never mind that those adhering to biblical precepts, with a few noted exceptions, are largely condemning unhealthy behaviors and policies, not "children and adults." The same kind of propaganda drives the misconception that GLBT-identified (many of them are still questioning) students face universal discrimination or relentless homophobic attacks in schools. The GLSEN-sponsored annual Day of Silence in public schools was organized to counter anti-gay discrimination and name-calling, but is supposed to cover all forms of bullying. Gay students and their sympathizers refuse to speak for an entire day, often wearing tape over their mouths to accentuate their protest. It is clear, however, that conservative Christians and pro-family advocates, many of whom are targeted by gay "moral agents" who unfairly blame them for much of the bullying, are increasingly being silenced in public schools.

Christian public schoolteacher Peter Heck, in a July 20, 2009 piece he wrote for OneNewsNow, made some disturbing observations about the 2009 convention remarks from retiring NEA general counsel Bob Chanin:

> With teachers, representatives, and affiliates to the National Education Association's annual convention gathered around, [Chanin] took to the stage to deliver his outgoing remarks. His inspiring and uplifting message asserted the profound commitment held by the NEA to the betterment of American society: "We are not paranoid; someone really is after us. Why are these conservative and right-wing b****rds picking on NEA and its affiliates? I will tell you why: it is the price we pay for success."
>
> As one of those right-wing "fatherless lads" Mr. Chanin was referring to, I found myself moved at how open-minded and inclusive his

speech sounded. But more than that, Chanin did a masterful job of demonstrating what the true priorities of the NEA are when he stated that what makes the group effective is, "not because of our creative ideas, it is not because of the merit of our positions, it is not because we care about children, and it is not because we have a vision of a great public school for every child. NEA and its affiliates are effective advocates because we have power."

Gay Politics in the Classroom

Is the power game just at the top levels of the NEA? Are pro-gay teachers really concerned with their students' welfare and education or are they more concerned about their own selfish political agenda? It's a fair question. Catholic journalist Allyson Smith photographed as many as eight elementary-aged students marching with teachers in a California gay pride parade in the summer of 2006. While she was unsure whether the children were the teachers' own children or their students, she was appalled at what they were exposed to during the parade—"floats that advertised hard-core, homosexual pornography" and more.[3] Other reports have alleged that GLSEN has brought middle and high school GSA students to at least one San Francisco gay pride parade in a yellow school bus, and also allowed them to march. *The San Francisco Chronicle* reported on an unusual field trip the parent of a charter school first grade class student arranged for the entire class in October 2008. It was to witness the lesbian wedding ceremony of their teacher, which Mayor Gavin Newsome officiated at City Hall. "It really is what we call a teachable moment," said the Creative Arts Charter School interim director Liz Jaroslow. "I think I'm well within the parameters."[4]

GLSEN's teacher's manual, "Tackling Gay Issues in School,"

in discussing GSA clubs says that exposure to pro-homosexual programs can't "create" or encourage homosexuality: "Contrary to the wholly unsubstantiated arguments of opponents, gay/straight alliances do not cause young people to become involved in sexual activity earlier than they otherwise would or to "choose" a sexual orientation that would otherwise not be their orientation."[5] But a lesson from the above-mentioned manual called "Bisexual Basics" for middle schoolers and older discusses the complexity of "sexual orientation." The lesson states: "Each of us should have the freedom to explore our sexual orientation and find our own unique expression of lesbian, bisexual, gay, straight, or any combination of these."[6] If that's not encouragement, I'd like to know what it is.

Not only is the NEA flagrantly pro-gay, but the national Parent Teacher Association (PTA) also appears to be pushing its own gay propaganda. While the NEA begrudgingly has to allow the Ex-Gay Educators Caucus to have a booth at its annual conventions—and they still endure taunts and ugly threats from gay educators—the PTA (as well as the NEA) has snubbed PFOX when requesting to have a booth at the PTA's annual convention several years running. PFOX lost a discrimination suit against the NEA, which a court ruled has the right to keep the ex-gay advocacy group out of its convention exhibit halls because their respective ideologies are at odds. The National PTA is the largest volunteer child advocacy organization in the United States. One of its stated purposes is "to be inclusive in its efforts to represent and assist all who nurture and educate children." That inclusion apparently does not extend to former gays or those who advocate for them. During recent annual conventions, the PTA has allowed PFLAG both to have a booth in order to distribute their materials and to present a workshop to PTA attendees. The National PTA has also allowed "It's Elementary," the gay-affirming video for schoolchildren, to be screened at its conference for several years now. National PTA President Ann Marie Weselak said in an interview with the American Family Association (AFA) *Journal* in 2006 the PFLAG booth was there "to help educate and inform parents on the topic of bullying in order to help make their children more safe in schools."[7] Even a cursory look at the PFLAG website confirms it is highly politicized and subversive in its quest for "equality" and educational programs that do not provide safe or accurate information for students. By the way, the theme of that 2006 PTA convention? Diversity. But once again, former homosexuals or anyone supporting change need not apply.

The NEA, through its teacher's manual, claims that our children are not ready for the universally tolerant society they envision. They maintain that our children "may need mental health care ... to conform to the planned society in which there will be no conflicts of attitudes or beliefs," in their brave, new, world without bounderies.[8] Who are they kidding? They may be right about our children needing mental health care, but it would be to undo the effects of years of liberal indoctrination in moral relativism, their postmodern religion. The NEA offers "values-free" sex education to elementary school children. It's called "Family Living." Homosexuality is taught as an acceptable lifestyle, with books such as *Heather Has Two Mommies*, *My Two Uncles*, *Daddy's Roommate* and *Who's in a Family*. Another recommended book in the California school system, *One Teenager in Ten: Writings by Gay & Lesbian Youth*, discusses (in explicit detail) a 12-year-old's first lesbian experience with her 23-year-old dance teacher.[9]

These classes and instructional materials are being mainstreamed into our public schools. When a 16-year-old student at Woodbury High School near St. Paul, Minnesota wore a shirt proclaiming "Straight Pride," he was singled out for his "intolerance," and he should have been disciplined for being divisive, the same as those pushing gay pride messages in school should be. Free speech and tolerance mostly go one way, however, in government schools. Many parents would be happy to see all politically charged messages removed from schools, since they have little to do with real education beyond serious civics. But the NEA even promotes condom distribution and contraceptives to children, along with abortion counseling without parental consent.[10]

In Massachusetts, the Provincetown school district caused quite an uproar in 2010 with its decision to distribute condoms even to elementary students, without parental knowledge or consent, as reported in *The Christian Post* on June 24, 2010. Even Gov. Deval Patrick was opposed to the policy. Parents opposed to these rights-usurping measures are justified in their anger. NEA lobbyists also have pushed for schools operating family planning clinics. Looks like they'll need them, given their views on allowing children to experiment with sex at ever-earlier ages.

How powerful and wealthy is the NEA? According to a 2006 report in *The National Review* examining 2005 union statistics, "One hundred top union executives made at least $280,000 annually, not counting benefits. ... NEA president Reg Weaver made $438,920, plus benefits. At his headquarters, 335 officers and employees scored $100,000 or more, averaging $140,977, before benefits."[11] Of course, only about 12 percent of NEA teacher dues is spent on cases where teachers need defending ("legal support") and the other 88 percent supports staff salaries ("administration") and a variety of nebulous causes, a full 45 percent of which are politically related.[12]

We can thank the Jimmy Carter-created federal Department of Education, the Washington bureaucratic gaggle largely under the political influence of the NEA, for many ill-conceived decisions that hamstring public education. Yes, our tax dollars are hard at work teaching Johnny how to use a condom and Susie that it's OK to experiment with bisexuality. "[For] the past dozen years, NEA resolutions have each year adopted more of the gay rights agenda," according to the August 2006 *Eagle Forum Education Reporter*. "Whereas, gay rights goals such as same-sex marriage are steadily losing at the polls [but have gained traction in a few pro-gay states since 2006], the gay rights agenda is moving ahead full speed in the public schools, with assistance from the NEA," the article states.[13] Among the resolutions passed at the NEA's 2006 annual convention in Orlando, Florida was A-14, which stated, "Funds must be provided for programs to alleviate race, gender, and sexual orientation discrimination and to eliminate ... sexual orientation and gender identification stereotypes in the public schools."[14]

X-Rated "Curriculum"

In consort with the NEA, GLSEN has gotten away with sponsoring trash in the guise of educational workshops. One particularly notorious education scandal involved a GLSEN-sponsored conference held on March 25, 2000, dubbed "Fistgate" by conservatives. Three Massachusetts Departments of Health and Education educators led a youth workshop titled, "What They Didn't Tell You about Queer Sex & Sexuality in Health Class" as part of the annual Boston-GLSEN "Teach Out" conference held at Tufts University. Massachusetts family advocate Scott Whiteman attended the "Queer Sex" session, for "youth only ages 14 to 21," and taped it while standing in the back of the room:

> In the workshop, instructor Michael Gaucher, prompted by a teen's question, verbally guided the students on the mechanics of "fisting"—a homosexual slang term for a sadistic sex act in which a man inserts his hand and arm into another person's anal cavity [or a woman into another's vagina]. Another instructor, Margot Abels, said fisting "often gets a

really bad rap," and described it innocuously as "an experience of letting somebody into your body that you want to be that close and intimate with." Abels and Gaucher also guided the students on techniques of oral sodomy and lesbian sex.[15]

The three state education employees were fired (one later was reinstated), but gay activists, represented by Gay and Lesbian Advocates and Defenders (GLAD), brought a lawsuit against Brian Camenker (of Mass Resistance), Scott Whiteman, and the Parents Rights Coalition. The suit was dropped in 2005. Another suit brought by one of the state employees was settled in 2006. The tape of the event, sealed by court order for several years, is now available to the public. Transcripts have revealed unbelievably shocking details.

Other panels at the Boston-GLSEN conference included:

- Ask the Transsexuals

- Early Childhood Educators: How to Decide Whether to Come Out [as a Homosexual] at Work or Not

- Lesbian Avengers: How to Promote Queer-Friendly Activism in Your Schools and in Your Lives

- The Struggles and Triumphs of Including Homosexuality in a Middle School Curriculum

- The Religious Wrong: Dealing Effectively with Opposition in Your Community[16]

Jennings published a book several years ago about growing

up in a "fundamentalist" Christian home and his abandonment by his pastor-father. It's no mystery where his disdain of conservative Christianity comes from. Interestingly, he is affiliated with a liberal New York seminary and claims to have returned to Christianity in some form. He actually revealed his goal to openly promote homosexuality in schools back in 1995. On March 5 of that year, Jennings gave a speech called "Winning the Culture War" at the Human Rights Campaign Fund Leadership Conference, parts of which are published at the Mass Resistance website (massresistance. com). Among other things, he said in that speech, "If the radical right can succeed in portraying us as preying on children, we will lose. Their language—'promoting homosexuality' is one example—is laced with subtle and not-so-subtle innuendo that we are 'after their kids.'" Jennings said the gay community must frame its education campaign around the issue of "safety" for GLBT students. "In Massachusetts the effective reframing of this issue was the key to the success of the Governor's Commission on Gay and Lesbian Youth. We immediately seized upon the opponent's calling card—safety—and explained how homophobia represents a threat to students' safety by creating a climate where violence, name-calling, health problems, and suicide are common," Jennings said. He has not stated how he plans to get across the message to public schools that trolling for sex encounters in public places is also unsafe for gay adolescents.

The education message goes beyond safety, of course. In 1997 at a regional GLSEN conference, New York teacher and GLSEN activist Jaki Williams led a workshop titled "Inclusive Kindergartens." Williams advised other teachers and fellow GLSEN activists on how to influence young, impressionable children with the gay agenda. Children in the kindergarten age are "developing their superego," Williams said, and "that's when the saturation process needs to begin. ... Five-year-olds really are very interested in the big questions. They're very interested in sex, death, and love, and they ask those questions, and they talk about them. And we want to help them find the answers ... on their level."[17] Parents, be advised that your real-world experience raising your own 5-year-olds does not count. Your children are, shall we say, unenlightened.

The NEA awarded Jennings the 2004 Virginia Uribe Award for Creative Leadership in Human Rights, amid protests from the Republican Educators Caucus and the newer Ex-Gay Educators Caucus. The two conservative groups cited Jennings' 1994 book, *One Teacher in 10*, in which he related that he chose not to report an alleged case of adult gay sexual abuse of a student to the proper authorities, as required by law. Jennings wrote of giving advice and sympathy in 1988 to a sophomore high school student in Concord, Massachusetts who confided to him his emotional distress over being involved "with an older man he had met in Boston."[18] Child protection laws in Massachusetts required a teacher to notify child welfare authorities within 48 hours if a child under 18 was "suffering physical or emotional injury resulting from abuse inflicted upon him ... including sexual abuse."[19] Jennings has sidestepped the allegations of wrongdoing. The student supposedly came forward, claiming he did not have sex in that incident and that he was 16, the legal age of consent in Massachusetts. Never mind that he was still younger than 18, and Jennings was mandated to report the alleged event as suspected abuse. The incident, nevertheless, raised red flags. Jennings may have manufactured at least some of the story to draw attention to the plight of gay teens as he saw it.

The conservative caucuses also cited Jennings' discriminatory statements against former gays. "Ex-gay messages have no place in our nation's public schools," he said in one GLSEN publication. "A line has been drawn. There is no 'other side' when you're talking about lesbian, gay, and bisexual students."[20] One wonders, then, just what the "line" is dividing. "If we are to be truly democratic in our support of each person's right to pursue his own happiness, then there would be no stigmatizing of any individual for choosing to leave a homosexual life or, for that matter, in choosing to reverse such a decision," Jeralee Smith, then-chair of the Ex-Gay Educators Caucus, said in a statement to NEA president Reg Weaver.[21]

Jennings came under close scrutiny after being appointed by the Obama administration to a high post within the Department of Education—Assistant Deputy Secretary for DOE Safe & Drug-Free Schools. As Jennings openly campaigned and organized for Obama during his presidential bid, many see this appointment as a payback. Politics as usual. The problem is this one truly flies in the face of many parents whose children attend public schools, given Jennings' history and connections to some of GLSEN's notorious activities and publications. Many outraged citizens have complained that Jennings is not qualified to hold the post he has been given.

Harmful to Minors? Yes!

It should be noted that Virginia Uribe, the lesbian (now-retired) Los Angeles teacher for whom the award given to Jennings is named, was founder of a controversial school program called Project 10, formed in 1984 to provide counsel to and protect the rights of GLBT students. The program takes its name from the discredited figure put forward by Kinsey supporters who claimed that 10 percent of the population is homosexual. Some of Uribe's infamous statements:

> The State Courts must be used to force the School Districts to disseminate accurate information about homosexuality. ... kids need to hear this. They need to hear the latest scientific information on homosexuality, and that's something that all

kids need to hear, not just gay and lesbian kids. Starting from kindergarten, again, and working its way all the way through high school. [This] idea of talking about it one time in high school ... well we know that doesn't work. We need to start tackling this at very early ages.[22]

Uribe was interviewed in 2001 for a "Life and Times" program aired by KCET-TV in Southern California. She said on the program, "The word 'faggot' is probably the most commonly-used derogatory remark, put-down, in the educational system and also, it's ... the least curtailed. To hear that simply compounds the shame that you feel about being part of that group, and each time you hear it ... it just compounds the feelings that you have of the lack of self-worth that you have as a member of that group."[23] I wonder how many vocabulary-challenged students today even know the outmoded word "faggot." They are more likely to say "fag" if they use the term at all. It's more common for students to use the more politically correct word "gay" as a general put-down term rather than a homosexual slur. Parents know this. So do teachers.

Would Uribe or other gay rights advocates in the education system be willing to acknowledge that the "lack of self-worth" experienced by gay-identifying students might be attributable, in part, to inherent unhappiness with being gay? Many adult gays say they had such feelings in their own younger lives. To deny gender-questioning adolescents equal access to information that would give them hope, or at least more than one way of coping, is an unkind cut of its own. Somewhere there is a commonsense line that even young people instinctively know ought not to be crossed when it comes to tolerance and self-esteem. Is there even a legitimate role these days for peer pressure among students to help them conform to a morally acceptable standard? Of course, that once-universal practice has been politicked out of existence when it comes to anything related to "gay rights."

Former educator and author Beverly Eakman points out the harm that is being done to students by liberal educators, in conjunction with wrong-headed mental health mandates:

> I cannot help wondering if much of the angst among teenagers surrounding sexual orientation doesn't come down to a sexual obsession, permitted to run rampant and unchecked by mental health "sexperts". ... Even though saner heads in the field have tried for years to rein in what they saw as over-sexualizing youngsters ... the majority of the mental health community since that time has been determined to provide young children with far more information about sex than they could possibly assimilate. ...
>
> [What] sex educators have done here is something very close to contributing to the delinquency of a minor—seizing, if you will, upon the perceived deficiencies of a vulnerable, under-age person and presenting him a set of non-negotiable options. ...
>
> It is ironic that in an age where sexual abuse of children is the only crime in which the person so accused is guilty until proven innocent, that sexualization of children is not a crime at all. The concept of age-appropriateness is gone with the wind, so it is no wonder that many children believe they are homosexual when, in fact, they are merely curious and even aroused by the nearly naked bodies all around them.[24]

We can expect parental rights and choices to come under increasing assault in the public education arena. The chilling 2005 decision of the U.S Court of Appeals for the Ninth Circuit in *Fields v. Palmdale School District* is a wake-up call. The court ruled that parental autonomy in raising children "does not extend beyond the threshold of the school door," and that a public school has the right to provide its students with "whatever information it wishes to provide, sexual or otherwise."[25] Small wonder, then, that so many parents were seriously concerned about President Obama having direct access to their children in his much-debated televised speech to the nation's students just after Labor Day in 2009. Why wouldn't they be wary of White House propaganda in such an address, given his dismal track record of appointments and policies in his first eight to nine months in office? Who really knew where he stood?

An increasingly liberal educational and legislative climate in states like California and Massachusetts continues to raise many concerns among parents. The signing into law of California's highly controversial SB 777 (that outlaws "discriminatory" statements in the classroom about homosexuality and allows students to be whatever gender they claim to be) only fueled an existing showdown between conservative and liberal forces in the Golden State. Because the bill was written in strategic language that makes it highly enforceable if gay students or parents sue the schools or educators, opponents have sought to overturn this law—problematic in a number of ways, actually. "The law alters the definition of the word 'sex' as being biological in nature and replaces it with the word 'gender' in California's Education Code," wrote *Washington Times* columnist Rick Amato on January 22, 2008. "It further defines 'gender' as 'sex' based upon a person's gender identity or gender-related appearance and behavior, and not upon their natural sex at birth," he pointed out.[26]

Jim Kelly, one of four board members of the Grossmont

Unified School District in San Diego, who lost one lawsuit challenging the legality of SB 777, says, "No one is arguing against anti-discrimination. There are current laws ... which protect students against the harmful effects of discrimination. ... [W]hat they have done here, however, is turn a disorder into a civil right. Gender identity issues are classified as a disorder by the American Psychiatric Association. This law makes it a civil right."[27] Though Kelly's use of the word "disorder" would be akin to waving a red flag at a charging bull, in the eyes of gay activists, he was referring to the one homosexuality-related classification still appearing in the DSM: Gender Identity Disorder (GID) or Gender Dysphoria. While "gender identity issues" may be a broad catchphrase, those responsible for the DSM have not yet determined GID is anything other than a disorder. Back in 1972-73, when gay activists were focused on getting the American Psychiatric Association to delete homosexuality as a treatable disorder from the DSM, the GID classification was allowed to stand. Today, however, more and more activists are pushing for antidiscrimination initiatives against transgender people or those who adopt a gender identity contrary to their assigned sex at birth—the T in GLBT. California's SB777 also applies to them. Truly intersexed people from birth—those with a Disorder of Sex Development (DSD)—fall into a gray zone the DSM is seeking to correct in its next revision.

The not-too-subtle push by educators to convince students that all GLBT behavior is normal and gay marriage is a step toward "equality and justice" is more than evident within the NEA. "It was during Bob Chase's [NEA] presidency that the Sexual Orientation Task Force was initiated, giving a whole arm of NEA leadership to gay-lesbian-bisexual-transgender (GLBT) causes," Jeralee Smith has said. "In 2002, a 60-page document detailing NEA's support of GLBT causes was adopted by the NEA executive committee, and handed to NEA delegates as a report which, technically, didn't even require a vote."[28]

While California's state legislature generates liberal pro-gay education bills, one after the other, WorldNetDaily reported in a 2002 article that when Republican Assemblyman Dennis Mountjoy introduced a bill (AB 1326) "aimed at prohibiting the promotion of homosexuality in public education," the measure was "summarily defeated without discussion."[29] In arguing for the bill during a committee hearing, Mountjoy expressed his outrage over sexually explicit curriculum materials proposed for California schools. Even after providing committee members with obviously offensive excerpts from some of the materials, his bill was killed.

A Florida school district took a bold step when faced with a situation in the 2006-2007 school year educators had never before encountered. That's when the country's youngest transgender child began attending school in the Sunshine State's Broward County. The boy's family enrolled him as a girl in kindergarten in the fall of 2006. The lad supposedly rejects his physical characteristics as a boy. According to *The Miami Herald*, mental health professionals diagnosed the cross-dressing boy with "gender dysphoria," or Gender Identity Disorder. The newspaper said the school planned to address the youngster by a unisex name. According to the *Herald* story, the boy's counselor said, "This would be one of the youngest children to be intentionally socialized as a transgendered child that I have ever seen. Courts in other jurisdictions have required children to be much older. In fact, accepted standards of care for gender dysphoria caution against this approach." Of course, pro-gay groups like Equality Florida and PFLAG praised the Broward and Miami-Dade county school systems for their "progressive policies."[30] Public school students have been exposed to pro-gay sentiment for so long that many will not bat an eye at having transgender students in their classes. Is this what educators refer to as "social justice"? Many educators fancy themselves wielders of a sword of justice that will right all wrongs, real or perceived.

Economist and social observer Thomas Sowell has come down hard on exposing social justice for the meaningless facade it is. In a September 14, 2010 Townhall.com commentary entitled, "The Money of Fools" (i.e., empty words, à la seventeenth-century philosopher Thomas Hobbes), Sowell said:

> Warm, fuzzy words and phrases have an enormous advantage in politics. None has had such a long run of political success as "social justice." ...
>
> While the term has no defined meaning, it has emotionally powerful connotations. There is a strong sense that it is simply not right—that it is unjust—that some people are so much better off than others. ...
>
> Some advocates of "social justice" would argue that what is fundamentally unjust is that one person is born into circumstances that make that person's chances in life radically different from the chances that others have—through no fault of one and through no merit of the others. ...
>
> None of these things is equal or can be made equal. If this is an injustice, it is not a "social" injustice because it is beyond the power of society.

Blatant Lies

On February 11, 2004, Kevin Jennings appeared on Fox News' "The O'Reilly Factor" to discuss what he called GLSEN's "new" marriage curriculum for schools, allowing students to explore the issue of same-sex marriage. When asked by Bill O'Reilly if it presented both sides of the issue, Jennings answered, "Absolutely."

Linda Harvey of Mission America, who reviewed the curriculum, had this to say:

> The reality is that Jennings is "absolutely" full of baloney.
>
> Once more, Jennings and GLSEN are not being honest. The curriculum is not at all objective but radically biased toward a pro-homosexual viewpoint. It distorts the information it provides, withholds vital additional information, and slickly manipulates student sympathies. The curriculum is also not new. We first reviewed this curriculum in 2001. It has been updated but is largely the same material.
>
> The limitations of the GLSEN curriculum are numerous, and this material is not at all appropriate to fashion into a teaching unit for students.[31]

Harvey went on to list ten detailed reasons why the curriculum, called "At Issue: Marriage," is "problematic." She maintains GLSEN takes a "spurious 'civil rights' approach toward homosexuality" and that they downplay or neglect to reveal the hazards of homosexual behavior." A pro-gay bias is obvious throughout the curriculum, she said, including a bias against traditional religious views on marriage. Further, most of the exercises are based on the assumption that homosexuality is as immutable as race. "Laws that once banned interracial marriage (miscegenation laws) are erroneously called a 'parallel' to the prohibition of same-sex marriage," says Harvey, while opposition to same-sex marriage is "depicted as needlessly fearful and backward." The United Nations "Declaration of Human Rights" is characterized as justifying same-sex marriage because "it calls for 'dignity,' marriage, and family rights and decries 'discrimination.'" In fact, this 1948 document was never intended to back any civil right for same-sex marriage, Harvey points out, despite gay activists' unsuccessful attempts to amend it to do just that. Nevertheless, students are told "to evaluate the actions of the Vermont legislature [which legalized civil unions in 2000] in light of this document in an attempt to bring the U.S. to 'justice' by international standards outside our country." Further, the curriculum resource list includes gay activist group websites (along with their accompanying soft-porn ads and links to worse sites, one would suppose) with no mention of sources that support traditional values.[32]

Harvey's entire assessment of the GLSEN curriculum can be found at the Mission America website (missionamerica.com). While I don't necessarily agree with some of its rhetoric or topics, Mission America has been following the incursion of pro-gay educational materials into public schools for quite some time, and concerned parents have found it to be a helpful tool in this regard. The organization completed a yearlong survey of American middle and high school students in 2003-2004, providing some interesting feedback about how the subject of homosexuality was being covered in the nation's schools. The questionnaire was distributed through the Mission America newsletter in the fall of 2003 and also appears on the website.[33] Schools are inargulably even more pro-gay today than in 2003.

Philadelphia was the first U.S. city to proclaim a GLBT History Month in its school system, amid vocal complaints from concerned parents. No doubt, other school districts have followed suit. According to an October 2, 2006 "Monday Briefing" editorial in the *The Amarillo Globe News* online, "One of the PR spinners for the [Philadelphia] district said the uproar by parents was not unexpected 'when you deal with diversity.' We're more interested in knowing if students in Philly can name any of the rights in the First Amendment, read on grade level or solve an algebraic equation.

We expect not. Then again, in the quest for diversity, perhaps it is more important to know whether Alexander the Great or Abe Lincoln were gay."

A gay rights spokesman appearing on "The O'Reilly Factor" on October 17, 2006 in support of GLBT History Month askedskeptical viewers to check out a supposed GLBT history website, glbthistory.com. He claimed this "educational" site highlightedhistoric contributions to society made by homosexuals. He mentioned Alan Turing, the gay Englishman who cracked the German Enigma Code during World War II. Was Turing prominently featured at (now-revamped) glbthistory.com? Nope. You had to know his name already to do a search via the news archives link, where three mentions came up. Not only was this site in its original form merely a gay political propaganda front, but it prominently displayed other site links that allowed students with one click to access gay porn, classified ads, and sex toy shops.

I thoroughly examined the site while it was first active. I saw no positive role models on the order of Martin Luther King Jr. or Booker T. Washington profiled. Just ridiculous stories claiming the Apostle Paul and a host of other historical figures were gay, along with profiles of drag queens, gay pedophiles, and a parade of social miscreants, one of whom was the late Harry Hay of NAMBLA fame. For a while, the site morphed into a total gay porn site. At least these "historians" finally chose to be honest about their real intent—to seduce innocent students and deceive their parents and teachers. It has returned to a semblance of a historical site as I write this, but is pretty short on information. It contains strange tidbits like this in its thumbnail sketch of gay history through 1972: "1941 - Word War II Began. The significance of this event to gay history is in the platooning of men and women in sex-segregated environments in which many men and women discovered their gay feelings. Historians attribute the growth of gay consciousness in the following decades to the sex-segregated environments." Apparently, the writers believed this was the first time in history the sexes had lived in segregated housing.

The idea for a gay history month was proposed in 1994 by Missouri high school teacher Rodney Wilson and gay journalist Paul Varnell. Interestingly, Varnell did not envision gay history month as a political statement. In a 1994 commentary he wrote for the *Chicago Free Press*, he said, "The obsession with politics by some activists amounts to a kind of tunnel vision bordering on pathology."[34] The NEA, not surprisingly, passed an amendment supporting Gay and Lesbian History Month in 1995.

Collegiate Antics

It isn't just elementary and secondary schools that have . been invaded by pro-gay activists. The realm of higher education has been home to many forms of socially liberal academic bias for decades. Writing in a special issue of the *Regent University Law Review* (deemed necessary because of the extent to which anything but pro-gay "research" is allowed to be published in most academic journals), Ty Clevenger, a Stanford Law School graduate, stated that "gay activists view anything but the slightest deviation from pro-gay orthodoxy as something akin to religious heresy."[35] Clevenger sums up the academic hypocrisy with regard to homosexuality thus:

> On the one hand, "mainstream" academic/ professional organizations publish research suggesting adult-child sex may not be harmful, and they endorse supportive therapy for individuals who wish to surgically alter themselves (some would say physically mutilate themselves) from one sex to the other. Yet, they denounce as unethical any healthcare professionals who offer therapy to

homosexuals who wish to become heterosexuals. In other words, it is ethical to counsel a man to have his penis removed so he can have sex as a heterosexual woman, but it's unethical to counsel a man to have sex as a heterosexual man even if he wants to have sex as a typical man.[36]

Clevenger also discusses the double standard for peer-reviewed academic journal articles. "The objectivity of researchers who are Christian, Mormon, Jewish Orthodox, etc., is open to question, while the fact that a researcher may himself or herself be a homosexual is not considered grounds for suspicion of bias.[37] Clevenger further states that academic bias has a negative bearing on court cases since courts regularly rely on published social science research, in addition to individual expert witnesses:

The aura of scientific objectivity clearly is long overdue for a challenge, particularly in the fields of psychology and psychiatry. Indeed, the law may, in many respects, be better equipped to insure the accuracy and fairness of social science research than the alleged scientists themselves, particularly in academic fields where political bias has overtaken empirical results. The rules of evidence, for example, allow counsel to examine rigorously a witness—even an expert witness—for evidence of bias, and the adversarial system of justice provides an opportunity for robust debate between competing points of view. Unfortunately, those attributes are increasingly rare in academia or the professional journals, where viewpoint discrimination and "political correctness" are the norm.[38]

As Clevenger points out, for many leftist academics the debate over gay rights is already over. One can see this gross bias in another incident at a Canadian university. In Canada, where saying anything that is not supportive of the gay rights agenda can qualify as hate speech, gay activists and professors protested the granting of an honorary doctorate to Canada's best-known ethicist, McGill Professor Margaret Somerville, in June 2006. Angry over Somerville's opposition to gay marriage, some professors who shared the stage with her at the graduation ceremony draped themselves in rainbow flags, with a few even turning their backs on her. Some carried signs reading, "Respectfully disagree" and "My Ryerson honours equal rights."[39] Somerville is no right-wing radical; she supports civil unions for gay couples, but also advocates for children's needs.

We also cannot overlook the role radical leftist librarians continue to play in academia. The ALA is in lock-step with the NEA in many ways. Conservative librarians are ostracized from their peers in the same way conservative teachers are. East Carolina University librarian David Durant wrote in a 2005 exposé on the ALA, "[I]n the wake of 9/11 and the war in Iraq, librarianship as a profession no longer simply leans to the left; it has become openly politicized. By 2004, to work in a major American public or academic library was to find yourself in a left-wing echo chamber."[40]

Given that public school children are indoctrinated from kindergarten on to accept homosexuality as normal, it is not surprising that by the time they reach college, they are collectively more accepting of the gay lifestyle. "[L]ast year's big UCLA survey of college freshmen found that 57 percent favor same-sex marriage (only about 36 percent of all adults do). Even as adult activists bicker in court, young Americans—including many young conservatives—are becoming thoroughly, even nonchalantly, gay-positive," observed John Cloud in *Time's* October 2005 cover story, "The Battle Over Gay Teens."[41] Similarly, a Zogby Poll of high school seniors as early as 2001found that roughly two-thirds of those responding believed that homosexual marriage and adoption should be legal.[42] Those numbers should be even higher now. The adult numbers are edging up, too.

Marvin Olasky, editor of *World* magazine, pointed out in a May 2007 commentary, "Surveys of political party affiliation show that Democratic professors outnumber Republicans at least 7 to 1 in humanities and social science departments across the land. That actually underestimates the tilt, because some northern Republicans are not conservative, and some professors eschew the Democrat label because they are further to the left." Added Olasky, "The situation isn't as bad as it could be, because some students expect professors to be propagandists and discount what they say, but many experience a slow toxic buildup."[43]

When enough parents realize the extent to which schools are engaging in political activism—particularly in the homosexual arena—when their priority should be providing students with a solid academic education, perhaps they will take steps to hold educators and administrators accountable to their primary mission. We can throw money at public education ad infinitum, but until we return schools to the role they were created for, we will continue to see a decline in the preparedness of our future leaders. Our education system has fallen prey to a gradual forgetting of history. C.S. Lewis sums it up well through the infamous demon Screwtape from *The Screwtape Letters*:

> "The Historical Point of View, put briefly, means that when a learned man is presented with any statement in an ancient author, the one question he never asks is whether it is true. He asks who influenced the ancient writer, and how far the statement is consistent with what he said in other

books, and what phase in the writer's development, or in the general history of thought, it illustrates, and how it affected later writers, and how often it has been misunderstood (especially by the learned man's own colleagues), and what the general course of criticism on it has been for the last ten years, and what is the 'present state of the question'. To regard the ancient writer as a possible source of knowledge— to anticipate that what he said could possibly modify your thoughts or your behaviour—this would be rejected as unutterably simple-minded. And since we cannot deceive the whole human race all time, it is most important thus to cut every generation off from all the others; for where learning makes a free commerce between the ages there is always the danger that the characteristic errors of one may be corrected by the characteristic truths of another. But thanks be to Our Father and the Historical Point of View, great scholars are now as little nourished by the past as the most ignorant mechanic who holds that 'history is bunk'."[44]

Seven

Christian Gay Movement:
"A New Thing" or Heresy?

A fter the Rt. Rev. Eugene Robinson was consecrated as the
first openly homosexual bishop by the Episcopal Church
in 2003, he stated, "The famous test pilot Chuck Yeager,
after breaking the sound barrier for the first time, in a speech said
something like: 'The plane shakes the hardest just before you break
through.' And I believe what we're experiencing from conservatives
right now is that shaking, and maybe the whole culture is shaking
before we break through this next barrier for gay and lesbian folks."
He then uttered his much-quoted sound bite: "I believe God is
doing a new thing in the world."[1] Many in the Worldwide Anglican
Communion and its American branch, the Episcopal Church,
disagreed, and still do. If what Robinson meant was a sanctioning
of non-celibate gay and lesbian clergy within the worldwide body of
Christ, he was speaking heresy to many. Others sincerely wanted
Robinson's "new thing" to be an attitude of loving redemption
that will bring a new era of harmony between conservatives and
progressives within the Church. But because an openly gay, non-

celibate clergyman spoke those words, he could only have meant one thing by them: homosexual acts between "committed" couples are not sinful. The earth did, indeed, quake that day.

Robinson's confirmation ignited a sizable firestorm among Episcopalians that has spread to other mainline denominations. In the summer of 2006, the rift in the Episcopal Church grew wider as a decidedly pro-gay woman, Katharine Jefferts Schori, was elected by a narrow margin as presiding bishop of the church. She stated in a CNN televised interview, "I believe that God creates us with different gifts. Each of us comes into the world with a different collection of things that challenge us and things that give us joy and allow us to bless the world around us. Some people come into this world with affections ordered toward other people, and some people come into this world with affections directed at people of their own gender."[2] Her remarks might have passed muster with a great deal more Christians had she not used the phrase, "come into the world," offering that the "challenge" of homosexuality is something people are born with, in her clerical opinion.

Ephraim Radner, rector of the Church of the Ascension in Pueblo, Colorado, and Andrew Goddard, tutor in ethics at Wycliffe Hall, Oxford, England, published a paper in November 2006 delineating what they viewed as an appropriate Christian response, civilly and biblically, to the gay cultural/theological debate. It is well worth reading (see endnote). Radner and Goddard point out the Anglican Church's previous resolutions, one of which (the Lambeth Resolution 1.10 in 1998) states, "... while rejecting homosexual practice as incompatible with Scripture, [this Conference] calls on all our people to minister pastorally and sensitively to all irrespective of sexual orientation and to condemn irrational fear of homosexuals. ..."[3] However, they also state, "Treating people like 'children of God' leaves unresolved, without further argumentation, from a Christian perspective, the moral and civil status of their actions. These may, as we know (in a range of cases from sexual predation to drug possession), even be viewed as criminal for one reason or another. The critical issue lies in these 'reasons,' and the analysis of such reasoning cannot simply be bypassed."[4] Therein lies the conundrum for the Church. Where do the Church's responsibility and authority begin and end in considering "the moral and civil status" of homosexuals within the body, as well as those on the outside to whom we have a Great Commission mandate to witness the truth of the gospel?

Until Robinson's confirmation "heard around the world," no openly homosexual man or woman had been granted a position of high ecclesiastical leadership in a traditional, mainline American church. Certain Catholic bishops long have been known within their jurisdictions and among senior leaders to be closeted homosexual men and even pedophiles, of course. Protestant denominations have had their share of closeted gay or struggling clergy with nowhere safe to turn for help except to a small fraternity or sorority of other closeted gays. The Vatican has been aware of the Catholic problem for some time as it has attempted to address—although rather poorly, in too many cases—the widespread incidences of both heterosexual and homosexual priests engaging in coerced sex acts with children and possibly even consensual sex with older teenagers or adults in the church. The vow of celibacy for priests has never been easy to maintain. It is also common knowledge that many troubled homosexuals become clergy in hopes that it will "cure" them, while others, gay and straight, become ordained in order to be closer to the objects of their sick pursuits. That has been particularly unfortunate for the many children who have been preyed upon by pedophile clergy of either persuasion. This problem is by no means limited to the Catholic Church.

Most Catholic and Protestant congregations in the U.S. are

uncomfortable with welcoming open, non-celibate homosexuals into their midst as they adhere to the biblically supported belief that homosexual behavior is sin, the same as all sex outside traditional marriage. That would put such folks on par with professing heterosexual fornicators or adulterers, were we to have any of those stand up within the church to claim such as a protected identity. The desire for gay-affirmed Christians—most believe God created them differently—to openly worship without discrimination led to the founding of liberal, gay-friendly churches. The largest denomination serving gay Christians is the United Fellowship of the Metropolitan Community Church (MCC), established in the United States in 1968. Many Christian gay-identified men and women have chosen over the years to leave their former churches and attend one of the 300 or so MCC churches around the world.

Gay "Fellowship"?

The MCC has faced a public perception of its churches being "gay pick-up joints" in the minds of some people. Of course, lots of average folks don't even know the MCC exists. An unsavory allegation appeared in a disturbing 2002 article written by Stephen Bennett (he is known as a formerly gay man), for WorldNetDaily. It certainly raised the specter of a sordid underside to at least some of these largely gay congregations. Let us hope, if this article was even half true, such churches have cleaned up their act. Bennett went behind the scenes of the San Diego MCC and discovered the church offering some peculiar "fellowship." Among the shocking examples he cited were a sadomasochist workshop sponsored by GLO (Gay Leathermen Only) at the church hall, called "Fisting For Beginners" and another workshop on "single tail whip and sensuous whip play."[5]

Concerned Women for America reported in an August 18,

2002 article on its website (ccwfa.org) that MCC communications director, Jim Birkitt, when asked if he knew MCC San Diego had held a "whip workshop with live demonstrations" in April of that year, replied, "My understanding is that that policy changed in April. None of our clergy do that." The MCC San Diego website places the San Diego LGBT Community Center link at the top of its gay links list, with another link provided for San Diego Pride, sponsors of the nation's fifth-largest gay pride festival and parade. Both sites are quite eye-opening. Gay Leathermen Only is listed on the LGBT Center's Social Groups Resources link with this disclaimer: "GLO is only a part of the leather/BDSM community and respects the fact that many of our members are members of other groups and organizations. We also respect all the other groups and organizations in our community; diversity is our strength and bond." Club X, the "pansexual leather/BDSM fetish group" mentioned in one of the San Diego MCC promos, has adopted "Safe, Sane, and Consensual" as its motto. The "consensual" part may raise an eyebrow, even more so when one sees this statement on the site: "If you are not legally an adult and interested in role empowerment, please visit HERE instead." The link goes directly to the White House official website. Draw your own conclusions. Those wishing to know about social events not listed on the site are advised to inquire further by e-mail. The "social calendar" is available only via the Club X Yahoo discussion group.

Should the MCC or any church that welcomes the gay community maintain the appearance of sanctioning the seamy underside of gay culture when many respectable gays want to advance their image of gay mainstream America? You decide. It seems the gay community has difficulty jettisoning its baggage, even in a church setting.

San Diego—"America's Finest City"—is fast becoming the next gay mecca, with a growing gay representation within city government, as well as a troublesome anti-Christian element. My family and I lived in North San Diego County for more than 17 years. Sadly, the San Diego area was the scene of my own rebellion. In and around many wonderful churches and active Christian communities in Southern California lies an underworld of confusion and depravity. It touches many communities the country, of course. This is not to diminish the hypocrisy in any other church where pastors and lay leaders believe they are committing sexual sin with impunity or are merely winking at it in others. All Christians, especially those in leadership, will have to answer for their sinful choices one day before God. "From everyone who has been given much, much will be required" (Luke 12:48).

Some churches have attempted to welcome GLBT Christians into their broader denominational fellowship. Several of these began in the seventies, with more added in the eighties and nineties. Joining these were various interdenominational groups, beginning with the Open Church Group and Evangelicals Concerned in 1975. Still, finding any common ground between gays and the rest of the body within any church denomination has been a painful and largely futile exercise. As Elizabeth Stuart put it in her 1997 book, *Religion Is a Queer Thing*:

> They have talked all day and all night. They have talked for days, weeks, months, and years. They have shouted at one another. They have walked out on one another. They have tried to conduct a civilized, Christian, loving debate. There have been small victories for all sides, which have given everyone a new energy to press on or oppose. But however hard they try and convince themselves otherwise they are deadlocked.[6]

The Lesbian and Gay Christian Movement (originally the Christian Gay Movement) was started in 1976. Soulforce, the interdenominational group of Christians identifying as GLBT or those who support them, was formed in 1999. Hoping to put a more politically correct face on the gay culture debate, liberal theologians have adopted a postmodern mantra that says homosexuality is just "another mystery of God's creation." Most conservative evangelicals and many mainline Christians are not buying that view, however. For them, pro-gay theology is a feeble attempt to deconstruct the truth of Scripture, which is sacrosanct: the world is fallen and homosexuality is but one manifestation of that brokenness. The compassion we ought to show the gay community has been lost in the blurring of lines that once were unthinkable to cross. "Out and Proud"? How can one be proud of sin? Isn't pride, itself, a sin? Perhaps "Out and Humble" or "Imperfect and Humble" would carry more weight, the latter applying to all Christians.

Scrutinizing the Church

"To the biblically ignorant, general pro-gay religious arguments can pass for truth. In the light of Scripture, however, they do not hold up under scrutiny," says Joe Dallas, a former gay activist who made the difficult trip out of that worldview and today is a Christian counselor helping other men who struggle with same-sex attraction. Dallas admits that the Church is facing a tough battle as it strives to win the hearts and minds of people who are searching for something more than what the world is offering. "When the divorce rate in the Christian community nearly parallels that of the secular community, when the use of pornography is epidemic among Christian men, when the scandals in our own leadership rival, and at times exceed, what we see in Washington ... why should the majority of Americans adhere to a moral standard that its own proponents seem unable to adhere to?"[7]

The Baptist Press reported that Richard Land, president of the Southern Baptist Convention's Ethics and Religious Liberty Commission (ERLC), said at the 2010 SBC annual meeting in mid-June, "Americans continue to practice this collective societal child abuse that we call divorce because we want to do what we think is best for us and it doesn't matter what promises we have made to our spouses and to God. It is flat-out rebellion against God." Land is known for not mincing words.

While many Americans found the James McGreevey scandal disturbing, those same Americans were more appalled when Rev. Ted Haggard, a prominent leader within the evangelical community, confessed to sexual immorality and drug use with another man in November 2006. Haggard wasn't seen as a self-righteous fanatic who one day would figuratively hang himself with his own rope, as we've seen others do. Yet, he found himself in a position of authority with feet of clay, and falling hard. Only God knows his motives. If anyone had been in a position to solidify the evangelical movement, it appeared to be Haggard. He has been in a restoration process since his fall. He is moving forward now with a home church, to the chagrin of those who feel he needs more time to heal. The Church, just as every individual, can benefit from a periodic, humbling self-examination. Leaders are subject to the same rise and fall of the culture around them unless they remain accountable to a higher source—Christ, himself. Other godly men and women must walk out that accountability with individuals, however.

Christian hypocrisy—apostasy, in the extreme—causes people to reevaluate the Church's role in modern society. Of course that role is not fluid, but the Church is made up of people who sometimes cling to fluid value systems and forget (or never learn) scriptural truth. This can create a wedge between different schools of Christianity that endlessly debate theology and biblical instruction to the Church where homosexuality and even HIV/AIDS prevention are concerned. Further, it fosters an atmosphere of mean-spiritedness and one-upmanship in the gay culture war. "So in addition to simply saying, 'The Bible condemns this behavior, it's unnatural, we're not built for it, these people are engaging in something they ought not to engage in,' we needed to pepper our statements with lurid, sometimes very false exaggerations and stereotypes about homosexual people themselves," Dallas points out.[8] Christians can forget that Jesus did not condemn the woman who was caught in adultery and about to be stoned (he would have treated a homosexual no differently), but the other side often forgets that he also said to her, "Go and sin no more."

All Christians are called to seek the truth of Scripture via a personal relationship with Jesus Christ. Yet, a great battle for the truth is being waged between gay Christians and their progressive supporters, who believe one thing, and conservative evangelical Christians, who believe another. Are we reading the same Bible? This debate is a critical part of the larger cultural war. If God can be portrayed as sanctioning homosexuality, what is to keep the more sordid elements of gayness and other fringe movements clinging to its coattails, from seeking to move forward into the mainstream? Will heterosexuals with warped lustful appetites begin to feel entitled to their share of mainstream approval? Some already do.

Gay Theology Exposed

I am focusing here primarily on two educated clergymen who represent both sides in this debate. Each presents his case in more detail than I can include here, and I invite readers to further evaluate them for themselves. One is the openly gay Rev. (Dr.) Mel White, former professor at Fuller Theological Seminary in Pasadena, California, and semi-retired co-founder of Soulforce. The other is Dr. Gordon Hugenberger, pastor of Park Street Church in Boston, who responded to questions from a congregant with a detailed letter of evangelical apologetics on October 26, 2007. I present highlights from Hugenberger's eight-point letter here over against the eight premises in White's pro-gay, eisegetical booklet, *What the Bible Says–And Doesn't Say–About Homosexuality*. The entire booklet, which includes some interesting personal asides by White, can be viewed at the Soulforce website (soulforce. org) while Hugenberger's open letter is at his church's website (see endnote).

Of course, these men are not the only ones to have evaluated theological views on homosexuality. Joe Dallas has provided an excellent and comprehensive response to pro-gay theology in his book, *The Gay Gospel?: How Pro-Gay Advocates Misread the Bible*. As a formerly gay Christian in the mold of White, Dallas' viewpoint is particularly pertinent. Robert A.J. Gagnon, associate professor of New Testament at Pittsburgh Theological Seminary, has written extensively on homosexuality. If you are seeking a more detailed hermeneutical approach, I recommend his book, *The Bible and Homosexual Practice*. Derrick Sherwin Bailey, Troy Perry, Elizabeth Stuart, and Mary Daly, to name a few, have written extensively for the pro-gay or lesbian feminist theological side.

While my heart goes out to White, given his very difficult journey to come to terms with his homosexuality–including at least one suicide attempt–he also is well aware that Christian apologetics compels us to counter his highly suspect theological arguments that so easily ensnare confused young people who may be questioning their sexual identity. In a sense, we are brother and sister in the Lord, but with adversarial doctrinal viewpoints. White presents eight premises to back his claim that homosexuality is not condemned in the Bible. The bulk of his discussion centers on the disputed passages of Scripture from both the Old and New Testaments that have been read for centuries as portraying homosexuality as sin. He presents himself as a biblical scholar and authority, declaring what God "really means" time and time again as he discusses the various Scriptures. He would have us believe the Holy Spirit has given him some unique insight that overrides what other respected theologians have—a kind of postmodern Gnosticism. His is an elitist approach that seeks to discount any apologetics viewpoint deemed unenlightened (message: "Fundamentalists" need not apply to his school of theology, even if they also know Hebrew and Greek).

I had planned to quote White's eight premises here, but Soulforce refused to give me permission do so, since they view this book as "oppressive to LGBT people."[9] Nothing was said in their missive about things deemed oppressive to former LGBT people. Readers can infer what the basic premises are from my response to each. Visit the Soulforce website for the whole picture.

Response to White's First Premise:

Given the high rate of biblical illiteracy among people who call themselves Christians, we can generally agree with White's assessment that most people have not carefully or prayerfully searched the Scriptures for God's instruction about homosexuality or life, in general. However, that does not negate the truth contained in those Scriptures. Be assured, God still hears the tree that falls in an unpopulated forest.

Response to White's Second Premise:

It is also true that the Bible has been misused to justify suffering and prejudice throughout history. The Crusades, the Inquisition and African-American slavery, particularly in America, are the most obvious examples. Again, this does not mean that

God did not condemn the practice of homosexuality in the Bible. It merely means that Christians are not always leaving the judgment to Him. There is a distinct difference between discernment and the postmodern definition of discrimination. And denying biblical instruction meant to help us can, indeed, lead to our harm.

Response to White's Third Premise:

Is there "new truth" in God's Word? The wisest man ever to live, King Solomon, insisted there is nothing "new under the sun." Absolute truth never changes; human interpretations to it can and do. Short-sighted and selfish humans have a narcissistic need to discover what they consider to be new truth.

Response to White's Fourth Premise:

The Bible is a book about *man's relationship with God,* as well as God's stated purpose for creating man and woman, starting in the Garden of Eden where marriage and godly sexual expression were born. From Genesis through the New Testament, God gives explicit instructions about marriage and the God-ordained, complementary relationship between husband and wife. "He made them male and female" and enjoined them to become "one flesh." This union is meant to reflect the entire image of God, and is even a metaphor of the relationship of Christ with his bride, the Church. Man cannot redesign what God has designed.

Response to White's Fifth Premise:

Again, this is a smokescreen meant to draw us away from the real truth about sexuality and how we are to honor God, in whose image we are made, with our whole being. The focus in biblical passages about sexuality is still on God and His truth.

Response to White's Sixth Premise:

Indeed, most biblical scholars believe that a homosexual

orientation, as opposed to homosexual *practice*, is not condemned in the Bible. We all have a sin nature that predisposes us to sinful behavior—call it an orientation—when we are tempted in our areas of weakness. When Paul wrote his first epistle to the Corinthians, he exhorted them to remain faithful in their new lives, stating that some of them were formerly doers of evil, including active homosexuality (1 Corinthians 6:11). Jesus stated he came to "fulfill" Old Testament law, not "abolish" it (Matthew 5:17), clearly meaning he would condemn the sinful acting out of homosexual desires while being compassionate toward the sinner, as he was toward the adulterous woman.

Response to White's Seventh Premise:

Both the Old and New Testaments have things to say about homosexuality *as we know it*. No matter how White and others try to twist the truth, it is clear that homosexual practice (not a predisposition toward same-sex attractions, as pointed out above) is sinful and subject to God's judgment. Jesus did not have to specifically talk about it as he came to "fulfill the law," which had been clearly stated. Sexual immorality is both an Old and New Covenant sin. Jesus could not have been clearer in speaking about God's definition of marriage in Matthew 19:4-6. In fact, marriage—obviously between a man and a woman—was so sacred for Christ that the Church is referred to as his "bride." A reading of John's Gospel leaves open the possibility that Christ did say things about homosexuality, as John says he both did and said many things that were not recorded. We are, first and foremost, to love God (meaning we will keep His commandments), then "one another." We can't fail in the second commandment if we obey the first. Conservative Christians view the Pauline and other apostolic letters to be doctrinal, just as the words of Christ are. Progressive Christians—especially those who are pro-gay—seek to canonize Christ's words above all other Scripture, while reinterpreting them to suit their needs, flying in the face of 2,000 years of documented church and canonical history in the process.

Response to White's Eighth Premise:

Of course, no one should use biblical injunctions against the practice of homosexuality as a justification for unjust discrimination against homosexuals or the usurping of their basic civil rights. The Bible does not allow for this kind of hate-mongering. Gays enjoy the same constitutionally protected rights as all other citizens in the U.S. There is no implicit "right" to civil marriage or official sanctioning of homosexuality handed down by our founding fathers. There is freedom of conscience for all individuals with a proviso that one person's "freedom" does no harm to another or to society. Finding something a personal affront is not the same as being harmed or deprived of life or liberty by it.

Hugenberger also has eight points to present. I have edited his comments for brevity's sake, with his approval. He gets more ink here because I am referring readers to Mel White's entire booklet, which is considerably longer, and because I have permission to quote him.

Dear Dr. Hugenberger,

We love the fact that Park Street Church stresses the gospel of Christ, but it doesn't get stressed out about so many of the secondary issues which seem to divide Christians (baptism, Charismatic gifts, style of worship, etc.). We sense, however, that there is not a similar openness to various points of view about the ethics of homosexuality. Why? Isn't this an issue over which sincere Christians disagree? After all, Jesus never condemned homosexuality, and Paul only condemned heterosexuals who engaged in homosexual acts, which were "unnatural" for them.

Sincerely,
Puzzled

Dear Puzzled,

Thank you very much for your thoughtful remarks and question about my recent comments regarding homosexuality. Let me say a few things about each of the main points you raise.

1. I tried to summarize as fairly as I could the principal convictions of modern evangelicalism and indicate a few areas where evangelicals in general, and Park Street Church in particular, recognize that there is room for honest differences of opinion. If we take [Hugenberger lists quite a few respected ministries and theological institutions] as well-known organizations which are representative of the convictions of the mainstream of evangelicalism in America today, ALL of these groups in official documents or writings by their leaders of which I am aware universally reject homosexual practice (NOT homosexual orientation) as a departure from the will of God. ... My point here, however, is simply to indicate that it would have been dishonest of me to suggest in my sermon on Sunday that evangelicals are agreed that this issue is comparable to baptism,

etc., on which evangelicals are found in large numbers on both sides of the question.

2. Since Paul was as well-educated and well-read as he was (he quotes secular authors like Epimenides, Aratus, etc.), he would have been quite familiar with the vast homosexual literature of the Hellenistic world in which tender, committed, nurturing homoerotic love was celebrated. No doubt, he would have known of Emperor Nero's own homosexual marriage to Sporus. Since Paul ministered for a length of time in Corinth, he may well have known firsthand of many other homosexual marriages. Despite all of this, at no point does Paul say even the slightest positive thing about homosexual practice. Instead, every time he addresses it, he rejects it as an option for Christians. ...

3. It is sometimes claimed, based on Romans 1, that Paul only condemned heterosexuals who were acting like homosexuals. This view has been frequently repeated since it was first invented by Derrick Sherwin Bailey in 1955 in his book, *Homosexuality and the Western Christian Tradition.* Unfortunately, however, it is mistaken. Virtually no New Testament scholar of any stature (regardless of his or her theology or sexual orientation) now supports it. ... [T]he present scholarly consensus is that, whether we agree with the New Testament or not, Paul rejected homosexuality in all of its forms as a violation of God's moral order for our lives. ...

4. The Old Testament prohibitions of homosexual acts are just as general as the New Testament prohibitions. They do not just condemn homosexual rape, or pederasty, or some other deviant behavior. Leviticus 18:22 says, "Do not lie with a man as one lies with a woman; that is detestable." The language of this prohibition could not be more general. It includes both one-night stands and life-long committed affectionate sex. It does NOT, however, include a homosexual orientation. I want to stress this since, in my opinion, the issues for homosexuals and heterosexuals are really not so different. Each of us, because of our decadent culture and our own sinful proclivities, faces sexual temptation in an endless variety of guises, and this is just as true for married persons as it is for single persons. This is why the Bible has as much to say about adultery and lust as it does about premarital promiscuity. In the end, every one of us has to decide day by day, to Whom do we belong? ...

5. You are right that Jesus nowhere explicitly condemns homosexual practice, but this is hardly evidence that he approves of homosexual practice. ... Really the safest conclusion is that Jesus never bothered to deal with a long list of sins because he did not need to. They were already condemned very clearly, whether explicitly or by implication, in the Old Testament. The main issues that Jesus addressed were areas where the Jews of his day had twisted or misinterpreted the Old Testament,

and they needed to be corrected. They thought, for example, that just because we are commanded to love our neighbor in Leviticus 19, this justifies us in hating our enemy. So Jesus corrects their misunderstanding. Otherwise, according to Jesus himself, his ethics are the EXACT same as the Old Testament. See the Sermon on the Mount, Matthew 5:17-20, where he makes this point.

6. Despite the lack of explicit teaching from Jesus on the topic of homosexual practice, I think we can safely infer that Jesus condemned it in any form. I say this based on the "law of excluded middle." In Matthew 19:1-12 Jesus takes up the matter of marriage and sex. He reminds his contemporaries that God's original plan for human beings was lifelong faithful marriage between a male and a female. Accordingly, Jesus condemns any who would break up "what God has joined together." Furthermore, Jesus insists that there is no approved ground for a divorce apart from sexual infidelity ("fornication," which includes willful desertion) on the part of one's spouse. ... In their shock the disciples exclaimed that if what Jesus was teaching is the case, it would be better to avoid marriage! Jesus surprises them again, perhaps, by affirming a life of singleness as a status that God approves, just like marriage. But what is notable for our discussion is that as far as Jesus is concerned, there is no THIRD option! One must either be chaste ("a eunuch ... for the sake of the kingdom") or one must be faithful in a heterosexual marriage ("male

and female" "united to his wife"). Surely if Jesus wanted to affirm life-long committed homosexual unions, here is where he needed to do it. ...

7. Park Street Church is blessed with many wonderful Christians who are now or have been homosexual in the past. As you may know, we have a significant ministry to the homosexual and lesbian community, including our weekly support meeting called Alive in Christ. ... What does it mean to be a new creature in Christ, if it does not mean that we can change in any way God wants? ...

The result is that we have become a kind of refuge for many. In fact, we have a number of key leaders in our church who are quite open about the fact that they were once in the gay life (in some cases before their marriages—their testimonies of transformation are amazing), while others admit that they still feel temptation in this area, but they are committed to giving their lives of singleness to God (to be eunuchs for the kingdom, as Jesus put it). ...

8. Finally, although I probably don't need to say this, I do want to emphasize that I do NOT consider homosexuality to be worse than any of the 'zillion sins I commit every day. In fact, it is tribute to the infinite grace and mercy of God that the sanctuary roof stays up each day that I walk into the room. In any case, we are not on some kind of crusade to single out those who may be dealing with this issue. Although I want the liberty

to be honest with the Bible and to address this topic from time to time, I have no intention of so stressing it that the many homosexual guests and visitors who are not interested in changing will feel put off or unwelcome (or at least no more put off or unwelcome than the many materialists who are not yet interested in changing). On the other hand, I want to say enough so that those who are trying to surrender this part of their lives to Christ will be encouraged, and also so that the rest will not be misled by a culture that increasingly is allowing only one side of the discussion to be heard.

I hope that this is helpful. Thank you again for your honest comments and for being a part of our church family.

Yours in Christ,
Gordon Hugenberger[10]

A majority of Americans supposedly now no longer believe in absolute truth. This percentage has been creeping up during the past decade, with the latest survey from the Pew Forum on Religion and Public Life indicating that even a majority of those who identify as evangelical Christians do not see Christ as representing the only way to salvation. "If 'absolute truth' no longer exists, even in the minds of half the 'born-again' population, it logically follows that doctrine, and the Bible itself, is given less credence," says Joe Dallas. Pollster George Gallup, Jr. noticed this in *The People's Religion: American Faith in the '90s.* "While religion is highly popular in America," he states, "it is to a large extent superficial. There is a knowledge gap between American's stated faith and the lack of the most basic knowledge about that faith. ..."[11] "If the notions of 'truth' and 'doctrine' are becoming unimportant to Christians, can the idea of 'sin' hope to survive?" asks Dallas. "Probably not; 25 percent of Christians polled in 1993 believed sin to be 'an outdated concept.' A desire for 'warm and fuzzy' without a commitment to truth makes the general religious arguments of the pro-gay theology all the more palatable. Unlike pro-gay social justice arguments, these general 'religious' arguments appeal to the themes of harmony and goodwill and bypass issues of mankind's fallen nature, sin, and obedience."[12]

Those who espouse gay theology and insist on santioning same-sex marriage are placing themselves in peril of being removed from God's grace. Again, I defer to C.S. Lewis' Screwtape:

> "The first job of their tempters was to harden these choices of the Hell-ward roads into a habit by steady repetition. But then (and this was all-important) to turn the habit into a principle—a principle the creature is prepared to defend. After that, all will go well. Conformity to the social environment, at first merely instinctive or even mechanical—how should a jelly not conform?—now becomes unacknowledged creed or ideal of Togetherness or Being like Folks. Mere ignorance of the law they break now turns into a vague theory about it—remember they know no history—a theory expressed by calling it conventional or puritan or bourgeois 'morality.' Thus gradually there comes to exist at the centre of the creature a hard, tight, settled core of resolution to go on being what it is, and even to resist moods that might tend to alter it. ... Here at last is a real and deliberate, though not fully articulate, rejection of what the Enemy calls Grace."[13]

Those who preach a gay-slanted gospel to impressionable young gay or gender-confused Christians have much to answer for. It is sad to think that many young men and women will be led into idolatry by this false teaching and many in the Church will be too afraid or politically correct to stand against it. "Gay pride" is a form of idolatry that places the "need" for homosexual intimacy above that of fellowship between mankind and God. We were created for God's pleasure and purposes, not our own. "For all that is in the world, the lust of the flesh and the lust of the eyes and the boastful pride of life, is not from the Father, but is from the world," wrote John (1 John 2:16). Paul warns us through his letter to the Colossians not to be taken "captive through philosophy and empty deception, according to the traditions of man, according to the elementary principles of the world, rather than according to Christ" (Colossians 2:8). In his book, *Stranger at the Gate*, Mel White insisted that it's not about sex. Yet he repeatedly refers to virile men he was attracted to throughout his life as "meeting his sensual grid."[14] Not God's grid and not even a human love grid, but a man's *sensual* one. Yes, all men and women have such a grid.

If there is one aspect of the Christian gay-affirming movement that is most damaging for those who espouse its tenets, it may be this: placing self-consciousness ahead of Christ-consciousness. No one has pointed this out quite as effectively as early twentieth-century Scottish preacher Oswald Chambers. Chambers is best known today for the book based on his Clapham, England chapel sermons and other teachings, *My Utmost for His Highest*. He said, "Beware of allowing self-consciousness to continue because by slow degrees it will awaken self-pity, and self-pity is Satanic. 'Well, I am not understood; this is a thing they ought to apologize for; that is a point I really must have cleared up.' Leave others alone and ask the Lord to give you Christ-consciousness, and He will poise you until the completeness is absolute."[15] I have observd an inordinate amount of self-pity at work in unsettled gays. It seems many of them seek happiness by enthroning self where God should be. That is true of all self-deceived Christians.

God never meant for us to build a religion around our sexuality. Sexual intimacy represents a real human need, but it does not surpass all needs. Many gays believe Christians are delighted to consign them to lives devoid of sexual intimacy with someone they love. Keeping God on the throne of our lives ought to be the real concern. "If God is for us, who can be against us"? (Romans 8:31). The very first Beatitude is "Blessed are the poor in spirit, for theirs is the kingdom of heaven." To be poor in spirit is to recognize one's utter dependence on God. He and he alone can fill the voids of our lives. "If I know I have no strength of will, no nobility of disposition, then Jesus says—Blessed are you, because it is through this poverty that I enter His Kingdom. I cannot enter His Kingdom as a good man or woman, I can only enter it as a complete pauper," said Chambers.[16] When we congregate in communities—be they gay enclaves or churches—that reinforce enthroning something other than God in our lives, we are refusing to accept the spirit-poverty that God demands of us. We are walling ourselves off from the very one we need the most.

C.S. Lewis said in *Mere Christianity*, "[God] is the source from which all your reasoning power comes. You could not be right and he wrong any more than a stream can rise higher than its own source."[17] Pro-gay "theologians" apparently have not yet had that epiphany. Pharisaic Christians also fail to read the entire Bible, which shows us how to love those we disagree with or see as deceived sinners.

Eight

Ministries of Reconciliation: Made Holy and Set Free

On a November 2005 morning in Lynchburg, Virginia, Liberty University students attending their mid-week convocation service—Wednesdays are usually the chancellor's day to speak—are treated instead to the captivating Kentucky drawl of guest speaker Melissa Fryrear, gender issues analyst at that time for Focus on the Family. It is a rare honor for any speaker to be standing in Jerry Falwell's stead during convocation, let alone a woman, as we Baptists know. Fryrear has come to Lynchburg from Colorado Springs via Boston where a few days earlier she was a key presenter at a Love Won Out conference in historic Tremont Temple Baptist Church. Even *The Harvard Independent* student newspaper has had to acknowledge that testimonies like Fryrear's are "intoxicating, a soothing narcotic in a chaotic world."[1]

Looking out at a sea of youthful faces in the packed LU Vines Center arena, Fryrear speaks with compelling transparency about leaving her former lesbian life and her present-day concerns about those struggling with same-sex attraction. "My whole world revolved around being gay," she tells them of her college and young adult years. "But God had other designs for my life."[2] Some students later respond by seeking counseling for their sexual identity struggles or choose to attend a recovery group at nearby Thomas Road Baptist Church. Fryrear and a growing number of formerly gay men and women believe in the call to minister God's truth and hope to those troubled by same-sex attraction with a "bold mouth and a compassionate heart."

Meanwhile, in another part of Lynchburg, a group of gay-identified students and supportive Christian activists from Soulforce is planning a cross-country media event called the Equality Ride that will take them to, among other places, the campus of LU the following spring—but not as invited guests. They, too, believe they have a corner on the truth. Soulforce co-founder Mel White, as previously noted, holds a doctorate in ministry from Fuller Theological Seminary and was a professor there. His story is somewhat the mirror opposite of Fryrear's, also seminary-educated. White fought his homosexual desires for 25 years or more before finally capitulating, accepting his sexual identity as "part of God's creative plan."[3] Each represents a separate Christian face of the larger gay (or formerly so) community.

Yes, We Do Exist

To those who are defined by the gay sexual identity they staunchly embrace, ex-gays—that's all of us who have seen eliminated or significantly lessened our struggles with same-sex attraction—are the red-headed stepchildren they are loath to acknowledge. Our existence, though the total number is unknown and our status is based largely on personal testimonies that gay activists love to refute, negates the linchpin of the born-gay, designed-that-way platform. Exodus and NARTH each attests to having led hundreds or even thousands of homosexual strugglers to some degree of help or change, either through individual therapy or recovery group work or both. Some "formers" say they have no more same-sex attraction at all, while others say they are in various stages of acquiring a heterosexual identity or learning to live in congruence with their faith, even if it means they may continue to experience some homosexual thoughts or temptations indefinitely. These folks realize that recovery from many forms of brokenness—and homosexuality is no different—is a long or even life-long process of transformation. Those who have bailed on that process because the quick fix was not there do not negate the successes of those who have stayed the course. Some of us never really saw ourselves as exclusively homosexual, but had substantial struggles with intermittent same-sex attractions, nevertheless. That is my story, in fact. Though some have referred to me as a "former lesbian" or bisexual, I never claimed either of those identities. "Broken," "sinner," or "prodigal" I could own.

Regardless of the degree of change they have attained, many former homosexuals say they are treated with far more contempt by the activist gay community than they ever were by Christians or über-conservative gay bashers while they were still active gays. Melissa Fryrear and Mike Haley, ex-gay colleagues at Focus on the Family for years (Fryrear has now moved on to other endeavors), have received death threats and tons of obscene hate mail. Most people never hear these stories. They are bombarded, however, with tales of threats or hate acts committed against gays.

The intolerant tolerance that gay activists tend to demand is one of their oddities that doesn't stand up to scrutiny. The other is the penchant that angry gays have for slanderous ad hominem attacks against those who dare to disagree with their way of seeing things. I cannot fail to point out at the same time that Christians have their own brand of destructive vitriol. However, one cannot cast aspersions on homosexual behavior without being perceived as negating the very humanity of gay people. I know my few diehard gay and lesbian friends and acquaintances are worthy individuals, created by God with a purpose, the same as I was. Sexuality, or how we choose to express it, is not our defining trait. It is only a part of who we are. Yet, what was sexual, emotional, and spiritual brokenness for me appears to be the very core of their identity. I, too, once thought it would bring me wholeness. I eventually saw it as a kind of "thorn in the flesh" that had the ability to either drive me away from God or draw me closer. I chose the latter course, though not without much painful struggle. In doing so, I realized God had never intended for me to embrace my temptations to homosexual behavior as being from him. That view is heretical since the Bible states clearly that God never tempts. Satan does. God uses human brokenness and temptation of all kinds to stretch us and grow us spiritually, if we are willing, and to demonstrate his glory and power in transforming us. I often have wondered if God bestowed the homosexual struggle on some because he was concerend their giftedness would lead to sinful pride and he wanted to stem that, as he did in Paul. Gay people are a gifted lot and the Church ought to be lamenintg the loss of much of that talent. Satan, of course, can tap into pride for his own purposes.

Homosexuality can be examined through the biological, the developmental psychological, or the theological lens, but any of those will confirm that God's creation is fallen, subject to the imperfection, pain, and rejection that come with human relationships. Homosexuality is neither a random, meaningless occurrence nor a God-designed gift. There are specific reasons that some individuals develop same-sex attractions, just as there are reasons that others become angry, depressed, substance-addicted, over-achievers—to name a few other crises, both overt and perceived, we are subject to in this fallen world. We speak of personality types and predispositions in other populations, but it has become politically incorrect in the extreme and tantamount to emotional genocide to do so with the gay community.

Soulforce members and others of their ilk rightly decry hateful discrimination and bigotry against the gay community, particularly if these acts are done in God's name. Is it true, however, that all messages from the pulpit that include homosexual sin among the many others worthy of rebuke represent, as Soulforce claims, psychological and spiritual "violence"? Not so, say many pastors who counter that such political correctness and theological gymnastics represent corporate insanity and biblical corruption. The net result of such reasoning is having the audacity to tell God he is wrong, with no apparent fear of his authority or judgment. Is that not what Job—as little responsible for his troubled state as anyone who awakes one day to the realization that he or she may be gay—was doing until God forced him to repent of his wrongful attitude? One can only conclude that the "god of this age has blinded [their] minds" (2 Corinthians 4:4). None of us is immune to that blindness, by the way. It is only cured by hearing and obeying the Word of God, which leads to a new "quickening" in our hearts and minds.

It is to organizations like Exodus that many pastors or concerned laypeople send the homosexual strugglers in their churches who are seeking information and help. And those inquiries have more than tripled in number in recent years, to 400,000 or more, according to Exodus. The Love Won Out conferences Exodus recently acquired from Focus on the Family—there are typically a half-dozen or so around the country per year—have drawn crowds of up to 1,800 people in some places, representing more than half the states in the country. The demand for conferences is now two years out. "That points to how desperately people need a Christ-like response on this issue and how gracious God is being toward those who are affected by it," Melissa Fryrear said, while still with Love Won Out and Focus on the Family.[4]

"Gay moralist" and philosophy professor John Corvino was invited to Focus on the Family in 2008 by Glenn Stanton, who is senior analyst for marriage and sexuality at Focus. The two men debate same-sex marriage issues around the country. Corvino's impressions surprised him somewhat:

> What impressed me is that the bulk of what they do ... is to help families. ... I expected to hear plenty about how Focus fights the "gay agenda." Instead, I heard plenty about how they help people with parenting issues, relationship challenges, and other basic life concerns. ... A second thing my visit made clear was that the people there tend to see God's hand in most aspects of their daily lives. "God led us here ... God blessed us with this ... What God has in store ..."—the language was constantly providential. This theme continued through my meeting with the ex-gays, whose stories typically included a strong sense of God's direction. Hearing their accounts made me realize that reconciling Christianity with a pro-gay stance will require more than simply addressing [B]ible verses. For it wasn't (merely) the [B]ible that convinced these people to renounce gay relationships. It was their understanding of their personal relationship with God.[5]

Though Corvino is now an atheist, his former faith gave him a lens through which to appreciate the power of a personal God in an individual's life. And he has rightly concluded that this is at the heart of the transformation experienced by those often referred to as ex-gays.

Reaching Out to Churches

Exodus has formed the Exodus Church Network to help churches bring a consistent, truthful message of love and compassion to those struggling with homosexuality. "Many sitting in the pews on Sunday are confused about what the Bible really has to say about homosexuality as well as the attitude we are to have towards those in the gay community," said Exodus president Alan Chambers, in announcing the outreach in 2006. "Former homosexuals, like me, have often experienced either harsh condemnation or theological misinformation in the Church—neither of which are helpful to those confused and personally struggling with this issue."[6] Many pastors may think same-sex attraction struggles do not affect their congregations. They should think again. This problem is no respecter of denominations, geographical areas, or ideologies. Youth are the most vulnerable to sexual experimentation of any kind in our churches. It's not a harmless game they are playing.

Bob Stith, former pastor of Carroll Baptist Church in Southlake, Texas, and currently head of the Southern Baptist Convention's Gender Issues Office, pushed for an initiative to address homosexuality through the SBC for years. He started the Living Hope ministry in his community under the Exodus umbrella. "I always thought we should set a standard of how churches should deal with this and have a game plan," he says.[7] That means teaching members how to interact with those in their churches who may be struggling with homosexuality, as well as having recovery or discipling resources for those who want to change. Discipleship or Christian mentoring is a vital part of any church's ministry. Even though there was no formal outreach or recovery program for same-sex attracted strugglers in the church she attended while she was seeking to change, Melissa Fryrear says she was mentored by an older couple who refused to judge her. "They met me where I was, accepted me with grace, loved me unconditionally, and prayed for me fervently."[8] It made all the difference for her. Any church can do that for a struggler. It's just old-fashioned love in action. Many churches feel undue pressure these days from activists or the mental health guilds to have a staff consisting of one or more licensed counselors and experienced lay leaders who are specifically trained to deal with the tough issues. It's wonderful when those resources exist, but how many churches can put such a program into place? For some, the option of a community program based at a larger church but shared by others is a viable way to go. Many don't have even that option. Traditional pastoral counseling or lay mentoring, assisted by good Christ-centered resources such as books, articles, and online ministries, can go a long way in mediating confusion and guilt in those struggling in any church. This book includes a list of recommended ministries and resources. Pastors also need to know who the reputable Christian counselors are in their area. Accountable online professional counseling or support groups are a growing resource that can be another tool in the pastoral kit.

'Fessing up to Our Mistakes

Not every struggling gay person meets with a warm reception from Christians in their churches, communities, or workplaces. Many are afraid of being made outcasts by their fellow Christians, whose slurs and general criticisms against homosexuals or "Sodomites" they have heard for much of their lives. This fear and anger formed the basis of Mel White's activist stance as a gay Christian today. White said he had a circle of seminary friends he confided in prior to his coming out, but he still received mixed signals from both the friends and the therapists he consulted. He condemned himself the most harshly of all, as is the case with many Christian gays. His turning point came when a Christian therapist told him it was okay to be a gay man and to pursue a same-sex relationship. "I didn't see shame or judgment in her eyes. I saw celebration. She was congratulating me. My Creator hadn't made a terrible mistake. ... I was a gay man. ... Her words brought pride!"[9]

That one word—pride—has been at the heart of much of the rift between the Church and homosexuals. Many are viewed as in-your-face proud of their identity, which is expressed sexually in sinful behavior, if the Bible is to be believed. That kind of unbiblical attitude doesn't sit well with most evangelicals, who claim their frosty reception of gays is a predictable response to this prideful preening. Several well-known godly injunctions against pride leap off the pages of the Bible for those who are biblically literate. "Pride goes before destruction, a haughty spirit before a fall," King Solomon wrote in the book of Proverbs.[10] "God opposes the proud, but gives grace to the humble," James wrote in the New Testament, echoing the Old.[11] And, of course, we are told that God hates "haughty eyes" (Proverbs 6:17). There are lots more biblical references to the sin of pride and worldly capitulation. Pride is "the deification of self," in the words of Oswald Chambers.

Is it this form of idolatry that makes homosexuality sit atop the hierarchy of sins in the minds of many Christians when they might wink at or pretend they are unaware of other more common sinful or unhealthy behaviors (social drinking, "innocent" lottery gambling or poker night, gossip, gluttony, petty theft of church or company supplies, pornography, heterosexual philandering, and more)? What about the prevalence in our churches of closeted incest between fathers or step-fathers (and even some mothers) and their own children that brings so many devastated young women and men years later into our recovery groups or therapists' offices, some of them confused about their sexual identities? Oh yes, it happens, far more than we want to know about. Hypocrisy, materialism—these are some of our biggest problems. And many Christians, unfortunately, tend to "shoot their wounded."

How do we address the need to minister to the hurts and fears of the walking wounded, particularly those living the private hell of sexual identity struggles and panicked over the possible retribution awaiting them at the hands of their fellow callous Christians, to say nothing of the God they feel must be angry with them? Are we pushing many of these precious people to inevitable identification with the secular gay community when they might really want or need to find wholeness and Christ-like acceptance within the Church? Too many people (on both sides) see the gay culture debate through one lens only—the black-or-white, all-or-nothing, us-or-them battle with only one victor. We either have to affirm homosexuality as a legitimate, healthy, alternate lifestyle or condemn all gays to hell and excommunication from the Church, in their view.

How sad that so many hurting people needing the love and healing ideally meant to exist in our church communities can't find it. Although I can't condone their pulling away from the necessity of repenting and I dislike the harsh way they tend to paint the entire evangelical community with one brush, I can understand why so many formerly struggling gay Christians believed the only option for them was to turn their back on their churches and form their own fellowships. They see it as a survival tactic while most evangelicals see it as heresy. Unchurched homosexuals do the same thing within the various gay enclaves they have formed. Bars or clubs become their surrogate "churches."

Getting it Right

Some pastors and lay leaders are well aware of these intra-church dilemmas while others are clueless. The church that effectively launched the small-group recovery ministry boon is Rick Warren's (of Purpose-Driven Church/Life fame) Saddleback Church in Lake Forest, California. Warren attests that the foundation of his mega-church has been the Celebrate Recovery program, developed by John Baker, a recovered alcoholic, in 1991.[12] Every Sunday, before and after their "seeker" services, church attendees may visit one of many information booths to check out small groups or resources or talk with a group representative. The groups for those desiring to overcome same-sex attraction have been heavily attended historically. Celebrate Recovery satellite programs have sprung up in churches all over the country. Soulforce, knowing this well, chose Saddleback Church as the church to stage its final 2008 American Family Outing "visitation" and church leadership meeting.[13] The basis of Celebrate Recovery is recovery applications of the eight Beatitudes from Jesus' Sermon on the Mount found in Matthew's Gospel.[14] Warren wrote them, in fact.

Other churches utilize a similar "Christ-centered" 12-step approach, slightly reminiscent of the 12 Steps of Alcoholics Anonymous, but with an emphasis on confidentiality and accountability instead of anonymity, and with a clear scriptural basis. In these types of recovery programs, participants are encouraged to give testimonies from their real-life experiences, sometimes before the entire church body and sometimes only among those in the recovery program. The "power greater than ourselves" that they acknowledge as being in control is Jesus Christ and not AA's illusive "God as we [understand] Him."[15] The Bible is heavily used as a teaching tool, along with other Christian recovery books and small-group interaction. The tenets of psychology that line up with Scripture may help shape the overall recovery vision, but it is biblically centered in focus. Groups may or may not encourage sponsors to help members with accountability. They are lay-facilitated by those who already have largely overcome the respective struggles addressed, and are generally under the supervision of a licensed clinical counselor or lay leaders trained and sanctioned by a guild organization such as the American Association of Christian Counselors (AACC).[16] Many, but not all, of the same-sex-attraction (SSA) groups are Exodus affiliates, meaning Exodus refers to them but they are not under Exodus oversight. There are separate groups for men and women, of course. The need for same-sex leadership of these groups is self-evident. While we must acknowledge that such programs are not perfect and that some leaders reflect Christ-like maturity and healing to a greater degree than others, they are a starting place for addressing brokenness in a meaningful way. I advocate for programs that would link recovery groups to follow-on discipleship—in small cell groups or one-on-one—with mature Christians.

The culture wars have taken an undisputed toll on the Church. "Gay activists have done exactly what they said they would do two decades ago," Bob Stith says. "The Church is way behind. Too many people in the Church won't discuss the issues publicly. But the culture is doing it." Stith has a great burden to see what he started reach its full potential. "I just believe if the Church learned to deal with this the way we should—being redemptive toward those who want to change—we could turn this around."[17]

Uncovering the Root of the Problem

I know the pain and guilt that come with being raised in the Christian tradition while experiencing sexual identity confusion. So do Mel White and Melissa Fryrear. Fryrear, like me, was a victim of childhood sexual abuse and has said other dysfunction existed in her family. According to her testimony, she had her first lesbian experience at 16 and decided to actively embrace a gay life when she got to college. She lived exclusively in that manner for ten years. Her church experience growing up was more nominal, something her family did out of obligation but with little or no passion or true commitment. Still, it had been enough to take root and it propelled her back to a new church "family" as an adult seeking answers. She did not truly accept Jesus Christ as her personal savior until then. As for her attitude toward the gay community, "There aren't any stones in my pockets," she has said. "How could I possibly cast a stone toward someone in sin, having lived as I've lived?"[18]

The more radical elements of both the pro-gay and anti-gay (not necessarily pro-Christ) camps are not hampered by biblical injunctions against throwing stones, of course. They maintain a ready arsenal of stones and even boulders. Again, we need to be reminded of Jesus' compassion toward the adulterous woman who was brought out to be executed by stoning, as the law required. "Let he who is without sin cast the first stone," he had said.[19] None of us qualify to condemn or throw stones as we all are sinners. God is the one who settles accounts with us all.

Much of what I know of Mel White, I learned from his book, *Stranger at the Gate*. I have read carefully other writings of his, and we have interacted some via e-mail and once briefly in person. He has shown me mostly graciousness, in fact, despite our disagreements. White's childhood was steeped in passionate fundamentalism and he was groomed from an early age to be a minister. He loved Jesus from childhood and was active in his church and in other youth activities as a leader while still in his teens. He kept his struggles with homosexual attractions largely secret and went on to marry and have children, praying that living a traditional life would "cure" him. There is no doubt, when reading his 1994 partly autobiographical book, that he very much loved his wife and children, and still does, though he eventually chose to leave his family and live as an openly gay man in another relationship. Like me, he did not have a real homosexual experience until in his late 30s, although he agonized over who he was and how he should live for decades. Clearly, White desperately wanted to be straight and whole in the eyes of God.

He was deeply depressed for years and is convinced that divine intervention prevented him from taking his own life.[20]

White's and Fryrear's two contrasting stories are equally authentic and painful, yet each followed a different path. White believes he is one of those for whom change has not been possible, and he has encouraged many other questioning gay Christians to accept that same belief about themselves. Did he lack the genuine repentance and identification with Christ that Fryrear or others have claimed? I cannot make that judgment. There are untold numbers of others who have been at the same crossroads, for some a life-and-death choice, and have gone in opposite directions. Even a number of those who once identified as ex-gay, including one of the founders of what is today Exodus, now call themselves ex-ex-gays, arguing that their attempts to change did them harm. Some of their stories are devastating. Most conservatives and devout evangelical Christians cannot bring themselves to accept homosexuality as a "gift" from God while die-hard liberals and gay activists (arguably adhering to their own fundamental "religion") refuse to accept ex-gays. So both are marginalized in their respective ways and are sometimes left to wonder who, except the God that created them, really cares.

Rev. Karen Booth, head of Transforming Congregations, a United Methodist Church outreach to homosexual strugglers wishing to change, and to churches that want to help them, has astutely observed a major difference between former gays and "ex-ex-gay" defectors:

> My anecdotal experience with ex-ex-gays has observed a consistent pattern of them reporting a laundry list of things they did to try to change and then indicat[ing] they expected God to take their temptations or desires away because

of their performance. In pastoral care, that's called "bargaining" or even "magical thinking," and it's often based on a "works righteousness" understanding of Christianity.

For many of the "formers" I know, it didn't work that way. Change happened when they willingly submitted their sexuality and discipleship/sanctification to the work of Christ and the Holy Spirit, come what may. I've never heard an ex-ex-gay talk that way.[21]

There are several perspectives that need to be examined when considering the impact of homosexuality on the culture and the individuals within it. I am only sharing here a few bits of stories representative of the painful inner struggles of people trying to come to terms with homosexuality or walk away from it. Sometimes there are children who also live through the pain of watching their home break apart while trying to understand something they are too young to grasp. Equally heart-wrenching are those spouses who feel betrayed as the very foundation of a life of promise is pulled out from under them. Confusion or guilt can be particularly harsh on parents as heartless folks point fingers at them for their supposed poor parenting of their gay children. Reparative therapy—again, it's not the only form of "change" therapy offered, though activists talk as if it is—might look at things as benign as normal temperamental conflicts between parent and child, or a separation such as that necessitated by a parent's profession. This therapy is bashed in its entirety in many circles. Some of the claims of its practitioners are suspect, but it deserves to be at least somewhere in the mix. Some parents ardently support their gay children while others are embarrassed or uncertain of how to relate to them. Various ex-gay ministries have reached out to parents and family members in recent years, and that is a good thing. The guilt many of them feel (for early parenting choices) is often without merit.

Another Testimony of Change

Joe Dallas might be viewed as an alter ego of Mel White. A former gay activist, Dallas was on staff at a Metropolitan Community Church before he made the trip out of homosexuality to become active in the ex-gay movement. He headed up Exodus for several years and now helps others who want to leave homosexuality through his Genesis Counseling center in Orange, California.

"I learned the pro-gay theology and became very adept at defending my lifestyle. No one would have guessed that, only a few years before, I'd been a married deacon in an evangelical church," Dallas says of his former life. Unlike White, he did not have a strong Christian foundation or a relationship with Christ in his younger days. He plunged into a secret gay life when he was only 15. Later, through the friendship and witness of a young Christian woman, he made the decision to become a Christian and got involved in one of the earlier Calvary Chapel fellowships (founded in California by Chuck Smith of Jesus Movement fame). He later married, but still was plagued by homosexual desires. Five years into his marriage, he fell back into gay acting out and he and his wife split up.[22]

Like White, Dallas bought the MCC's pro-gay theology hook, line, and sinker. After a while, he "lost interest in the Church, dropped out and became wildly promiscuous," according to his testimony. It was around the time that the AIDS epidemic was coming to light as a problem among gay men in the early-to-mid-1980s. Dallas became scared as some of his gay friends were dying. After seeing an old friend on TV speaking about leaving his former gay life, Dallas decided he was ready to make that change for good.

He began seeing a Christian counselor for help. A year later, he met a young, divorced mother and, after falling in love with her, he confessed his former struggles. She trusted and encouraged him and they eventually married.[23]

Dallas speaks clearly and lovingly to both sides of the gay cultural divide. He does not spare the Church the rebuke it needs to hear, and he calls judgmental and misinformed Christians to total scriptural authority, which includes Christ-like compassion for all sinners in need of healing and redemption. White seeks a tolerance that affirms the misguided choices of the gay-identified community and is all too ready to censure those who refuse to bend a knee to those demands. Dallas calls for evangelical sermons that are more redemptive toward gays, while realizing we who see the destructiveness in homosexuality cannot throw the baby out with the bathwater. Here's his message to the Church and to those of an evangelical activist bent:

> To listen to some of us talk, you'd think it's more important to defeat these people politically than it is to see them won into the Kingdom of God. And that ought not to be. And my wife and I are unapologetically politically active. We are unapologetically a part of that vast right-wing conspiracy. But we are also aware of what Jesus, himself, said, having been presented with a political out, a short cancellation of what he was facing, "My kingdom is not of this world." There are more important things than defeating the gay rights movement. There are the souls of the lesbian women and homosexual men themselves, of infinite value to God, of much more value than any political gains we may make or losses we may suffer.[24]

Those are words all Christians need to take to heart, prayerfully and honestly examining ourselves before God.

"If we say we hate something we should have evidence that indeed we do and if we say we love someone, there should be tangible evidence that we do that as well," Dallas also told an audience he was addressing at a Love Won Out conference. "Now, I think we've got the hate part down. I think we've got plenty of good, verifiable, clear evidence that we hate the sin of homosexuality." He went on to say, "As the body of Christ we are not given the luxury of addressing issues out of our own passions, out of our own opinions, representing our own biases one way or another, but rather, we have the mandate to represent a viewpoint that adequately expresses God's heart and his mind towards a particular issue."[25]

Christians might try this on for size: "What I do find to be effective and redemptive is for each of us to love all sinners and hate our own sins. If we hate our own sins more, we might not be so distracted by the sins of others. If we hate our own sins more, we might actually abide in Christ at a depth that HE would multiply the power of the gospel to call other sinners to forsake their sins, too." That comes from Bill Hensen of FOTOS (Fish on the Other Side) Ministries. He shared it in a blog post (billhenson.blogspot.com) on February 24, 2010.

Like many men—Christian or otherwise, gay or straight—Joe Dallas once visited bars to find acceptance and nonjudgmental company. There he learned a lesson applicable for the Church as he observed his bar mates:

> After a while, I came to notice something these people had that I really came to envy, and that was their easy camaraderie with each other. You'd see them swing through that door of the cocktail

lounge, look at each other and say, "Oh, thank God, it's just you. Here I can be honest. Here I am safe. Here I can really be authentic and say what I feel and be what I am and not have to hide and repress and pretend." And I began to think, why can't the body of Christ be more like a bar? When is the last time we heard somebody say, "I am two steps away from having an affair with my secretary." "I stepped into an adult bookstore last week and I cannot get the imagery out of my mind and I swear I feel compelled to go right back there." "I am homosexually tempted. My God, I've fallen in love with another man at the Church. What do I do with this? Somebody help me, pray for me, hold me accountable, be with me."[26]

Of course, that's exactly what authentic recovery ministry is all about. It is the one real place in the Church where the pretentious masks can come off, where people are truly transparent and supportive of each other. Those ready to be transformed "by the renewing of their minds" also realize they are desperate sinners—true spiritual paupers—that they are in a "hospital" designed just for them and not the proverbial museum for saints. Oh, that more churches would get this, whether in old-fashioned, one-on-one discipleship or in a more formal recovery group setting!

And what of authentic outreach to the gay community? Dallas maintains there are three primary types of gay people we all will encounter at some time or another. One category is militants, or those with a "rigid agenda to normalize homosexuality." These are the ones who seek to win what often becomes a shouting contest when given an opportunity in a public or media forum— "guerrilla theater." There is no shouting contest, of course, unless they are set against equally militant anti-gay mouthpieces. Then there are the moderates in the GLBT community, which describes most gays and lesbians who are not agenda-driven. "They live basically as we live, work 9 to 5, pay the bills, mow the lawn," says Dallas. "There are differences, of course, but the differences really don't supersede our commonality." That last assertion engenders some deep thought and soul-searching. Lastly come repentant gay people who will "hear the message of the gospel and will say, 'Yes, I respond to that. I know God intended something different for me. And I want that. I agree with that. So here I am. Now what?'" The response to each group must be tailored to the specific place each group is in, he says.[27]

I submit that conservative Christians and those opposed to the gay sociopolitical agenda can be viewed in similar categories. Some are militants, seeking to stomp out "the hated enemy," while many just want to live and let live. Still others, especially those of us who have known the pain or confusion of a homosexual struggle, are in a place where lovingly, compassionately, and patiently, we can help repentant gays to find wholeness. People who feel called to minister to the homosexually broken or their families come from all walks of life. Almost to a person, they have either overcome their own battles or have faced issues with family members who identify as being gay.

A Time Such as This

One battle-tested veteran hoping to change the oft-vitriolic Christian response to gays is Nancy Heche, D.Min., a Christian counselor based in Chicago, and author of *The Truth Comes Out: The Story of My Heart's Transformation.* If the name Heche sounds familiar, that's because she is the mother of well-known actress Anne, whose much-publicized lesbian affair with comedienne Ellen DeGeneres during the late nineties brought her additional notoriety. That is but one element of Nancy Heche's story, however. Married for 25 years to a Christian music minister who, as she found out shortly before his 1983 death from AIDS, also had lived a secret, homosexual life, Heche watched her family slowly disintegrate from the deep emotional wounds of a betrayal that none of them could understand. She writes in the introduction to her book, "The journey has tested me and twisted me and humbled me and broken me." Heche's Job-like saga (her losses included a child who died in infancy, her only son being killed in a car crash and her oldest daughter dying of cancer) took her ultimately to a place of healing and gave her a changed heart toward the gay community, all of whom she admits she had hated for years. Now she says, "I truly believe that I have 'come to the kingdom for such a time as this,'" in the biblical words of Queen Esther. "God has confirmed that I am to administer the healing oil."[28]

One such opportunity of ministering was the simple desire of a young man attending a Love Won Out conference in Toronto. He encountered a small group of protestors as he was leaving the conference, and asked if he could buy them some donuts. Instead, they invited him to join them for pizza. "Mostly, I just listened to their frustration and felt it with them. They said they often feel abandoned by the older gay community because people get into relationships, their jobs, and moving around a lot and don't really work to promote tolerance for gays. One of the guys shared quite personally almost right off the bat of how his life is 'choosing between one of two hells.' Meeting someone with his kind of hurt and pain made me realize how much their gay identity is a part of them and yet how difficult it is to live with."[29] For this young man, that was at least a start.

The most unorthodox Christian outreach to homosexuals has to be that of Andrew Marin and the Marin Foundation. Based in Chicago's Boys Town gay community, Marin has spent countless hours talking face-to-face with gays and lesbians, listening to their painful stories, and trying to forge a bond of trust with them. His outside-the-box outreach began as a quest to understand why three of his closest friends had all come out to him as gay or lesbian within a short period of time. Needless to say, this shook his foundations and caused him to re-examine some of his prejudicial views about homosexuals. Marin leads Bible studies for GLBT folks and engages both the Christian and gay communities in his blog. He has written a groundbreaking book called *Love Is An Orientation: Elevating the Conversation with the Gay Community*. Some Christians take strong exception to the book and Marin's approach. He is a relatively young man, and I believe his ministry is still finding itself, but his book got me to stop and really think about some notions I had been holding onto. It began a process of reevaluation of "the gay question" for me.

The Marin Foundation has undertaken a first-of-its-kind study on religion and spirituality within the GLBT community. It examines subjects from all 50 states, the District of Columbia, and other countries. It is called "Religious Acculturation within the Gay, Lesbian, Bisexual, and Transgender (GLBT) Community," and I was one of the respondents as a one-time same-sex-attracted individual. I very much desire to see the results of this research, a four-year project.[30] Other researchers have looked into various aspects of faith as it intersects with the gay community. Prior to this study, the most recent such look had come from The Barna Group, which found that the same percentage of homosexual men and women self-identify as Christian as do heterosexual people (70 percent). Gays registered noticeably lower on the scale for specific faith questions than did their straight counterparts. Nevertheless, George Barna noted, "A substantial majority of gays cite their faith as a central facet of their life, consider themselves to be Christian, and claim to have some type of meaningful personal commitment to Jesus Christ active in their life today." The survey showed that gays tend to shun the local church, however.[31] That presents a challenge every church ought to take up.

Folks like those mentioned here, along with many other unsung formerly gay and straight servants of Christ, are the selfless ones who seek to help when most others walk away. They seek to offer love, reconciliation, and clarity to the fractured individuals and their families who seek their counsel or who flock to the churches that host outreach conferences or recovery ministries. This growing, compassionate army seeks to move the Church away from an uneasy, reactive stance to more of a loving, proactive one through education and support. It isn't easy in the wake of ridicule and criticism from the gay community, and even a few extremists on the right.

Speaking of active or activist gays, Mike Haley told *The Harvard Independent*, following the October 2005 Love Won Out conference in Boston, "If they decide that homosexuality is for them, then they have a right in America to embrace that. But I also want a right as a person who doesn't want homosexuality in my life ... to walk away from homosexuality."[32]

If an ex-gay or any compassionate person can choose to love and pray for someone actively engaged in homosexuality, refusing to throw them under the church bus, then the self-righteous crowd probably also can tone down its rhetoric about folks sincerely seeking balance in addressing the issues "going over to the dark side." God holds all people who confess to being Christians to a higher standard than those in and of the world. He will continue to reserve his harshest censuring for those who are acting as hypocrites. Scripture is clear in this. Again, Christ is the bridge. He means for us to be somewhere on it. 1 Corinthians 13 ("If I speak in the tongues of men and of angels, but have not love, ... I am nothing") is not an optional part of Christian living. It is an imperative as we have been taught the original model for love and have fellowship with Christ.

Nine

Marriage Conundrum: "A House Divided ..."

Of all the offensives mounted by aggressive gay activists, none has galvanized traditionalists and conservative Christians more than the campaign to redefine marriage as including the "right" to same-sex unions. The debate reached a crescendo in recent years as more states have voted to add one-man, one-woman marriage amendments to their constitutions, believing this to be the only way to prevent liberal activist judges from annulling the laws already in place when inevitably challenged in the courts by gay petitioners. And gay lobbyists, who patiently waited through the years of both moderate Democratic and Republican dominance, moved swiftly during the first two years of the Obama administration to take advantage of the political and ideological power shift in Washington and increasing numbers of backtracking Republican lawmakers. Democrats have adopted gay rights as an indispensable plank in their political platform, and they have celebrated having a president in the White House who they know is quite capable of enacting long-coveted parts of the gay social agenda, regardless of the will of the people or the more sensible voices of caution. He has been at work to do just that, in fact. It remains to be seen how the widespread Republican mid-term election victories will impact this agenda.

Just how imposing is the Christian, conservative, pro-family sleeping giant these days? Are people growing weary of doing battle on the culture front? Will we see another spiritual Great Awakening that will overshadow the culture war? We truly need "good leaven" to counter the effects of all the bad we have endured. Christ has some committed servant-warriors within his true Church who are "rightly dividing the word of truth" and have had enough of milquetoast theology and toothless servanthood. God's banner of truth goes with his servant/warriors as they minister to a dying world and address a postmodern culture that seeks to cast the Church as effete and impotent. We must remember that the one carrying the banner ahead of us is Christ. He is armed with a two-edged sword of truth and grace. It always cuts both ways. We cannot be squeamish about acknowledging just how much of the Church's undoing has come from within. The big "D"—divorce—ought to be exhibit A. Sexual sins of all sorts are rife within our churches. Four fingers are pointing accusingly back at us when we point hypocritically at the gay community.

Just how much of a threat are same-sex unions to the health of marriage and to the Church? How do we take a balanced look at this movement without erring on the side of hypocrisy? Where do the civil and the sacred intersect? Despite the strong support voters have shown for state marriage amendments, gay activists will never tire in their quest for same-sex marriage as it represents legitimacy for homosexuals like nothing else does. Diehard activists are convinced they can wear down the opposition, and history is on their side. Although Massachusetts' lawmakers and Supreme Judicial Court were far outside the mainstream in declaring homosexuals have a right to marry each other in 2003, California's even more liberal judicial stance, with no state residency requirement for gay couples seeking to wed, opened the door for an all-out assault against traditional marriage in state and, now, federal courts—most assuredly all the way to the highest court in the land. New England, once the seat of staunch Puritan values and faith-based Ivy League universities, has seen gay marriage affirmed at an unprecedented rate, with only Maine and Rhode Island—the latter still largely Catholic—yet to capitulate. Maine's temporary gay-marriage law was challenged and defeated by voters. New Hampshire's same-sex marriage law may be in similar jeopardy. Iowa's unanimous Supreme Court ruling to affirm gay marriage shocked the heartland, but voters struck back in 2010 and refused to retain three of those judges. New York turned back a legislative push for gay marriage and New Jersey, having already legalized gay civil unions, seeks to make those full marriages, as Vermont did. The Illinois legislature recently voted to join those few states that sanction civil unions.

California's voter-upheld gay marriage ban (and constitutional marriage amendment) was the first to be challenged in federal court, and was thrown out by an activist judge. The ruling is under appeal. Meanwhile, 40 states have laws explicitly prohibiting same-sex marriage, and 31 of those have constitutional one-man, one-woman marriage amendments, which now are in danger of being ruled unconstitutional in violation of the 10th Amendment, argue some legal scholars. A growing wave of mostly lesbian former partners battling each other for child custody in family courts—the most infamous and longest so far pitting staunchly pro-gay-marriage Vermont against equally staunchly anti-gay-marriage Virginia—adds additional drama to the scene. Who could have predicted such goings-on a mere decade ago?

Actually, a few people perceived then as criers of "Wolf!" did make such predictions. Their most ardent voices have been loudly represented in the pro-family Arlington Group, the most powerful evangelical lobby in American history, whose behind-the-scenes work is detailed in Dan Gilgoff's book, *The Jesus Machine: How James Dobson, Focus on the Family, and Evangelical America Are Winning the Culture War.* The problem is, many perceive the culture to be more and more in the control of anti-family forces. Is this perception a media sleight-of-hand ("all the stage is a world") or a growing reality? Are culture warriors laying down arms because of the effectiveness of this psychological warfare or because they truly have become complacent? Does this mean the battleground will shift back to the Church, where it belongs, at least in part?

While much of the country is well aware of the dire need to stand firm in the worldwide war against terror, a good number of us also understand the vital importance of the other ideological war we are fighting—the one against secularism and moral relativism. This generation also must stand firm in that war if marriage and social order are to be preserved as our Creator intended them to be. Christians have legitimate concerns over how best to engage in this battle. Do they fight it from the top down—politically—or from the bottom up—socially and spiritually, man-to-man, woman-to-woman, heart-to-heart? Should they be doing both? Do they have a right to do either if they are not also standing up to preserve marriage against the onslaught of divorce and "self-actualization"? I fall more within the Great Commission camp, but I preface that with the Sermon on the Mount's underpinnings. Jesus implied we were entitled to examine the actions of others through a God-informed lens, only after we had first dealt with our own hypocrisy, i.e., removed the "planks" from our own eyes. We can acknowledge our duty as citizens to engage where we must in the political realm, to the extent that we can find godly men and women willing to stand up for principle and the good of the people rather than for self-interest. Our government, from top to bottom, is riddled with unprincipled officials who can barely read our Constitution. It stands to reason that when enough people see these charlatans for who they are, they will exercise their rights as citizens to throw them out of office. It happens periodically. But it also is true that we have shot ourselves in the collective foot for more than a generation by forgetting how to raise up our future leaders and by abandoning the eternal truths to which our leaders held this nation accountable for much of its relatively young history.

I daresay most Americans are willing these days to suffer gay-identified men and women to live in whatever partnerships they desire—save state-sanctioned marriage—if that is their "pursuit of happiness" behind closed doors. But the tension between the poles has become wearisome and worrisome. Many but certainly not all, whether gay or straight, just want to quietly go about their business and blend into society as law-abiding, contributing citizens. We will have to accept that carefully and patiently crafted public sentiment in favor of certain gay "rights" is not going away. Those bent on forcing the rest of us to accept same-sex marriages on an equal footing with traditional marriage have thrown down the gauntlet. The traditional family concept has been under siege for decades because of the ill-conceived social experiments of no-fault divorce, unrestricted welfare, and the mainstreaming of vice industries such as gambling, pornography, and alcohol. Selfishness and materialism have undercut our altruistic nature, to the detriment of family cohesiveness. Yet this vital institution—the family headed by a father and a mother in gender-complementary roles—has been the backbone of all civilized societies since the dawn of time. It is still the best model—the only one in God's scheme—for ensuring that both current and future generations will be healthy, happy, and productive. Still, how do we shore up the traditional, biblical concept of family on a national scale when we have all been complicit in damaging it? Even more to the point, can we ever accomplish such an objective with political machinations? Clearly, one cannot legislate changed hearts. Laws are necessary in a fallen, sinful world. We need much more than jurisprudence to guide us, however. We need God's all-but-forgotten commandments written across our hearts and not sitting within the closed pages of our dust-gathering Bibles.

No, the family is not in the best of health these days. But why would we allow it, embattled as it is, to suffer another blow that would leave it on life support? Gay activists have convinced large numbers of the mainstream population that allowing them the right to marry is no threat whatsoever to the rest of us since we've already messed up marriage well enough without it. Multiple wrongs don't finally arrive at a right, however. We can't mince words over what is at stake here.

Same-Sex Marriage Under the Microscope

I am especially indebted to two men whose cogent analysis I will refer to in this chapter, along with others: Glenn Stanton and Bill Maier, authors of *Marriage on Trial: The Case Against Same-Sex Marriage and Parenting.* Stanton, as earlier noted, serves as senior analyst for marriage and sexuality at Focus on the Family while Maier is their resident psychologist and vice president. These men have a legitimate take on the issues. Yes, they have an ideology to uphold and gay activists have taken issue with the validity of some of the studies they cite. Of course, there always will be differing interpretations of statistical data, so it can't always be viewed as conclusive proof. Studies, some of which are more scientific than others, are an indicator of a pulse. It is impossible to eliminate all bias from the minds of any study's authors, just as some bias will remain in the minds of those interpreting the data. That's why the best arguments rely on the unwavering standards of truth that came from the Creator's mouth, even though human interpretation sometimes muddies those waters for people lacking wisdom or spiritual discernment. The "natural man" or the one for whom divine truth is "foolishness," in the words of the apostle Paul, still resides within all of us to some extent. Read Romans 6-8 to grasp this dual-nature struggle, and God's solution to it. God's truth is there for all to see if we are willing to open ourselves to the Holy Spirit's illumination through prayer and meditation on the Scriptures. Those who will undertake the discipline of reading the Bible with a teachable mind will gain the ability to see that truth and let it pierce them with a searching light, just as David entreated God to do at the conclusion of Psalm 139: "Search me, O God, and know my heart; test me and know my anxious thoughts. See if there is any offensive way in me, and lead me in the way everlasting."

To understand the big picture, we need to take a brief excursion down the road of sociology/anthropology. Stanton and Maier point out that man's perception of homosexuality has evolved over the ages. Originally, we tended to view it as sodomy, an act. From there, sociologists in the 19th Century convinced us homosexuality was a condition. In more recent years, we have come to acknowledge there is a gay community and political ideology, with the term gay meaning an identity.[1] Naturally, something accepted as an intrinsic part of one's nature will have a stronger impact on the way we interact with that person and view his or her needs. Gay rights activists know this, of course. It has been part of their evolving strategy to win hearts and minds. While our views of homosexuality have evolved over time, it is not true that society has likewise evolved to a point where it can consider gay marriage as an intrinsic right. It is quite a stretch for homosexuality to be perceived as "a mechanism for facilitating evolutionary human progress," as Stanton and Maier point out.[2]

The question that needs to be settled in the minds of

thoughtful and concerned citizens is this: Do homosexuals have the fundamental human right to marry each other, with the full sanction of government and all the legal entitlements thereof? If the answer is "yes," then we have no option but to uphold that right. If it is "no," as is my position and that of every citizen who understands the potential harmful outcomes of so radical a social experiment, then we have an obligation born of our collective national conscience and a biblical mandate to oppose that experiment vigorously. Since the prevailing, historic, Judeo-Christian view of marriage is not that of a human-created institution but a God-ordained one, we don't have the autonomy to tamper with its basic definition at this whim and that. If we allow homosexuals and their advocates to redefine it for their purposes—no matter how emotionally compelling their stories are—what is to prevent any other social extremist group from further conforming marriage to fit its "needs"? We already know one organized lobby waits in the wings, hoping they also get their shot at making polygamy legal. Why stop there? Open group marriage (polyamory) is the stated preference of others, and they also have their fratri-sororities. Could child-adult marriages also be in the offing? When the American Psychological Association says that pedophilia is not harmful, that idea begins to dangerously burrow itself into mainstream thought. Redefining marriage is a slippery slope that may lead to places we don't want to go. Any minority or individual in this country can issue a challenge to the common good by claiming they have been offended by the status quo. It happens all the time. And, somehow, fair-minded people who are loath to offend—they forget about the offense to the sensible majority, of course—feel compelled to consider their "plight." This is how unconscionable laws become reality.

As pointed out earlier, economist and political commentator Thomas Sowell advises us to be wary of those "who are promoting envy under its more high-toned alias of 'social justice.' He further observes, "Those who construct moral melodramas—starring themselves on the side of the angels against the forces of evil—are ready to disregard the Constitution rights of those they demonize, and to overstep the limits put on the powers of the federal government set by the Constitution."[3]

Our founding fathers spoke of natural law and "Nature's God" with the same breath as they did "unalienable rights." Christian philosopher Edward Feser is another outspoken opponent of same-sex marriage, maintaining that it violates natural law:

> According to natural law theory, marriage is a natural institution. That means it has a nature, an essence, just like Euclidean triangles, dogs, cats, lead, gold, and other natural substances have. Therefore it isn't something we can change just by changing a legal definition, any more than the legislature or a judge could decide that cats by nature ought to have five legs or that the Pythagorean theorem ought no longer to apply to right triangles. Moreover, according to natural law theory, given the nature or essence of marriage, it is inherently heterosexual.[4]

One irony in the gay quest for marriage is that in those countries that have already legalized it, many same-sex couples still don't bother to wed. That is outside the traditional norm for heterosexual marriage. In the Netherlands, where same-sex marriage was legalized in 2001, only 12 percent of all cohabiting gay or lesbian couples are married and the numbers of gay marriages have been declining every year.[5] The numbers are similar in Canada and the few other countries where gay marriage is legal. Has there been a declining trend in Scandinavian countries for all marriages and a corresponding rise in out-of-wedlock births among cohabiting couples since homosexual registered partnerships and marriages became legal? This point is being debated by social scientists. The evidence does not appear to be clear-cut at this point in time, and may be tainted by political posturing on both sides. "Gay-marriage advocates rejected the idea that marriage is intrinsically connected to parenthood, and the Dutch public bought that argument," wrote Stanley Kurtz for the *National Review*. Kurtz is a research fellow at the Hoover Institution and has painstakingly studied Dutch gay marriage issues. "Once marriage stops being about binding mothers and fathers together for the sake of the children they create, the need to get married gradually disappears," he says.[6]

Today the out-of-wedlock birth rate in the U.S. is at an all-time high, with cohabiting couples being the major culprits, followed by single mothers over 20. Unmarried women give birth to 38.5 percent of all children born in the U.S., according to the Centers for Disease Control and Prevention's most recent data, from 2006. Is this an anomaly that has statistically bottomed-out or is it a growing trend? We don't yet know. A group of Dutch academics who have called for a national debate on the health of marriage have said, "There are good reasons to believe the decline in Dutch marriage may be connected to the successful public campaign for the opening of marriage to same-sex couples in the Netherlands. The introduction of gay marriage paved the way to a greater acceptance of alternative forms of cohabitation," they concluded.[7] Americans should be concerned about that possibility. According to the National Center for Health Statistics (NCHS), the Netherlands has seen a dramatic rise in out-of-wedlock births, from 4 percent to 40 percent—the highest increase by far among industrialized nations—since 1980. Clearly, something unusual is going on there.

What the Camel Wants To Bring into the Tent

It only took four years for the first polygamous (polyamorous, actually) challenge to the Dutch same-sex marriage law to take place. In September 2005, Victor and Bianca de Bruijn, already married, and Mirjam Geven (the two women claimed to be bisexual) were joined in a private cohabitation ceremony (a contract, not a state-registered partnership or a full-fledged marriage). Their three-way union may have been more of a media stunt than a blip on the radar of real concern, but it already appears to have made some legal, political, and cultural waves in the Netherlands. Is the de Bruijns' ménage-a-trois union a step down the road to legalized polyamorous marriage? Some social observers on both sides of the gay marriage debate think it is possible. Bisexuality and polyamory have gained momentum as a combined social movement, as we already have seen, although die-hard gay activists are not fully comfortable with granting bisexuals co-equal status with those who are exclusively homosexual.

Certainly worth noting is an organization that promotes public acceptance of polyamory in association with the Unitarian Universalist Church. Unitarian Universalists for Polyamory Awareness (UUPA) was established in the summer of 1999. Their aim is to become the welcoming arm for polyamorists much as the MCC has been for homosexuals. What has long been known as a subculture in the sordid world of pornography and sexual deviancy is angling for mainstream status. Radical activists support a sexual continuum model, believing we all have a disposition toward being "poly" to some extent. Even prominent professors at Ivy League schools—most notably, Kenji Yoshino, formerly a law professor at Yale, now at New York University Law School—have taken up the bisexual cause. In a 2000 *Stanford Law Review* article ("The Epistemic Contract of Bisexual Erasure"), Yoshino argued that bisexuality is far more prevalent than presumed. The bisexuality/polyamory movement is problematic for both sides in the cultural debate. Valerie White, founder of the UUPA with her brother, Harlan, told *Bi* Magazine in 2003 that the UUPA planned to keep its polyamory movement low-key for the time being. "It would put too much ammunition in the hands of the opponents of gay marriage. ... Our brothers and sisters in the LGBT community are fighting a battle that they're close to winning, and we don't want to do anything that would cause that fight to take a step backwards," she said.[8] Those backing polyamory have shown their hand prematurely, at any rate. They have given us a preview of what could be in store for us if same-sex marriage is legalized across the U.S.

In the summer of 2006, *The Baltimore Sun* had a sizeable feature on the polyamorists' national conference, held in Maryland that year. In October 2005 the documentary, "Three of Hearts: A Postmodern Family," was released. It is the story of the 13-year relationship of two men and a woman, and aired on BRAVO (the network that gave us "Queer Eye for the Straight Guy," "Boy Meets Boy," and "Gay Weddings") in the spring of 2006. Longtime lesbian activist Paula Ettelbrick, a law professor at New York University and Columbia University, also is a spokesperson for the poly movement. Her take:

> Marriage will not liberate us as lesbians and gay men. In fact, it will constrain us, make us more invisible, force our assimilation into the mainstream and undermine the goals of gay liberation. ... Marriage runs contrary to two of the primary goals of the lesbian and gay movement: the affirmation of gay identity and culture and the validation of many forms of relationships. ... Being queer means pushing the parameters of sex, sexuality, and family and in the process transforming the very fabric of society.[9]

Just who speaks for the gay-rights movement on marriage and other issues is at times unclear. Any serious observer of the gay community will see an undercurrent, a rift between gay men and lesbians or bisexual women, with both sides at times angling to be the more representative voice.

It should be noted that a surprising number of homosexuals, at least in the United States, are opposed to gay marriage. The more radical of them have no desire to identify with what they consider a socially oppressive institution. They want to be totally liberated and free to express their sexuality as they please, a holdover view from the old sixties sexual revolution. How has this knocking down of established pillars worked in the Netherlands? "The Netherlands changed from one of the most religious countries in Europe to one of the most secular. Today, nearly three-quarters of the Dutch under 35 claim no religious affiliation," Kurtz wrote in a 2004 article for *The Weekly Standard*.[10] A Dutch socially liberal government came to power in 1994—the first time since 1913 that no representatives of the socially conservative Christian Democratic Party were included. Will the rest of Europe follow in the Netherlands' footsteps? Given the rate of secularization across the European Union, it would appear so. Let me be clear in stating that gay marriage is a symptom of and not a cause of this decline. But a clear correlation exists.

How else does "pushing the parameters of sex" manifest itself in same-sex unions? *The New York Times* ran an interesting article in January 2010 entitled, "Many Successful Gay Marriages Share an Open Secret." The secret? Open and mutually accepted "play" with other partners. The article centered on a study at San Francisco State University that gives "a rare glimpse inside gay relationships and reveals that monogamy is not a central feature for many." This Gay Couples Study tracked the relationships of 556 male couples for three years and discovered 50 percent of them had other sex partners, with the approval of their "conjugal" partners. "With straight people, it's called affairs or cheating," said Colleen Hoff, the study's principal investigator, "but with gay people it does not have such negative connotations." Is this what gay marriage advocates really want to bring to the table? Of course, none of the dozen "open-marriage" gay couples contacted by *The Times* would give their names, worrying that being equally open about their little secret "could undermine the legal fight for same-sex marriage." If you think the situation itself is a tad bizarre—and lest we forget, "open marriage" has been going on with a small percentage of straight couples for a long time—consider this off-the-wall statement by the aptly named Joe Quirk, author of *It's Not You, It's Biology*: "The traditional American marriage is in crisis, and we need insight. If innovation in marriage is going to occur, it will be spearheaded by homosexual marriages."[11] Satire grows more real.

Interestingly, a smaller number of homosexuals do not wish to alter the basic fabric of traditional marriage, realizing that it does serve the common good and is nature's way of preserving a healthy and productive society. One of the more outspoken gay critics of gay marriage has been Paul Nathanson, a professor of religious studies at McGill University in Toronto, Canada. He accuses fellow homosexuals who advocate gay marriage of being selfish and short-sighted. In "Marriage à la Mode: Answering Advocates of Gay Marriage," a paper examining Canada's same-sex marriage law, first presented at Emory University in Atlanta in 2003, Nathanson and co-author Katherine Young stated:

> This indifference to society as a whole is made clear by those who defend gay marriage. Allowing gay people to marry, they say, would be beneficial to gay individuals (or to the gay community). How could that, they ask, harm straight individuals

(or the straight community)? But advocates of gay marriage have made no serious attempt to consider the possible harms and object to those who want more time to assess the evidence from other periods or other cultures.[12]

Nathanson and Young went on to publish an article in the *Journal of Family Studies* in November 2007 ("Redefining Marriage or Deconstructing Society: A Canadian Case Study") that continued to solidify the case for traditional marriage. The article was written "to alert countries still struggling with this topic to the rational and substantial grounds for maintaining the historic definition of marriage—specifically, the rational connection between heterosexuality and the purposes of marriage—and how to do this with minimal impairment to gay couples and their children."

Disposable Children?

Since a primary purpose for marriage is to bear and nurture children in a safe, healthy, moral environment, we are compelled to consider the impact of same-sex marriage on the children growing up in families headed by either two dads or two moms. When motherhood and fatherhood are stripped of their unique significance, children suffer the consequential gender-model confusion. Advocates of same-sex marriage are expecting children to accept that mothers and fathers are dispensable or interchangeable. That is an absurd notion. We only need to look at the problems encountered by children living in single-parent homes or stepfamilies to see that intentionally creating homes lacking either a mother or father or blending divorced parents and their children into same-sex-parented homes can only compound these problems. Some social scientists who have studied blended families have concluded that children being raised in same-sex-parented families and stepparented families face similar obstacles. Children living in single-parented and stepparented families—some of them are essentially raising themselves—experience an abnormally high degree of emotional, behavioral, and academic problems.[13] Research indicates that preschool children living with one biological parent and a stepparent are 40 times more likely to be abused than children living with both biological parents.[14] In fact, "stepparenthood per se remains the single most powerful risk factor for child abuse that has yet been identified," according to researchers Martin Daily and Margo Wilson.[15] A 1993 *Psychology Today* article entitled "Shuttle Diplomacy" concluded, "Stepfamilies are such a minefield of divided loyalties, emotional traps, and management conflicts that they are the most fragile form of family in America."[16]

Gay and lesbian parents will counter—and they can trot out studies to support their claims—that they can contribute a more stable environment for children. In some ways, they can. Most are fairly stable emotionally and economically, and choose to be involved in their children's lives. But there the advantages they may claim over mom-dad households end. The crux of the debate seems to be which is more essential for a child's wellbeing and development—gender-role-bending adults who care and can provide materially for the child or gender-complementary mothers and fathers who provide the time-honored security of traditional role models. Traditional families may face hardships, and divorce is a specter that certainly looms large for them statistically. Yet the conservative view—backed by reams of sociological data—is that they provide better environments for children, all things being generally equal, than same-sex-parented families. Same-sex parents also know their children are subject to being harassed by peers for having two mommies or daddies. Why place that unnecessary burden on kids when growing up is tough enough? Can gays really turn that phenomenon around? Consider that traditional families with gender-confused children face isolation and harassment, too. The discomfort that "otherness" generates within social settings for both children and adults seems to be a universal thing. And where are the statistics that establish gay couples as more divorce-proof than straight couples? The data show more strikes against gay parenting, when all is said and done.

Divorce has a far greater and longer-lasting impact on children than liberal social scientists or activists care to admit. Children being raised in same-sex-parented homes, the majority of which are with two lesbian "mothers," generally have been conceived with the help of anonymous or familial donor sperm/eggs or are the products of at least one prior divorce. Others are adopted. While one can sympathize with what may be the altruistic motives of gay couples wanting to adopt, it is harder to justify deliberately allowing children to be born into such relationships or dragging children from one marriage or home setup to another, the same as it is in straight marriages. The gender role confusion element inserts another problem into the equation.

Interestingly, the American Academy of Pediatricians (AAP) in a 2002 "Technical Report" concluded that children "of divorced lesbian mothers—they were referring to mothers with children from previous marriages who later took lesbian partners—grow up in ways very similar to children of divorced heterosexual mothers."[17] The AAP's report was meant to cast same-sex parenting in at least a normative light, and gay marriage advocates use it to back their stance. However, the report, by implication, has just the opposite effect. One of the better-known long-term studies begun in the 1970s to assess the impact of divorce on children was conducted by Dr. Judith Wallerstein and a team of researchers at the University of California at Berkeley. The study specifically concluded:

> [C]hildren from divorced and remarried families are more aggressive toward their parents and teachers. They experience more depression, have more learning difficulties, and suffer far more problems with peers than children from intact families. Children from divorced and remarried families are two to three times more likely to be referred for psychological help at school than their peers from intact families. More of them end up in mental health clinics and hospital settings. There is earlier sexual activity, more children born out of wedlock, less marriage, and more divorce.[18]

The existing body of research is still too small for sufficiently conclusive evidence as this social experiment is still relatively new. There is one ongoing study that has followed lesbian couples and their deliberately conceived children since 1986. It is called the National Longitudinal Lesbian Family Study (NLLFS). This group maintains that its periodic interviews with the children at several age intervals have shown them to be as well-adjusted as heterosexually parented children, on average.[19] The most recent report on the now-17-year-old children from these families, released in November 2010, indicates some underlying problems, however. The abstract of the latest findings reports that "18.9 percent of the adolescent girls and 2.7 percent of the adolescent boys self-rated in the bisexual spectrum, and 0 percent of girls and 5.4 percent of boys self-rated as predominantly-to-exclusively homosexual."[20] The sampling is not representative of the overall lesbian parent population, but these results are telling, nonetheless.

Psychologist Trayce Hansen has uncovered some other evidence that appears to confirm the down side of the NLLFS study. She reviewed nine studies she says "suggest that children raised by homosexual or bisexual parents are approximately seven times more likely than the general population to develop a non-heterosexual sexual preference."[21] It stands to reason that same-sex parents would more readily affirm gender-bending identities in their children. As early as 2001, pro-gay sociologists Judith Stacey and Timothy Biblarz concluded that children raised in lesbian-parented homes are more likely to engage in homosexual behavior themselves, that daughters of lesbians are "more sexually adventurous and less chaste," and that lesbian couples are more likely to break up than heterosexuals.[22] Despite these red flags, the AAP came to the conclusion that children raised by same-sex parents would not be harmed to any significant degree, at least not any more so than children from divorced and remarried families already were. Such conclusions will only exacerbate a social problem we already know exists while paving the way for those we have not yet fully learned about. In the abortion debate, the advent of ultrasound technology has begun leveling the playing field. Expectant mothers who view ultrasound images of their babies are far more likely to go through with the birth, even if they choose to give the baby up for adoption. Will the sad and confused faces of the children of estranged same-sex "parents," especially when one of them has renounced homosexuality, become the "ultrasound" of the gay marriage debate?

Stanton and Maier point out that another danger in sanctioning same-sex marriage is it destroys the significance of gender. In other words, it dehumanizes both men and women by suggesting that masculinity and femininity are meaningless. "A woman is reduced to a womb and its practical function" while "the one important thing about manhood will be sperm."[23] They further state, "Gender in a society that accepts same-sex marriage can only refer to meaningless, impersonal, interchangeable parts. A socially equal—and not just tolerated—same-sex marriage does damage at a very fundamental level."[24]

Be Careful What You Hope For

The ugly reality of divorce and child custody battles, the same trap that many heterosexual couples fall into, is the inconvenient truth proponents of same-sex marriage fail to acknowledge. Studies of gay marriage in Sweden indicate there is a much higher percentage of divorce among homosexual married partners than that found in heterosexual marriages. "Gay male couples were 50 percent more likely to divorce within eight years and lesbian couples 167 percent more likely to divorce than heterosexual couples," according to the gay website loveandpride.com. Child custody battles already are and will continue to be harsh reminders of where we have gone wrong in making marriage individual adult needs than about the needs of children.

Consider the case of "divorced" same-sex partners Janet Jenkins and Lisa Miller, who had joined in a civil union in Vermont in late 2000 while residents of Virginia. In 2003, after moving with Jenkins to Vermont, Miller began seeking to have the union officially dissolved in Vermont courts. In 2002, she had given birth (in Virginia) to a daughter conceived via artificial insemination. She was initially willing to grant supervised visitation with the child to Jenkins. The Vermont Supreme Court recognized Jenkins as a parent, even though she had no biological connection to the child and had not adopted her, and ordered Miller to allow unsupervised visits. A major bone of contention was that Miller had renounced her fling with homosexuality (she said a counselor had once convinced her she was a lesbian) and had reclaimed and deepened her Christian faith. Living and attending church again in Virginia, she regretted her past life of sin and wanted a healthier life for herself and her daughter. For Miller to honor her onetime misguided commitment to a same-sex union was now anathema to her and harmful, in her view, for her daughter. Despite the ongoing risk of being in contempt of the Vermont court's order, Miller eventually felt compelled to deny visitation to Jenkins. She drew the line at protecting her daughter from the influences of Jenkins' active lesbian life and her stated anti-Christian views. Both states' courts continued to remain largely unsympathetic to her parental autonomy, yet affirmed her as the custodial parent. Miller alleged in court testimony that Jenkins had been emotionally and verbally abusive to her while they lived together and that the few visits Isabella had had with Jenkins had also been emotionally traumatizing for her. Angry at being deprived of a court-granted parental "right," despite the two states' dueling laws, and actually citing Miller's evangelical Christian faith as harmful to the child, Jenkins began petitioning the court for sole custody and even sought in 2009 to have Miller jailed for contempt.

The case grew into an ugly, protracted battle—now seven years long—with activists and sympathizers on both sides using it to wage an ideological and political war. Virginia's Marriage Affirmation Act and state constitutional marriage amendment have not been enough so far to stop Jenkins' march through the courts. She succeeded, to the delight of gay marriage activists who have made the case their cause célèbrè, in having a Vermont family court award her sole custody of a child she barely knows and has no biological or adoptive ties to. Miller refused to recognize Vermont's rulings, firmly believing Virginia's laws supported her stance. So far the higher courts (the Supreme Court of the United States has not yet agreed to hear any appeal) have ruled in Jenkins' favor, all but ignoring the best interests of the child. Miller has said that, through her constant prayers, God repeatedly impressed on her she was not to allow visitations to take place. Her actions may be to her a form of civil disobedience, something she believes her faith demands in this case. She apparently believed it necessary to carry it all a step farther sometime prior to January 1, 2010, the date she was to have relinquished custody of her then-seven-year-old daughter to Jenkins.

Lisa and her daughter, Isabella, disappeared and their whereabouts have not yet been confirmed. A new firestorm of media coverage and gay activist outrage ensued. It periodically erupts when some report of their alleged location surfaces on a gay blog or the Associated Press covers the latest court update.

I enjoyed a friendship with Lisa and Isabella Miller for a little over a year. I had learned about their case the year before they moved to the Lynchburg area and began attending my church. I know Lisa was deeply conflicted over what was the right thing to do. She desperately sought to honor God. I am convinced she would make any sacrifice she deemed necessary to protect her daughter and retain the freedom to raise her in the Christian faith. There has been much debate over how she has handled it all. She had to be aware, as she and her attorneys continued to square off with her former partner and the courts, that all her decisions would bear long-term consequences. Her faith and the strong desire to conform her life to God's purpose, realizing she had been the recipient of his amazing grace, held her steady. Presumably, she remains so resolved. She cut off all contact with me, and everyone else I knew to be mutual friends, to my knowledge, when she determined to take flight. I knew nothing of her plans, and remain in the dark, despite some unfounded and hysterical accusations to the contrary.

This travesty represents the tip of the iceberg in legal nightmares that still await us. Other similar cases are going on all around the country and many more will follow if same-sex marriage is widely recognized as a basic right. More and more court rulings are affirming the parental status of same-sex partners with no biological or adoptive relationship to the children. Same-sex marriage activists are pursuing a state-by-state, domino-toppling strategy to achieve their goals. In fact, New York Sen. Chuck Schumer said before a group of gay activists on October 22, 2009: "Equality should know no bounds, and we must not rest until we have [gay] marriage in all

50 of these United States."[25] Are the rights and needs of children being consigned to the dustbin of political correctness, however? That would be a short ideological hop, since so many people already have decided that unborn children are expendable appendages of women's bodies they can "amputate" for any reason.

Life After "the Curse"

Other than for procreation and nurturing of future generations, traditional marriage serves to protect women from predatory men and to provide men with a "social station" of proper restraint. Respected sociologists have drawn similar conclusions. Of course, some women also have predatory notions. Men are less prone to monogamy, which is a flashpoint in any discussion about gay male sexual behaviors. Society has imposed the need for men to remain monogamous through marriage. We already know that the gay view of marriage for many men and women allows for few boundaries. As Christians, we can surmise that the fall of man and God's curse all the way back in the Garden made philandering an issue, since the Genesis account set up marriage before sin entered human history. To render traditional marriage insignificant is to invite social anarchy. It is the uniting of the two genders that perfectly answers the basic needs of men and women and teaches children how to behave toward the opposite sex. Marriage is not just about companionship or a joining of two people who are reflections of each other. That would make it a narcissistic undertaking. Husband and wife are meant to focus outwardly, each on the needs of the other, rather than seeking to have their individual needs met. They have a common aim—begetting a family—that benefits society. Fathers teach sons how to love and respect women. Same-sex marriage would only lower the bar for heterosexual marriage. Why should men marry women and remain monogamous when gay men are notoriously promiscuous? If women marry each other, what does that say about the need for men at all? There is always the sperm bank. In short, there is nothing good to be gained from same-sex marriage. Who within the Church really wants to facilitate the hastening of this darkness?

Children raised in a family headed by a mom and a dad learn about the essential differences between the two sexes, and develop within a healthy, balanced framework that combines the particular strengths of each gender. Even single mothers have tended to encourage their children to participate in gender-appropriate activities while lesbian mothers' "preference for their child's play was gender-neutral," according to Stacey and Biblarz.[26] Many studies have concluded that a loving, nurturing, involved father is as essential to the health and well-being of a child as a loving, nurturing mother. The unique styles of parenting that both fathers and mothers bring to a family help children in all aspects of development, whether verbal, motor, social, or analytical. Another study found that children who feel close to their fathers are twice as likely to attend college, 75 percent less likely to become teen parents, 80 percent less likely to be incarcerated, and half as likely to be depressed.[27] The Progressive Policy Institute, affiliated with the Democratic Leadership Council, has reported that the relationship between crime and fatherless families is "so strong that controlling for family configuration erases the relationship between race and crime and between low-income and crime."[28]

Other troubling studies show that homosexual sexual abuse may be significant within families raising foster children. One study developed from data provided by the Illinois Department of Children and Family Services and the Minnesota Department of Human Services (two states that allow gay foster parenting) appears in the August 2006 online issue of *Pediatrics*. The study concluded that 35 percent of the reported sexual abuse cases in foster homes involved homosexual foster parents, with most of the sexual assaults committed by lesbians.[29] Only 3 percent of foster children are in homes with gay foster parents, according to The Urban Institute. Not that heterosexual-parented families don't have major problems with sexual abuse, as I have pointed out. We need to clean up that act. If homosexuality was once considered the "sin that dare not speak its name," child sexual abuse remains the crime that dare not speak its name. Society turns a blind eye to it, in large measure.

With such overwhelming evidence in favor of traditional marriage, imperfect as we have made it, why are we facing such a widespread challenge from radical gay activists and liberal social engineers to redefine marriage? Actually, as Stanton and Maier point out in their book, a move toward gay marriage and other socially engineered forms of marriage has been inevitable, given the social climate that began with the widespread availability of contraception when the birth control pill was developed. It was particularly pushed by Margaret Sanger, founder of Planned Parenthood. The pill gave rise to the sexual revolution and cavalier attitudes about having children. That, in turn, brought about the clamor for a woman's "right to choose" that led to *Roe v. Wade* and abortion on demand. "For the first time, parenthood didn't demand protection of a child but rather allowed for the child's destruction."[30] Sociologist Pitirim Sorikin predicted in the 1950s that a sexual revolution would "destroy the real freedom of normal love; and in lieu of enriching and ennobling the sexual passion, [reduce] it to mere copulation."[31]

Gay Political Strategies

Polls and voter referenda indicate that gay marriage still has a long way to go to be widely accepted. But gay activists are a long-suffering lot. They press on. In July 2006, *The Washington Blade* reported that the Democratic National Committee had a "five-point plan" to fight proposed state marriage amendments. Voters cast ballots on eight such amendments in the fall of 2006, approving seven by an average 64-percent margin. Arizona became the first state among 31 to date to narrowly reject an amendment limiting marriage to one man and one woman, but voters there passed a revised version in 2008. *The Blade* said the Democrats would portray the marriage amendments as "divisive ploys by Republicans ... to deflect voter attention from other important issues" and was training Democratic "operatives in all 50 states" to campaign against the state ballot measures.[32] Two major gay lobbying groups, the Human Rights Campaign and the National Gay and Lesbian Task Force, pledged several million dollars toward the fight, but the opposing conservative groups prevailed. The pro-gay groups bought ads in 50 newspapers featuring five homosexual couples and proclaiming, "Marriage matters. They're committed. So are we." Voters overwhelmingly disagreed. Whenever the people have had their say, this has been the case. Because California took its marriage fight to federal court, where no state has been yet, some prognosticators fear the Golden State could sound the death knell for all 31 state constitutional marriage amendments, unless the Supreme Court of the Unites States refuses to hear an appeal, in which case it will only apply to California. Some legal scholars believe pushing for overturn of the California judge's Proposition 8 ruling all the way to the nation's highest court would not succeed.

Of the many screeds that appeared from conservative pundits opposed to Judge Vaughan Walker's ruling on Proposition 8, one was well reasoned. It came from commentator Dennis Prager. He referred to the studies that Walker apparently believed gave him the license to rule as he did. "That many Americans believe these studies—studies that are in any case based on a small number of same-sex couples raising a small number of children, during a short amount of time (a couple of decades), based on the researchers' own notions of what a healthy and successful young person—only proves how effectively colleges and graduate schools have succeeded in teaching a generation of Americans not to think critically but to accept "studies" in place of common sense."[33]

An interesting 2004 *New York Times* op-ed piece by Shari Motro, a University of Richmond (Virginia) law professor, pointed out that, although marriage benefits are "seen as proxies for helping families with children," such benefits do not extend to the one-in-three children born out of wedlock. "If 50 percent of marriages end in divorce, 50 percent of marriage-based 'rewards' are nothing but an expensive mistake."[34] If the gay community wants to rally around those same-sex couples that remain in serious committed relationships and accord them whatever honor they may wish to, that is fine. The rest of us may wish them well and allow them space to live free of discrimination in an open society with entitlement to the basic rights every citizen deserves. That is as far as our recognition need go. Again, I would love to see half the energy that is spent fighting gay marriage expended on strengthening and divorce-proofing traditional marriages.

Interestingly, following the state of Washington's decision in favor of traditional marriage, gay lobbyists appeared to switch tactics. A website called BeyondMarriage.org appeared with the new message seeking "legal recognition of a wide range of relationships, households, and families—regardless of kinship or conjugal status." This statement was signed by 260 gay activists. They also sought "access for all to 'vital government support programs' including health care, housing, Social Security and pension plans, unemployment insurance, and welfare assistance."[35] Clearly, some gay lobbyists are sensing the necessity of linking gay marriage to other causes in order to move it forward. Their true colors are showing, of course, as one of the categories of marriage protection in their new campaign is for "queer couples who decide to jointly create and raise a child with another queer person or couple, in two households" and "committed, loving households in which there is more than one conjugal partner."[36] Still have doubts about the ulterior motives of some gay marriage advocates? This organization aims to soften the unsavory parts of its message by including other benign-sounding, minority family arrangements—the two little, old grannies on "fixed incomes" helping each other, or siblings forced by economic circumstances to live together, etc.

While the media provided considerable coverage to the summer 2006 failure of the Senate to approve a federal Marriage Protection Amendment, barely any coverage was given in the same time frame when the 20th state (Alabama) passed its own version by a margin of 81 to 19 percent. Focus on the Family's James Dobson was the rare media exception as CNN allowed him to voice his opinion in a July 2006 commentary. Even though few people expected any serious congressional action at that point in time, Dobson assailed the senators, including some prominent Republicans, who fell back on the states' rights argument:

> All of these senators are smart enough to know that, first, it would create utter chaos to have 50 different definitions of marriage in one country, where every state is required by the Constitution to support the laws of the other 49. Come on, Senator McCain and company. You and your colleagues know better than that.
>
> Second, senators wanting the states to define marriage are fully aware that the people will not be permitted to make their own decisions. Arrogant activist judges, most of them appointed by President Bill Clinton or President Jimmy Carter, will simply overturn the will of the electorate.[37]

Dobson's words proved to be prophetic, as his concerns have been justified in seven gay-marriage-affirming states so far, with several others percolating. At last count, 18 states now recognize same-sex partners as de facto non-biological parents to children living in those unions.

Judicial Bullying

Precedent still remains on the side of traditional marriage. That is why many gay activists have warned against making a surge toward the courts to seek legal recognition by other states of same-sex marriages under the U.S. Constitution's Equal Protection clause (14th Amendment) and to challenge DOMA. That may not last long, however, given recent history. In July 2010, a federal court in Massachusetts ruled that DOMA violates "states' rights" and federalism in defining marriage. It seems the courts want to have it both ways—to have both federal oversight over marriage and to allow states to define marriage for themselves, a double standard that will never work. Both sides have seen victories, but most observers would not have predicted the progress of same-sex marriage or civil unions so far, especially in Iowa. New York still has some staunch conservatives in the mix, but its decision to uphold traditional marriage so far may not stand for that long as it is home to some of the most liberal judges in the nation and a pro-gay-marriage governor. New York City Hispanic pastors (as many Hispanics had done in California earlier) rallied for a protest that drew as many as 10,000 to City Hall one Sunday in May 2009.[38]

Openly lesbian justice Virginia Linder was elected to Oregon's Supreme Court in 2007. She joined fellow gay justice Rives Kistler, who was added to the court in 2003. It is difficult to say how many other states may be facing openly homosexual or gay-sympathizing judicial appointments, but they have the best shot ever under an Obama administration. Liberal Democratic governors and state legislators dot the American political landscape a bit less now than they did prior to the 2010 mid-term elections, but they will not retreat. Growing numbers of elected officials are openly gay—and some remain in the closet—with many others decidedly pro-gay in their politics. Has the time come when only a federal marriage amendment can preserve marriage as a legal union between a man and a woman? Is such an amendment even possible?

Finding Our Backbone

Have we come to the point where we have no effective apologetics by which to defend the traditional family? Never before now has a society been asked to articulate a facts-based defense for a foundational institution always inherently known to be right and best. Many who should know better falter as the new false doctrine proclaiming same-sex marriage as equal to traditional marriage takes center stage and wins more and more people to its side through deception and faulty logic. We are strongest when we acknowledge our godly heritage, weakest when we ignore or forget it.

For millennia marriage has been the basic building block of civilization—the microcosm of society. Families are little societies that exist for the mutual benefit of all members. Many families intersect to build enclaves and towns and spread out from there. It is, therefore, not far-fetched to say that as the family goes, so goes all of civilization. Although the Judeo-Christian ethic teaches us that "the same Lord is Lord of all" (Romans 10:12), and America's Declaration of Independence declares that "all men are created equal," there is something deeper to ponder. Consider Isaiah 29:16. "You turn things upside down, as if the potter were thought to be like the clay! Shall what is formed say to him who formed it, 'He did not make me'? Can the pot say of the potter, 'He knows nothing?'" Those who disregard the significance in why God "made them male and female" and warned us not to "put asunder" what he had joined together are, indeed, telling the potter what to make of them. That casts culpability on both sides in this debate.

In previous chapters, I have expounded on the biblical foundations of human relationships, the most intimate of which is marriage. Here's how C.S. Lewis put it:

> The Christian idea of marriage is based on Christ's words that a man and a woman are to be regarded as a single organism—for that is what the words "one flesh" would be in modern English. And the Christians believe that when He said this He was not expressing a sentiment but stating a fact—just as one is stating a fact when one says that a lock and its key are one mechanism or that a violin and a bow are one musical instrument. The inventor of the human machine was telling us that its two halves, the male and the female, were made to be combined together in pairs, not simply on the sexual level, but totally combined.[39]

From a biblical perspective, the denial of the Creator's design for marriage is open rebellion against his authority and his very image in the world. Of course, God is most perfectly reflected in the "one flesh" of husband and wife, a melding of the masculine and feminine into a complete, life-giving whole. God means for us to have meaningful same-sex friendships with a brotherly or sisterly kind of intimacy. Obviously, the marriage bond is based on gender complementarity, with each spouse helping and completing the other in a unique way, as C. S. Lewis so beautifully illustrated. This kind of bond simply cannot happen within same-sex unions.

I have been blessed with wonderful, sisterly friends; they

encompass every generation and are in addition to my friendships with my mother and my adult daughters, the most important female relationships I have. I have only brothers for siblings, although I do have sisters-in-law who are like sisters to me. No friend I have in this world is like my husband, however. Our relationship exceeds them all because it touches every level of human desire or need, including the one at the very core of my nature—the God-given desire for intimacy with someone not like me but uniquely created to be one with me. That God can take two very different beings, man and woman, and join them through the mystery of marriage into "one flesh"—a union that is stronger than any other save that with Christ, himself—is an incomprehensible marvel. But it works when we allow God to be at the center of it. With so much focus on the problems with marriage in this postmodern age, we hear far too little about the good marriages or those that have come back from the brink of ruin to flourish and give hope to others struggling. That is part of my story, as well. How desperately we need such couples to reach out and mentor those who are hurting and about to go under, or to counsel young people who are considering marriage, but are unprepared for it. Wouldn't it be wonderful if we could see a far-reaching marriage-building movement that would help to slash the divorce rate dramatically? Our churches are the places where such an effort can flourish, if we have the heart for it.

If the Church opens itself to the possibility of sanctioning or blessing homosexual marriages, it is no longer the true, confessing church of Christ. Church reformer Martin Luther warned long ago against capitulating to the world: "If I declare with loudest voice and clearest exposition every portion of God's truth except for that one little bit which the world and the devil are at that moment attacking, I am not confessing Christ no matter how boldly I am professing Christ." Dante said it even more strongly: "The hottest places in hell are reserved for those who in time of great moral crisis maintain their neutrality."[40]

God has given us choices. They apply to the individual as well as to all of society:

> This day I call heaven and earth as witnesses against you that I have set before you life and death, blessings and curses. Now choose life, so that you and your children may live and that you may love the Lord your God, listen to his voice, and hold fast to him (Deuteronomy 30:19-20).

Suggested Resources

American Association of Christian Counselors (AACC)
1639 Rustic Village Road
Forest, VA 24551
www.aacc.net
1-800-526-8673

Courage (Catholic Ministry)
www.couragerc.net
210 West 31st Street
New York, NY 10001
212-268-1010

Cross Ministry
www.crossministry.org
P.O. Box 1122
Wake Forest, NC 27588
919-569-0375

CrossOver Ministries
www.crossover-inc.org
120 N. 3rd St., Ste. 206
Danville, KY 40422
859-608-7176

Desert Stream Ministries
www.desertstream.org
706 Main Street
Grandview, MO 64030
1-866-359-0500

Evergreen International (LDS Ministry)
www.evergreeninternational.org
307 West 200 South, Ste. 4006
Salt Lake City, UT 84101
1-800-391-1000

Exodus International (Love Won Out)
www.exodus-international.org
P.O. Box 540119
Orlando, FL 32854
1-888-264-0877

First Stone Ministries
www.firststone.org
1330 N. Classen Blvd., Ste. G80
Oklahoma City, OK 73106
405-236-4673

Focus on the Family
www.focusonthefamily.com
Colorado Springs, CO 80995
1-800A-FAMILY (232-6459)

Genesis Counseling
www.genesiscounseling.org
17632 Irvine Blvd., Ste. 220
Tustin, CA 92780
714-508-6953

JONAH - Jews Offering New Alternatives to Homosexuality
www.jonahweb.org
P.O. BOX 313
Jersey City, NJ 07303
201-433-3444

Living Hope Ministries
http://livehope.org
P.O. Box 2239
Arlington, TX 76004
817-459-2507

Love in Action International
www.loveinaction.org
4780 Yale Road
Memphis, TN 38128
1-800-201-4129

The Marin Foundation
www.themarinfoundation.org
700 W. Bittersweet Pl., Ste. 208
Chicago, IL 60613
773-572-5983

National Association for Research and Therapy of Homosexuality
(NARTH)
www.narth.com
1-888-364-4744

One by One
www.oneby1.org
106 East Church St.
Orlando, FL 32801
407-423-3441 (ext. 1489)

Outpost Ministries
www.outpostministries.org
P.O. Box 22429
Robbinsdale, MN 55422
763-592-4700

Portland Fellowship
www.portlandfellowship.com
P.O. Box 14841
Portland, OR 97293
503-235-6364

Regeneration Ministries
www.regenerationministries.org
P.O. Box 9830
Baltimore, MD 21284
410-661-0284

Sheer Faith Ministries
www.debbiethurman.com
P.O. Box 385
Monroe, VA 24574
434-929-8002

Transforming Congregations
www.transcong.org
2412 Second St.
Monroe, WI 53566
608-325-5712

The Way Out
www.sbcthewayout.org
1290 E. Highland St.
Southlake, TX 76092
817-424-9121

Witness Freedom Ministries
www.witnessfortheworld.org
7595 Sunstone Drive
Atlanta, GA 30236
678-519-5110

Worthy Creations
www.worthycreations.org
P.O. Box 93
Fort Lauderdale, FL 33302
954-970-990

Recommended Reading

The Bible and Homosexual Practice: Texts and Hermeneutics, by Robert A.J. Gagnon

The Broken Image by Leanne Payne

Coming Out of Homosexuality by Bob Davies and Lori Rentze

City of Man: Religion and Politics in a New Era by Michael Gerson and Peter Wehner

The Complete Christian Guide to Understanding Homosexuality: A Biblical and Compassionate Response to Same-Sex Attraction by Joe Dallas and Nancy Heche

Desires in Conflict: Hope for Men Who Struggle with Sexual Identity by Joe Dallas

The Divided States of America?: What Liberals AND Conservatives Are Missing in the God-and-Country Shouting Match! by Richard Land

Emotional Dependency by Lori Thorkelson Rentzel

Ex-Gays?: A Longitudinal Study of Religiously Mediated Change in Sexual Orientation by Stanton Jones and Mark Yarhouse

The Game Plan: The Men's 30-Day Strategy for Attaining Sexual Integrity by Joe Dallas

God's Grace and the Homosexual Next Door by Alan Chambers

Growth Into Manhood by Alan Medinger

The Heart of Female Same-Sex Attraction by Janelle Hallman
Homosexuality and the Politics of Truth by Dr. Jeffrey Satinover

Homosexuality: The Use of Scientific Research in the Church's Moral Debate by Stanton L. Jones and Mark A. Yarhouse

Into the Promised Land: Beyond the Lesbian Struggle by Jeannette Howard

Leaving Homosexuality: A Practical Guide for Men and Women Looking for a Way Out by Alan Chambers

Love Is An Orientation: Elevating the Conversation with the Gay Community by Andrew Marin

Loving Homosexuals as Jesus Would by Chad Thompson

Marriage on Trial:The Case Against Same-Sex Marriage and Parenting by Glenn Stanton and Bill Maier

Out of a Far Country: A Gay Son's Journey to God. A Broken Mother's Search for Hope by Christopher Yuan and Angela Yuan

Out of Egypt: One Woman's Journey Out of Lesbianism by Jeannette Howard

Portraits of Freedom by Bob Davies and Lela Gilbert

Restoring Sexual Identity: Hope for Women who Struggle with Same-Sex Attraction by Anne Paulk

Someone I Love Is Gay by Anita Worthen and Bob Davies

Strength in Weakness: Healing Sexual and Relational Brokenness by Andrew Comiskey

Surviving Sexual Brokenness: What Grace Can Do by Thom Hunter

The Truth Comes Out: The Story of My Heart's Transformation by Nancy Heche

When Homosexuality Hits Home by Joe Dallas

Notes

Chapter 1

1. E.C. Green, V. Nantulya , R. Stoneburner, J. Stover, "What Happened in Uganda? Declining HIV Prevalence, Behavior Change, and the National Response," Washington, D.C.: USAID, 2002.

2. Zak Szymanski, "HIV Campaigns Spark Debate," *Bay Area Reporter*, www. ebar.com, November 9, 2006.

3. Craig Timberg. "Speeding HIV's Deadly Spread." *Washington Post* Foreign Service: March 2, 2007; p. A-1.

4. UNAIDS 2008 Report on the Global AIDS Epidemic.

5. James D. Shelton, "A Tale of Two-component Generalised HIV Epidemics, *The Lancet*, Volume 375, Issue 9719, 964-966, March 20, 2010.

6. James D. Shelton, "HIV Myths Should Not Be Resuscitated—Author's Reply," *The Lancet*, Volume 370, Issue 9602, 1809 - 1811, December 1, 2007.

7. Lionel Wright, "The Stonewall Riots—1969," *Socialism Today*, No. 40, July 1999.

8. Ibid.

9. James H. Jones, *Alfred C. Kinsey: A Public/Private Life* (Darby, Pennsylvania: DIANE Publishing Co.,1997). Cited in Nicholas Cummings and Rogers Wright's, *Destructive Trends in Mental Health: The Well-Intentioned Path to Harm* (New York: Brunner-Routledge, 2005), p. xii.

10. Ibid.

11. Nicholas Cummings and Rogers Wright, *Destructive Trends in Mental Health: The Well-Intentioned Path to Harm* (New York: Brunner-Routledge, 2005), p. xii.

12. *Destructive Trends in Mental Health*, p. xxx.

13. Josh Montez, "Medicaid Leaves the Sex-Change Business," CitizenLink.org, August 10, 2006.

14. Marshall Kirk and Hunter Madsen, *After the Ball: How America Will Conquer*

its *Fear and Hatred of Gays in the 90's* (New York: Doubleday/Plume, 1989), pp. 148-154, 248-251, 254-258.

15. Anton N. Marco, "Gay 'Marriage'?" *The Journal of Human Sexuality,* George A. Rekers, Ph.D., ed., Lewis & Stanley Publishers, 1996.

16. Mike Royko, "Gays' Problems Not all that Bad," *Colorado Springs Gazette-Telegraph,* April 30, 1993.

17. Vic Pollard, "Gay Rights Backers Cheer Flood of Bills," *The Bakersfield Californian, September 9, 2006.*

18. Pete Winn, "California Pro-Gay Education Bill Stalls," CitizenLink.org, June 29, 2006.

19. Dan Walters, "With Gay Marriage Duel in Courts, Capitol Faces Curriculum Fight," *The* Sacramento Bee, July 14, 2006.

20. Elizabeth Saewyc, Ph.D., RN, PHN, Carol L. Skay, Ph.D., Patricia Hynds, Sandra Pettingell, Ph.D., Linda H. Bearinger, Ph.D., MS, RN, Michael D. Resnick, Ph.D., and Elizabeth Reis, MS, "Suicide Ideation and Attempts in North American School-Based Surveys: Are Bisexual Youth At Increasing Risk?" *Journal of Adolescent Health,* 2008 February; 3(2): 25–36.

21. Warren Throckmorton, "Bill O'Reilly is Right About Gay Teens," *The Conservative Voice,* October 14, 2005.

22. Denise D. Hallfors, Martha W. Waller, Daniel Bauer, Carol A. Ford and Carolyn T. Halpern, "Which Comes First in Adolescence—Sex and Drugs or Depression?" *American Journal of Preventive Medicine,* 29(3): 163-170.

23. Ibid.

24. Helen Gao, "Scouts Seek New Places for Meetings: Troops Won't Pay School District Fees," *The Union Tribune,* September 12, 2005.

25. Family Research Council Commentary: "Philadelphia Chooses Political Correctness over Scouts," Washington Watch Daily Radio, August 7, 2006.

Chapter 2

1. Elisabeth Elliot, "The Essence of Femininity: A Personal Perspective" in *Recovering Biblical Manhood and Womanhood: A Response to Evangelical Feminism,* edited by John Piper and Wayne Grudem (1991: Wheaton, Illinois: Crossway Books), p. 395.

2. "'Gay' Activist Says 'We Will BURY You': Threats Made Against Christian Workers Opposing Homosexual Agenda," WorldNetDaily, May 5, 2007.

3. David W. Virtue, "Inclusion, Inclusion ... Not," Virtue Online, July 7, 2006.

4. Issac Bailey, "Homosexuality Seen Differently Through Faith," Faith & Ethics page, *The Sun News*, July 2, 2006.

5. Elizabeth Birch (Human Rights Campaign), Address given at the "Exposed" Conference, University of California, Santa Cruz, February 7, 1998.

6. Dr. Gordon Hugenberger, "Questions and Answers on Issues Related to Homosexuality and Same-Sex Marriage" (at parkstreet.org), June 15, 2004.

7. "Seven Out of 10 Say Beliefs Should Not Be Abandoned Over Gay Rights," *Evening Standard* ("This Is London" Entertainment Guide), November 29, 2006.

8. Brian Fitzpatrick, "Media Ignore Impending Collision: Gay Rights vs. Religious Liberty," Townhall.com, June 10, 2008.

9. Jonah Goldberg, "Canada's Thought Police," Townhall.com, June 18, 2008.

10. Pete Vere, JCL, "Catholicism — A Hate Crime in Canada?" *Catholic Exchange*, June 4, 2008.

11. *After the Ball*, p. 179.

12. From discussions with Darrell Massie, author of book pending publication. Used by permission.

13. Malcolm Muggeridge: *Christ and the Media*, 1979 (reprinted by Regent University Publishing, 2003), p. 15.

14. Ibid.

15. *Christ and the Media*, p. 67.

16. *Christ and the Media*, p. 14.

17. "ABC's Nightline Airs Pro-Gay Media Bias," American Family Association Action Alert, June 6, 2002.

18. *After the Ball*, p. 148.

19. *Christ and the Media*, p. 29.

20. Daniel Gonzales, "Question of Bias in MSNBC Coverage of Ex-Gays," Ex-Gay Watch, July 4, 2005.

21. Bob Unruh, "Now It's EX-Gays Getting Pummeled: Verbal to Violent, Attacks Rise Against Former Homosexuals," WorldNetDaily, May 27, 2008.

22. Kyle Rice, "I Hate Being Gay," *The Advocate*, September 15, 2006.

23. "Larry King Live," CNN, June 15, 2006.

24. Interview with Daryl Pitts, D.Min., on July 5, 2006.

Chapter 3

1. Robert L. Spitzer, "Can Some Gay Men and Lesbians Change Their Sexual Orientation? 200 Participants Reporting a Change from Homosexual to Heterosexual Orientation," *Archives of Sexual Behavior*, Vol. 32, No. 5, October 2003, pp. 403-417.

2. Roy Waller and Linda A. Nicolosi, "Spitzer Study Published: Evidence Found for Effectiveness of Reorientation Therapy," National Association for Research and Therapy of Homosexuality (NARTH).

3. Ibid.

4. Benjamin Kaufman, M.D., "Why NARTH? The American Psychiatric Association's Destructive and Blind Pursuit of Political Correctness" *Regent University Law Review*, Vol. 14:423.

5. Ibid.

6. Joyce Howard Price, "APA Denies Any Retreat on Gay Therapy," *Washington Times*, September 3, 2006.

7. "Homosexuality and Sexual Orientation Disturbances," in Alfred M. Freedman, Harold I. Kaplan and Benjamin J. Saddock, eds., *Comprehensive Textbook of Psychiatry II*, second edition (Baltimore: The Williams & Wilkins Co., 1975), p. 1519.

8. WThrockmorton.com blog entry, September 19, 2007.

9. Warren Throckmorton, "New Book Details Benefits and Limits of Gay Change," The Center for Vision and Values, Grove City College, September 20, 2007.

10. Warren Throckmorton, "Interview with Dr. Robert Spitzer," March 2004, drthrockmorton.com.

11. Ibid.

12. Ibid.

13. Human Rights Campaign, "A Resource Guide to Coming Out."

14. Jeffrey B. Satinover, M.S., M.D., "The Trojan Couch: How the Medical Health Guilds Allow Medical Diagnostics, Scientific Research and Jurisprudence to be Subverted in Lockstep with the Political Aims of their Gay Subcomponents," 2005 NARTH Conference Report, pp. 1-2.

15. Satinover, p. 11.

16. Edward O. Laumann, John H. Gagnon, Robert T. Michael and Stuart Michaels, *The Social Organization of Sexuality: Sexual Practices in the United States* (University of Chicago Press, 1994), p. 283.

17. Satinover, p. 19.

18. Waller and Nicolosi, op. cit.

19. Wayne R. Besen, *Anything But Straight: Unmasking the Scandals and Lies Behind the Ex-Gay Movement* (New York: Harrington Park Press, 2003), p. 234.

20. *Anything But Straight*, p. 42.

21. Elizabeth Saewyc, Ph.D., RN, PHN, Carol L. Skay, Ph.D., Patricia Hynds, Sandra Pettingell, Ph.D., Linda H. Bearinger, Ph.D., M.S., RN, Michael D. Resnick, Ph.D., and Elizabeth Reis, M.S., "Suicide Ideation and Attempts in North American School-Based Surveys: Are Bisexual Youth At Increasing Risk?" *Journal of Adolescent Health*, 2008 February; 3(2): 25–36.

22. Beth Gorham, "B.C. Researcher Says American Group Distorting Her Research on Teen Suicide," CBC News, June 19, 2006.

23. "Elite Schools Face the Gay Issue," *The New York Times*, June 13, 1997.

24. Jennifer Thurman and Art Toalston, "Activists Attack SG Nominee: Homosexuality Stance Targeted," *The Baptist Press*, June 22, 2007.

25. Ibid.

26. Chad McBride, "The 12th Annual Conference of the National Association for Research and Therapy of Homosexuality Held in Washington, D.C.," narth.com, December 16, 2004.

Chapter 4

1. "The O'Reilly Factor," Fox News, November 18, 2003.

2. Warren Throckmorton, "O'Reilly Is Right About Gay Teens,"drthrockmorton. com, October 14, 2005.

3. Warren Throckmorton, "Brokeback Syndrome: More Than One Way Off the Mountain," *The Conservative Voice*, February 13, 2006.

4. "In CNN Guest Column, Dobson Mischaracterized Same-Sex Marriage Debate, Suggesting Public Support for Constitutional Ban," Media Matters, June 30, 2006.

5. Julie Hollar, "Media's Gay Marriage Consensus: Insider Critics Charge

Press Didn't Play it Straight," Fairness and Accuracy in Reporting, September/October 2004.

6. Ibid.

7. Ibid.

8. Ibid.

9. Robert Knight, "Networks Ignore Crushing of Marriage Vote in Massachusetts," Culture and Media Institute, June 15, 2007.

10. "Hardball with Chris Matthews," MSNBC, November 23, 2003.

11. "The O'Reilly Factor," Fox News, November 18, 2003.

12. L. Brent Bozell III, "Gay-Biased Times," *Pittsburgh Tribune-Review*, July 16, 2006.

13. Michelangelo Signorile, "Power Outage," *New York*, March 5, 2001.

14. Ed Thomas, "'Fair and Balanced' Fox News Called on Alleged Pro-Homosexual Support," *Agape Press*, September 13, 2006.

15. Rob Mall, "Against the Ex-Gays," *Christianity Today* Blog, April 13, 2006.

16. Mark Penn, "America's Newest Profession: Bloggers for Hire," *The Wall Street Journal*, April 21, 2009.

17. Paul Greenberg, "Confession," Townhall.com, January 30, 2008.

18. Richard A. Viguerie and David Frank, *America's Right Turn: How Conservatives Used New and Alternative Media to Take Power* (Los Angeles: Bonus Books, 2004), p. 335.

19. Peter Wehner, "This Is 'Diminished Power'?" *National Review*, January 23, 2008.

20. Jim Daly, "Cultural Warriors," *The Washington Times*, January 9, 2008.

21. Viguerie and Franke, p. 336.

22. Bob Moser, "The Crusaders: Christian Evangelicals Are Plotting to Remake America in Their Own Image," *Rolling Stone*, April 8, 2005.

23. "Lesbian, Gay, Bisexual, and Transgender Pride Month, 2009 by the President of the United States of America: A Proclamation," June 1, 2009.

24. "Some Evangelicals Look to the Left," CBS Evening News, September 21, 2006.

25. Ibid.

26. "Openly Gay Mayor Blasted For 'Christian Courtesy,'" CBS News,

September 23, 2006.

27. "Palm Springs Fumes Over 'Ex-Gays' Welcome," *The Advocate*, September 1, 2006.

28. "Openly Gay Mayor Blasted For 'Christian Courtesy,'" op. cit.

29. Melissa Fryrear, quoted in a newswire release, September 21, 2006.

30. Marcia Ford, "Two Books Reveal a Diversity that Might Surprise Many," "Religion BookLine," *Publishers Weekly*, August 2, 2006.

31. Ibid.

32. "Readers Respond: Letter from Rick Warren," TheSimon.com, July 28, 2006

33. "Rick Warren Responds to Newsweek," GetReligion.org, June 12, 2008.

34. John Cloud, "The Battle Over Gay Teens," *Time*, October 10, 2005.

35. Stanton L. Jones and Mark Yarhouse, *Homosexuality: The Use of Scientific Research in the Church's Moral Debate* (Downers Grove, Illinois: InterVarsity Press, 2000), p. 97.

36. Associated Press: "Gen. Pace Says Gay Sex Immoral," September 27, 2007.

37. Cal Thomas, "The Olbermann Factor," Townhall.com, November 10, 2010.

38. Cloud, "The Battle Over Gay Teens."

Chapter 5

1. *After the Ball*, p. 149.

2. Paul E. Rondeau, "Selling Homosexuality," *Regent University Law Review*, Vol. 14:443-485, 2002.

3. Rondeau, p. 452 footnote.

4. Rondeau, p. 454 footnote.

5. Ibid.

6. Cloud, "The Battle Over Gay Teens"

7. Ed Vitagliano, "Confronting Gay-Straight Alliances in the Public Schools," *Agape Press* (now *AFA Journal*), June 28, 2005.

8. *After the Ball*, p. 146.

9. Anastasia Toufexis and Edward M. Gomez, "Is The Gay Revolution a Flop?"

(A Review of *After the Ball*), *Time,* July 10, 1989.

10. National Coalition of Anti-Violence Programs (NCAVP) Report, "Anti-Lesbian, Gay, Bisexual and Transgender Violence in 2005."

11. "Gay Domestic Violence Finally Measured," *Journal of the Family Research Institute,* Vol. 16 No. 8, December 2001.

12. "Violence Against Gays On The Rise, 365gay.com, April 26, 2005.

13. Matt Foreman's State of the Movement Address to the National Conference on LGBT Equality in Denver, Colorado on February 8, 2008.

14. From Amazon.com editorial description of Mel White's *Religion Gone Bad: The Hidden Dangers of the Christian Right* (New York: Tarcher, 2006).

15. NCAVP 2005 report.

16. Ibid.

17. Reuters, "Elton John Wants Religion Banned," November 12, 2006.

18. Dan Harris, "Film Shows Youths Training to Fight for Jesus," ABC News, September 17, 2006.

19. Ibid.

20. Marilyn Geewax, "Rights Group: Big Companies Growing More Gay Friendly," Cox News Service, October 1, 2006.

21. Human Rights Campaign Foundation, "Corporate Equality Index: A Report Card on Gay, Lesbian, Bisexual and Transgender Equality in Corporate America," 2008.

22. Josh Montez, "Gay Chambers of Commerce Pop Up Around the Country," CitizenLink.org, October 17, 2006.

23. Ibid.

24. 1 Samuel 16:7.

25. Cloud, "The Battle Over Gay Teens"

26. Ibid.

27. Jon Dougherty, "Report: Pedophilia More Common Among Gays," WorldNetDaily, April 29, 2002.

28. Ibid.

29. Ibid.

30. Ibid.

31. Henry Clough, "Covering Up for Harry: Our Dishonest News Media," weirdrepublic.com, June 16, 2004.

32. Art Moore, "Meet the Women's Auxiliary of NAMBLA," WorldNetDaily, July 22, 2002.

33. Ibid.

34. Ibid.

35. Eli M. Oboler, "The Grand Illusion," *Library Journal* (March 15, 1968), Vol. 93, No. 6, p. 1279.

36. Marjorie Fiske, *Book Selection and Censorship: A Study of School and Public Libraries in California*, (Berkeley: University of California Press, 1959), p. 24.

37. Wilhelm Reich, *The Mass Psychology of Fascism* (New York: Farrar, Strauss and Giroux, 1946), 1970 (first German edition, 1933), p. 146.

38. Loretta Haroian, Ph.D., "Child Sexual Development," *Electronic Journal of Human Sexuality*, Volume 3, Part I, February 1, 2000.

39. The article referenced is: Bruce Rind, Philip Tromovitch, and Robert Bauserman, "A Meta-Analytic Examination of Assumed Properties of Child Sexual Abuse Using College Samples," *Psychological Bulletin*, 1998, Vol. 124, No. 1, 22-53.

40. Making Daughters Safe Again, mdsasupport.homestead.com.

Chapter 6

1. Policy Statement: "Homosexuality and Adolescence," American Academy of Pediatrics, 1993, as quoted in "Just the Facts About Sexual Orientation & Youth: A Primer for Principals, Educators and School Personnel," National Educational Association, et al, 2000.

2. Alan Sears, "The Curious Case of NEA Priorities," Townhall.com, August 26, 2006.

3. Josh Montez, "Kids Used to Promote Homosexual Agenda," Family News in Focus, August 23, 2006.

4. Jill Tucker, "Class Surprises Lesbian Teacher on Wedding Day," *The San Francisco Chronicle*, October 11, 2008.

5. "GLSEN Encourages Youth Experimentation," MissionAmerica.com.

6. Ibid.

7. "Struggling Gays and Lesbians Welcomed: PFOX Reaches Out With Message of Hope," *Agape Press* (now *AFA Journal*), September 14, 2006.

8. "The Education Crisis," *Real Truth*, September-October 2003.

9. Ibid.

10. Ibid.

11. Deroy Murdock, "Unholy Unions: Exploiting Labor," *National Review*, September 1, 2006

12. "Union Dues," *NEA Today*, April 2005.

13. Education Reporter (Eagle Forum), August 2006.

14. Ibid.

15. Lambda Report on Homosexuality (April-May 2000), reprint of Whiteman affidavit, submitted April 18, 2000 to Hon. Martha Coakley, District Attorney for Middlesex County, Massachusetts, pp.1-4.

16. Brian J. Burt, *Lambda Report*, January/February 1998, p. 5.

17. *Lambda Report*, p. 4.

18. "Child Abuse and Neglect Reporting: A Guide for Mandated Reporters," Massachusetts Department of Children and Families, 2009.

19. George Archibald, "NEA Groups Protest Award to Gay Studies Activist," *The Washington Times*, July 3, 2004.

20. Ibid.

21. Ibid.

22. Transcript of video, "Gay Rights/Special Rights: Inside the Homosexual Agenda" (Jeremiah Films) at christian-apologetics.org.

23. "Life and Times" program archives, KCET-TV.

24. Beverly Eakman, "The Power of Suggestions about 'Gay-ness,'" NewsWithViews.com, October 14, 2004.

25. Phyllis Schlafly, "NEA Agenda Is Frightening to Parents," Eagle Forum, July 26, 2006.

26. Rick Amato, "Learning About the 'Three Sexes," Townhall.com, January 22, 2008.

27. Ibid.

28. Susan Brinkmann, "Gay History Month in City Schools Seen Part of Trend,"

The Catholic Standard and Times, November 6, 2006.

29. Diana Lynne, "Lawmakers 'Sanction' Use of District-Approved 'Porn,'" WorldNetDaily, 2002.

30. "Transgendered Child Set to Enter Florida School System," *Agape Press*, July 14, 2006. (Note: *Agape Press* is now *AFA Journal*.)

31. Linda Harvey, "The Top 10 Reasons to Protect Students from GLSEN's Deceptive 'Marriage' Curriculum," MissionAmerica.com.

32. Ibid.

33. "Mission America Student Survey Results," MissionAmerica.com.

34. Paul Varnell, "Why We Need Gay History Month," *Windy City Times*, March 24, 1994.

35. Ty Clevenger, " Gay Orthodoxy and Academic Heresy," *Regent University Law Review, Vol. 14:244, 2002.*

36. Clevenger, p. 243.

37. Clevenger, p. 244.

38. Ibid.

39. John-Henry Westen, "In Canada Even 'Moderates' Are Tarred as Extremists,"LifeSiteNews.com, June 20, 2006.

40. Michelle Malkin, "Laura vs. Unhinged Librarians," *Jewish World Review*, June 21, 2006.

41. John Cloud, "The Battle Over Gay Teens," *Time*, October 10, 2005.

42. Nicholas Jackson, "Children at Risk," *The Conservative Voice*, September 3, 2006.

43. Marvin Olasky, "No Student Is an Island," Townhall.com, May 31, 2007.

44. C.S. Lewis, *The Screwtape Letters* (New York: HarperCollins Publishers, 1942 (1996 HarperSanFrancisco edition), pp. 150-151.

Chapter 7

1. Deborah Caldwell, "God is Doing a New Thing in the World," Interview with Eugene Robinson, BeliefNet.com, May 3, 2003.

2. Pete Winn and Jessica Headley, "Episcopal Leader: Homosexuality Not a Sin," CitizenLink.org, June 20, 2006.

3. Ephraim Radner and Andrew Goddard, "Human Rights, Homosexuality

and the Anglican Communion: Reflections in Light of Nigeria," VirtueOnline, November 22, 2006.

4. Ibid.

5. Stephen Bennett, "Sex, Torture and Erotic Electrification in America's "Gay" Churches," WorldNetDaily, July 18, 2002.

6. Elizabeth Stuart, *Religion Is a Queer Thing: A Guide to the Christian Faith for Lesbian, Gay, Bisexual, and Transgendered Persons* (Cleveland, Ohio: The Pilgrim Press, 1998), p. 1.

7. Joe Dallas, "Responding to Pro-Gay Theology: General Religious Arguments," Focusonthefamily.com, August 31, 2005.

8. Joe Dallas, "How Should We Respond?" Plenary address at (undated) Love Won Out conference.

9. E-mail from director of Soulforce, December 15, 2009.

10. Dr. Gordon Hugenberger, Park Street Church, Boston: "Questions and Answers on Issues Related to Homosexuality and Same-Sex Marriage," parkstreet.org, June 15, 2004.

11. Dallas, "Responding to Pro-Gay Theology," Exodus-International.org.

12. Ibid.

13. *The Screwtape Letters*, p. 191.

14. Mel White, *Stranger at the Gate: To Be Gay and Christian in America* (New York: Simon & Schuster, 1994), pp. 34, 73, 88, 129, 178.

15. Oswald Chambers, *My Utmost for His Highest* (Grand Rapids, Michigan: Discovery House Publishers, 1963), August 20th reading, p. 170.

16. Chambers, August 21st reading, p. 171.

17. C.S. Lewis, *Mere Christianity* (New York: McMillan Publishing Company, 1943), pp. 52-53.

Chapter 8

1. Jon Liu, "While the Crimson slept ... Boston Becomes the Hub of the Universe, and a Challenge Is Issued," *The Harvard Independent*, November 3, 2005.

2. Address by Melissa Fryrear at Liberty University, November 2, 2005.

3. *Stranger at the Gate*, p. 29.

4. Interview with Melissa Fryrear.

5. John Corvino, "The Gay Moralist: Behind Enemy Lines," JohnCorvino.com, Ma y 2008.

6. Press release from Exodus International, June 2006.

7. Interview with Rev. Bob Stith on July 5, 2006.

8. "... And a New Seed Was Planted," Focusonthefamily.com.

9. *Stranger at the Gate*, p. 156.

10. Proverbs 16:18.

11. James 4:6.

12. John Baker, *Celebrate Recovery Leader's Guide* (Grand Rapids, Michigan, 1998), p. 14.

13. American Family Outing promo at soulforce.org.

14. *Celebrate Recovery Leader's Guide*, p. 9.

15. "The 12 Steps: Living the Recovery Program," Alcoholics Anonymous.

16. The AACC offers lay recovery curriculum called "Caring for People God's Way," including a certificate for those who complete the course.

17. Interview with Bob Stith.

18. Interview with Melissa Fryrear.

19. John 8:7.

20. *Stranger at the Gate*, p. 174.

21. Blog entry on WThrockmorton.com, September 21, 2007.

22. Testimony of Joe Dallas as told to Bob Davies, stonewallrevisited.com.

23. Ibid.

24. Joe Dallas, "How Should We Respond?" (Undated) Love Won Out Conference Plenary Address.

25. Ibid.

26. Ibid.

27. Ibid.

28. Interview with Nancy Heche, June 20, 2006.

29. D.K. DeKlerk, "Love Wins Out ... for Everyone: The Story of One Man

and Fifteen Protesters," New Direction Ministries testimonies, NewDirection.ca.

30. Andrew Marin has discussed the forthcoming study on his blog.

31. Liu, *The Harvard Independent*.

32. "Spiritual Profile of Homosexual Adults Provides Surprising Insights," Barna Group, Barna.org, June 20, 2009.

Chapter 9

1. Glenn Stanton and Dr. Bill Maier, *Marriage on Trial: The Case Against Same-Sex Marriage and Parenting* (Downers Grove, Illinois: Intervarsity Press, 2004), p. 15.

2. *Marriage on Trial*, p. 39.

3. Thomas Sowell, "Dismantling America, Part 4," Townhall.com, August 20, 2010.

4. Interview with Dr. Edward Feser, Lifesite.com, August 19, 2010.

5. "50,000 Gay Couples in Netherlands," expatica.com, November 14, 2005.

6. Stanley Kurtz, "The Marriage Mentality," *National Review*, May 4, 2004.

7. "Academics Raise the Alarm Over Marriage," The Heritage Foundation, July 2, 2004.

8. Stanley Kurtz, "Here Come the Brides: Plural Marriage Is Waiting in the Wings," *The Weekly Standard*, December 26, 2005.

9. Paula Ettlebrick, "Since When Is Marriage a Path to Liberation?" from *Same Sex Marriage: Pro and Con*, ed. Andrew Sullivan (New York: Vintage Books, 1997), p. 120.

10. Stanley Kurtz, "Going Dutch? Lessons of the Same-Sex Marriage Debate in the Netherlands," *The Weekly Standard*, May 31, 2004.

11. Scott James, "Many Successful Gay Marriages Share an Open Secret," *The New York Times*, Jan. 28, 2010.

12. Paul Nathanson and Katherine Young, "Marriage á la Mode: Answering Advocates of Gay Marriage," Presented at Emory University on May 14, 2003.

13. Ellen C. Perrin, "Technical Report: Co-parent and Second-Parent Adoption by Same-Sex Parents," *Pediatrics*, Vol. 109, No. 2:341, 2002.

14. Martin Daly and Margo Wilson, "Child Abuse and Other Risks of Not Living with Both Parents," *Ethology and Sociobiology*, Vol. 6:197-210, 1985.

15. Martin Daly and Margo Wilson, *Homicide* (New York: Aldine de Gruyter, 1988), pp. 87-88.

16. "Shuttle Diplomacy," *Psychology Today*, July-August 1993, p. 15.

17. Perrin, p. 341.

18. Judith Wallerstein et al., *The Unexpected Legacy of Divorce: A 25 Year Landmark Study* (New York: Hyperion, 2000), p. xxvii.

19. Stephanie Levin, "New Research Finds Children of Lesbians Thriving and Equal to National Norms," *UCSF Today* (University of California, San Francisco), November 3, 2005.

20. Nanette K. Gartrell, Henny M. W. Bos, and Naomi G. Goldberg, "Adolescents of the U.S. National Longitudinal Lesbian Family Study: Sexual Orientation, Sexual Behavior, and Sexual Risk Exposure," *Archives of Sexual Behavior*, published online November 6, 2010.

21. Trayce Hansen, Ph.D., "A Review and Analysis of Research Studies Which Assessed Sexual Preference of Children Raised by Homosexuals," drtraycehansen.com.

22. Judith Stacey and Timothy J. Biblarz, "(How) Does the Sexual Orientation of Parents Matter?" *American Sociological Review*, Vol. 66, No. 2:159-183, 2001.

23. *Marriage on Trial*, p. 57.

24. Ibid.

25. Schumer's remarks, Empire State Pride Agenda dinner, October 22, 2009.

26. Stacey and Biblarz.

27. Frank Furstenberg and Kathleen Harris: "When and Why Fathers Matter: Impacts of Father Involvement on Children of Adolescent Mothers," in *Young Unwed Fathers: Changing Roles and Emerging Policies*, ed. R. Lerman and T. Ooms (Philadelphia: Temple University Press, 1993).

28. Elaine Kamarck and William Galston, "Putting Children First: A Progressive Family Policy for the 1990s," White Paper from the Progressive Policy Institute, September 27, 1990, pp. 14-15.

29. "35 Percent of Foster-Parent Molestations Homosexual," Christian Newswire, August 10, 2006.

30. *Marriage on Trial*, p. 122.

31. Pitirim A. Sorokin, The American Sex Revolution, (Boston: Porter Sargent, 1956), p. 88.

32. Lou Chibbarro Jr., "Marriage Fight Heads to Legislatures in N.Y., Calif.," *The Washington Blade*, July 14, 2006.

33. Dennis Prager, "Same-Sex Marriage and the Insignificance of Men and Women," Towhnall.com, August 17, 2010.

34. Shari Motro, "Single and Paying for It," *The New York Times* (Op-Ed), January 25, 2004.

35. "Beyond Same-Sex Marriage: A New Strategic Vision For All Our Families and Relationships," BeyondMarriage.org, July 26, 2006.

36. Ibid.

37. James C. Dobson commentary: "Media Provides Cover for Assault on Traditional Marriage," CNN, July 6, 2006.

38. Jennifer Riley, "Thousands of NY Christians Protest Gay Marriage," *Christian Post*, May 18, 2009.

39. *Mere Christianity*, p. 95-96.

40. As cited in "In Defense of Marriage," by Phil Thrailkill, pastor of Duncan Memorial United Methodist Church, 2003.

Index

More Titles by Debbie Thurman

From Depression To Wholeness: The Anatomy of Healing

Hold My Heart:
A Teen's Journal for Healing and Personal Growth

Sheer Faith: A Teen's Journey to Godly Growth

A Teen's Guide to Christian Living: Practical Answers to
Tough Questions about God and Faith
(co-authored with Bettie B. Youngs and Jennifer Youngs)

12 Months of Faith: A Devotional Journal for Teens
(co-authored with Bettie B. Youngs and Jennifer Youngs)

Outsmarting Depression: Surviving the Crossfire
of the Mental Health Wars

Books may be purchased via www.debbiethurman.com.

About the Author

Debbie Thurman is a Christian journalist, award-winning columnist and author of seven nonfiction books. She has written scores of articles and commentaries published in a variety of newspapers and magazines over her 35-year writing career. She has been a church teacher and ministry leader for more than 25 years. She is also the founder of Sheer Faith Ministries.

Married for 29 years, Debbie and her husband reside in Central Virginia and have two married daughters. She holds an A.B. degree in English from Sweet Briar College in Virginia and served eight years as a public affairs officer in the U.S. Marine Corps.

Debbie's ministry mission has been to educate and encourage families battling emotional and spiritual brokenness, whatever form that takes, and to help facilitate the Church's outreach to them. She was a founding group facilitator of Freedom Ministry at Thomas Road Baptist Church in Lynchburg, Virginia. Mostly, Debbie seeks to fulfill the Christ-given "ministry of reconciliation" the Apostle Paul speaks of in 2 Corinthians 5:18 through her writing, speaking, and discipling efforts.

Debbie's ministry website is debbiethurman.com.